How to Do Everything

How to Do Everything

Everything you should know how to do

Rosemarie Jarski
Illustrations by Milena Jarski

THE LYONS PRESS
Guilford, Connecticut
An imprint of The Globe Pequot Press

Dedication
To Our Perfect Mum and Dad

First Lyons Press Edition 2007
Originally published in 2006 by New Holland Publishers (UK) Ltd

Copyright © 2006 text: Rosemarie Jarski
Copyright © 2006 illustrations: New Holland Publishers (UK) Ltd
Copyright © 2006 New Holland Publishers (UK) Ltd

The Lyons Press is an imprint of The Globe Pequot Press

10 9 8 7 6 5 4 3 2 1

Printed in the United States of America

Design: Paul Wright
Illustrations: Milena Jarski
Production: Hazel Kirkman

ISBN 978-1-84537-415-0

Library of Congress Cataloging-in-Publication Data is available on file.

Note:
The author and publishers have made every effort to ensure that all instructions given in this
book are safe and accurate, but they cannot accept liability for any resulting injury or loss or
damage to either property or person, whether direct or consequential and howsoever arising.

CONTENTS

— INTRODUCTION —

"I might give my life for my friend, but he had better not ask me to do up a parcel."
—*Logan Pearsall Smith*

We all have gaps in our knowledge when it comes to everyday skills, and most of us would rather do anything than tackle them—without going quite as far as Mr. Pearsall Smith, perhaps. But no one is born knowing how to do wrap a package. It's only easy if someone shows you how. The problem these days is that parents are so busy earning a living that they don't have time to pass on their wisdom, and such skills don't form part of the school curriculum, so there really is no one to show you—that is, till now.

How to Do Everything is your essential guide to daily living, offering a thorough grounding in the practical skills everyone should know how to do. Whatever your personal blind spot—ironing a shirt, sewing on a button, packing a suitcase, or wrapping the notorious package, you'll learn how to master this, and many more useful skills.

Your guide does not pretend that placing a designer lemon-squeezer on your kitchen counter is the key to domestic bliss. Nor does it presume that you have an army of maids and nannies to do your chores for you. Advice is down-to-earth and hands-on, focusing on those household problems and challenges you are most likely to encounter in real life: how to cure a dripping tap, combat condensation, and unclog a sink. You'll also get to grips with a power drill, a plumb line, and a paintbrush. And find the answers to Life's little frustrations, like how to remove sticky labels, open supermarket plastic bags, and fit a duvet cover onto a duvet without being swallowed.

Making light work of drudgery is only part of the story. There's also the chance to enhance your personal style. Try some fashionable new ways to tie a tie or a silk scarf. Look stylish in a sarong. Shine your shoes. Braid hair. Floss.

With your image and home polished to perfection, what better way to show them off than with a fabulous dinner party? Your guide comes in handy here, too, helping you create a beautiful table, cater for guests with different dietary needs, and carve meat like a culinary Zorro. There's also advice on how to open a bottle of bubbly like a Grand Prix racing driver. Not.

Such a variety of subjects needs careful organization and your guide is designed to be user-friendly. Information is mercifully jargon-free and presented in bite-sized pieces that are easy to digest, fun to browse, and quick to access when you need a solution fast; after all, a red wine stain on your favorite outfit won't wait. Step-by-step instructions are enhanced, wherever necessary, by line drawings, so you can see at a glance what to do. The aim is to demystify and simplify. Where other household manuals leave you feeling daunted and inadequate, this guide will instill you with the confidence and enthusiasm to jump right in and give it a try.

And once you've embarked on a project, you won't be abandoned halfway through. Too many manuals offer only cursory directions. For example, they'll explain how to hang a single piece of wallpaper and then just leave you to it. Which is fine if your room has no windows, doors, corners, or light-switches. This guide holds your hand every step of the way, particularly through the tricky parts.

Another failing of many home references is that they tell you *how* to do something without telling you *why*. What is the point of a detailed explanation of how to bleed a radiator if you have no idea why it's necessary? And who, in their right mind, would attempt the origami puzzle that is a hospital corner on a bedsheet without knowing why it's worthwhile? You'd take one look and think, "Life's too short. Why bother?" This guide is different because it takes the time to tell you why a particular technique is needed or beneficial. When you understand that hospital corners a) make your bed cosier; b) keep your toes toastier; c) guarantee you a better night's sleep; and d) make your bed easier to make in the morning, you'll be itching to get at those bedclothes and start folding.

"If a job's worth doing, it's worth doing well," Mother used to say. As the title of this guide implies, old-fashioned standards are not sacrificed on the altar of convenience. You'll learn how to do things just so, in a way that would pass muster with Mom.

Not that the intention is to turn you into a Stepford Wife or Husband. Heaven forbid! Once you've learned how to do things "by the book," you can bend, and even break, the rules, according to your own personal preferences. But it's certainly worth remembering that James Joyce learned the basic rules of grammar before he wrote *Ulysses*.

Housekeeping manuals, as a genre, are often accused of belonging to the School of what Basil Fawlty called "the Bleeding Obvious," patronizing readers with information that is basic common sense. Well, common sense is not as common as is commonly supposed. If flossing your teeth is common sense, why do dentists report soaring levels of gum disease? If cutting your toenails is common sense, why do chiropodists report soaring levels of ingrown toenails? If unclogging your toilet is common sense, why do plumbers rank it their number-one reason for a call out? As the host of *Who Wants to be a Millionaire* likes to remind us, "It's only easy if you know the answer." This guide makes no apologies for taking you back to basics, showing you how to wash your hair, how to wash your hands, and even how to wipe your bottom—surely the *reductio ad absurdum* of all instructional advice—until you discover there are also tips on how to breathe. The crucial word to add in each case is *correctly*.

The guide may be pitched at entry level, but that doesn't mean there's not plenty to interest and even challenge experienced divas of domesticity, who will enjoy finding ways to improve their techniques. They'll also pick up new hints and unusual ideas, like how to make a crystal ice bowl, wrap a parcel Japanese-style, and decorate a Christmas tree upside down (you or the tree? Turn to page 289 and see). Domestic pedants will savor the hard-core domestic facts, such as the exact number of strokes to vacuum over a carpet, the precise angle to place a teaspoon on a saucer, and the exact number of inches a tablecloth should overhang the table. "God is in the detail," as Ludwig Wittgenstein said—or was it Martha Stewart?

How to Do Everything is that rare thing in the world of home references: a manual that is suitable for both sexes. Most manuals are segregated along gender lines. The guys get complicated-looking diagrams and macho facts about how a microwave works, and the gals get a sparkly pink cover and girly tips on throw pillows. Odd, really, since when last observed, men and women were both seen to inhabit similar environments—called "homes"—sometimes, even, together. Both have laundry to sort, stains to remove, dishes to wash, and the techniques don't differ according to whether you wear a pink apron or a blue. In this guide, there are no areas off-limits to either sex—with the possible exception of how to shave your face.

Male, female, or gender-neutral, all home references ultimately fall into two camps: those that consider housekeeping a chore, and those that consider it a thing of beauty and a joy forever. This guide assumes that you would rather lie on the couch than vacuum under it, and that it would have to be dipped in chocolate before you could find joy in a dust cloth. The emphasis is on how to do the best job as quickly and efficiently as possible, so you can start having some real fun. That said, it does acknowledge the pride and satisfaction in a job well done or a new skill mastered. And it positively encourages jumping up and down, punching the air, and shouting, "Eureka! I'm a genius!" when you learn how to tie that bow tie, darn that hole in your sweater, or unclog that toilet (though in the last scenario, you'll probably be jumping up and down anyway).

Hopefully, you'll experience many air-punching moments as you sweep, shine, and stitch your way toward domestic enlightenment. By the end, your life won't be perfect—whose is?—but it will be easier, happier, and more gracious in little ways. Sometimes, it's the little things in life that make the biggest difference.

P.S. Memo to Mr. Logan Pearsall Smith: Please turn to page 283 so your friend will never have to have your demise on his conscience.

– GET ORGANIZED –

"All I need is room enough to lay my hat and a few friends."

—DOROTHY PARKER

— THE TWELVE-STEP PROGRAM TO DE-JUNKING —

Take away the mess and you take away the stress.
If you're a junk-ie, follow this simple twelve-step program to recovery . . .

Step 1

Recognize the junk. Broken gadgets, last year's calendars, old watches, dried-up mascara and shoe polish . . . and will you honestly ever finish crocheting that afghan?

Step 2

Divide and conquer. Get four boxes and label them: Throw Away, Recycle, To Keep, and Maybe. Go from room to room and work your way through every cupboard and drawer. It's tough, but the first cut is the deepest.

Step 3

Do the clutter test. If you can't decide about an object, ask yourself these questions: Do I love it? Do I use it? Does it make me happy? Any item that scores a no, has to go.

Step 4

Rearrange your closet. Most people wear 20 percent of their wardrobe 80 percent of the time. Tailor your wardrobe to the season and your size. Any garment you haven't worn in the last year, put in a bag and donate to charity. (See "How to organize your closet," pages 14–15.)

Step 5

You've got a friend. Enlist the help of a friend and do a deal: you help them with their decluttering, and they help you with yours. Sometimes you need a dispassionate eye to tell you that fluorescent lime green poodle skirts are never likely to come back into fashion.

Step 6

Climb off the consumer merry-go-round. I want it all, and I want it now. Fine, but where are you going to put it? No matter what you buy, you will never be satisfied. That's what consumerism is all about. So where's it all going to end? The problem with possessions is that they can become like comfort blankets offering a false sense of security. We think we need them more than we do.

Step 7

New for old. Make a pact with yourself: "If I buy that new pair of shoes, I promise to dispose of an old pair or donate them to charity." Apply this principle to all new purchases.

Step 8

Toss it. Keep a large wastebasket in every room and empty it daily. Shred any document containing your personal details. (See "Shredding," page 235.)

Step 9

Conquer the paper mountain. Sort through paperwork. Create a filing system. Clear the junk in your office and on your computer— consign old files to the recycle bin.

Step 10

Thanks for the memo-ry. Put up a memo board— but don't clutter it! Do you really need the 11 takeout menus? Well, yeah, come to think of it . . .

Step 11

No hoarding place. The spare room, the attic, the basement, the garage, the shed . . . think of them as spaces to store items not currently in use, rather than places to stash and hide the junk.

Step 12

Repeat the mantra: A place for everything and everything in its place.

TIP: Don't be tempted by freebies. Most of them will end up in the bag for donation sooner or later.

— STORAGE —

It's not always possible to move to gain extra space, but there are often better ways to exploit the space you already have. It's just a matter of looking at a room with fresh eyes. Just because a room has always been arranged a certain way does not mean that's the best use of space. Be flexible. Sometimes it's as simple as changing the way a door hangs. Or, where every last square inch of space has been exploited, adding a mirror to create a sensation of more space.

Types of storage: Built-in storage makes the best use of the space available and frees up valuable floor space. If your rooms are an irregular shape, custom-built cupboards can be made to fit an awkward space perfectly. You can't take them with you when you move, but potential buyers will regard them as an asset, so they should increase the resale value of your property.

GIVE IT A TRY: Instead of buying new storage containers, adapt existing furniture to make maximum use of space. Put new internal shelves into an old cupboard; put new shelving units in an old-fashioned pantry.

TOP TIP: Make use of dead space under the bed, under the stairs, above and under windows. The space under the stairs can often be converted into separate cupboards to store cleaning equipment, sports gear, wine bottles, etc. It may even be opened out into a small office.

— ORGANIZING AROUND THE HOME —

Sort out your living space and your mind will follow. If your home is more health-hazard than haven, follow the one true path to organizational nirvana . . .

— HALLS AND LANDINGS —

Often overlooked, but can provide valuable storage space for outdoor clothes, cleaning equipment, DIY tools, etc. Line the walls with shelves to house your book collection or turn the walls into your art gallery.

— KITCHEN —

Move out larger appliances such as the washing machine and freezer into a utility room to create more cupboard space.

Hang brooms and brushes on the inside of a cupboard door.

Free up valuable surfaces in the kitchen by hanging utensils on the wall. Racks for spices, herbs, and mugs can also be fixed to the wall.

Suspend an old-fashioned clothes airer to make use of ceiling space. Hang pots and pans from it—or dry bunches of herbs and roses on it.

TIP: Buy storage containers only when you know how you will use them; otherwise, they themselves become part of the clutter.

Replace a kitchen table with a breakfast bar with built-in storage.
And use folding chairs or stools.

Fix screw-in hooks under shelves to hang mugs.

Buy an iron organizer, which enables you to hang both your iron
and ironing board from the inside of a door or wall.

Use drawer organizers to keep drawers clutter-free.

— LIVING ROOM —

Use a combination of open shelving and cupboard storage.

A custom-made unit to house your stereo and television equipment
is nice, but what happens when you want to
upgrade to a larger set?

Instead of tables and nests of tables, go for small, freestanding cupboards that can
be used for storage.

Buy a dining table with drop-down leaves.

Choose glass-fronted cupboards to display collections and avoid dust.

— BEDROOM —

After your bed, clothes are likely to take up the most room,
so ensure adequate closet space.

Choose a daybed with built-in drawers,
for storing linen and larger items.

Replace bedside tables with built-in shelving
around and above the headboard.

— BATHROOM —

Box in baths or pedestal basins to create useful storage space for cleaning equipment,
toilet rolls, etc.

Install a cabinet on the wall above the toilet.

Swap the bathroom mirror for a medicine cabinet where you can stow
all your lotions and potions.

*TIP: If you're tired of pulling the plug on the TV instead of the vacuum, you can buy (or make) stickers
to put on your plugs to identify which appliance is which.*

Limit the number of bottles and packets hanging around by transferring cotton balls into attractive storage jars and soap into pretty dishes.

Fix glass shelves across the window and fill with plants.

— CLOSETS —

"The hotel I'm in has a lovely closet. A nail."—Henny Youngman

— MAXIMIZING CLOSET SPACE —
If space is limited, fit sliding doors on the closet.
Folding doors also help if floor space is tight.

If the units have no back, ensure the wall is wallpapered or
painted with paint that will not rub off on your clothes.

Don't lay carpet on the floor of your closet;
if it becomes infested with insects, your clothes will be at risk.

Install fluorescent lights if your closet is deep
so you don't have to root around in the dark.

Use the space on the inside of the closet door: install rails made
out of curtain wire and hang ties or belts from it.

If you have plenty of closet space and not enough drawers,
set up wire basket racks in the cupboards. They are better than drawers
because you can see at a glance what's inside and they keep clothes aired.

— HOW TO ORGANIZE YOUR CLOSET —

Have a good sort-out of your closet: discard any items that no longer fit, are out of style, were unwanted presents (he'll never know), are not flattering, or were "mistakes" (aka bargains).

Get into the habit of hanging up your clothes as soon as you take them off (and also encourage the family to do the same).

Ensure clothes are clean before putting them away. Use a clothes brush to remove dust and stray hairs.

As a general rule, hang up all clothes except sweaters and underwear.

Don't hang woolen or knit garments, as they will stretch. Fold and store flat (see page 37).

Remove items from pockets before hanging or they could stretch garments.

Fasten all buttons and zippers on clothes to help maintain their shape.

TIP: Recycle your old clothes. Those old T-shirts make great cleaning cloths, and those silk undies will buff up your windows to a perfect shine.

Wooden or padded coat hangers are preferable to flimsy wire—though wire hangers are good for unclogging the vacuum cleaner!

If you must use wire hangers, make them non-slip by winding several elastic bands around each end of the hanger where you hang your clothes. There's nothing more annoying than clothes that are always slipping off their hangers.

Pad the shoulders of coats and jackets with white acid-free tissue paper to help them keep their shape.

Don't hang jackets by the loops as it will distort the shape of the shoulders. Hang on sturdy wooden hangers.

Hang trousers from the waist rather than over the bar of a hanger.

Hang skirts from the loops on the waistband.

Hang belts from the buckle rather than rolled up, as they could crack.

Hang all shirts together, all skirts together, etc., and group according to color.

Group long clothes at one end of the closet and short clothes at the other, so that the space below can be used for shelves or drawers to store folded clothes.

Hang black garments and evening dresses inside out to keep them cleaner.

Don't fill your closet too full. Allow the air to circulate between clothes, and open the door to let fresh air in.

Shelves are more practical than drawers. Clothes are more accessible and less likely to wrinkle.

Line drawers and shelves with wallpaper or lining paper and slip in a scented sachet to keep moths at bay.

Buy drawer dividers so you can keep socks, tights, and undergarments separate in your underwear drawer.

Never store clothes in dry-cleaning plastic bags. They will be susceptible to condensation leading to mold.

Store heavy items at waist height so you don't have to bend down or stretch up to reach them and risk injuring your back.

If they came in a box, store shoes in that. Use a hole-punch to make holes in the box so air can get to them. Don't store shoes in plastic bags.

Take a photograph of your shoes and stick it on the front of the box so you can identify the pair you want at a glance.

Use shoe-trees in leather shoes and boots to help them keep their shape.

Pack winter clothes away for the summer and summer clothes away for the winter. Clean clothes to be stored but iron only when you take them out again. Store in a dry place with herbal or chemical moth-repellent.

TIP: One person's clutter is another person's treasure. Sell your unwanted stuff on eBay, have a garage sale or donate it to charity.

— HOME LAUNDRY —

*"My mother from time to time puts on her wedding dress.
Not because she's sentimental. She just gets really far behind with her laundry."*

—BRIAN KILEY

— WASHING —

In a spin with your laundry? These tips might not make washday your favorite day of the week, but they will certainly help banish those laundry-day blues . . .

— SORTING —

They can put a man on the moon, they can build an entire car using only robots, but no one has yet found a way of washing clothes together without dyes running. The only way to avoid that all-pink fashion parade is to sort your laundry. Group clothes by color—whites, darks, colors (bright or pastel prints), and separate delicates to be hand-washed.

To test a garment for colorfastness: Choose a hidden area, such as an inner seam, dampen a cotton wool pad, and leave it on the fabric for 5 minutes. If any dye comes off on the cotton wool, wash separately.

— PREPARING THE WASH —

• Turn clothes inside out before washing to reduce risk of fading and pilling.

• Check that all pockets are empty: an illegible winning lottery ticket is worthless.

• Mend any rips or loose seams or you'll be landed with a tougher repair job later.

• Close all buttons, zippers, bra-hooks, and tie belts so they don't snag or catch.

• Button up the duvet cover—a favorite hiding place for odd socks and undies.

• Wash delicate items, such as tights, in a pillowcase tied with a plastic-bag tie.

TIP: For sparkling collars and cuffs: Before washing, dampen and rub household soap into dirty marks. Use a toothbrush to work the soap into a lather. Rinse and wash as normal.

— PREWASH SOAKING —

If you've been draining the sump on your Harley, or wolfing spaghetti off a white tablecloth, a prewash soaking is essential for your clothes—and you. Submerge your filthy clothes in a bucket or bath and forget about them for as long as you can. No, you shouldn't actually go away on vacation and leave them. But whites can be left overnight. On stubborn stains, rub detergent directly into the stain.

Always test for dye stability before soaking.

TIP: Train kids from an early age to deposit their dirty laundry in their own laundry bag. Hang it on the back of their bedroom door to save space and afford easy access so there can be no excuses. (Also works for grown-ups!)

Your Guide to Fabric Care Symbols

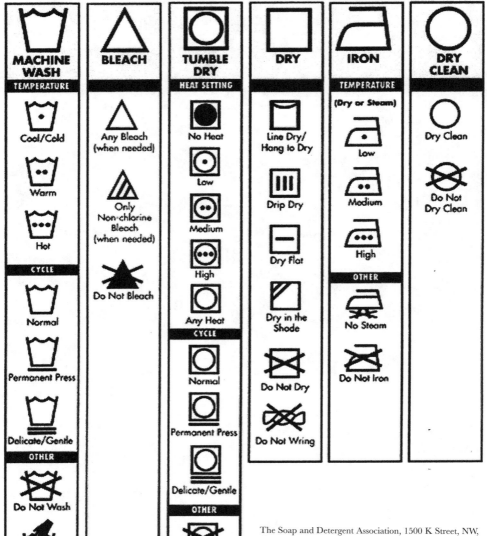

MACHINE WASH	BLEACH	TUMBLE DRY	DRY	IRON	DRY CLEAN
TEMPERATURE		**HEAT SETTING**		**TEMPERATURE** (Dry or Steam)	
Cool/Cold	Any Bleach (when needed)	No Heat	Line Dry/ Hang to Dry	Low	Dry Clean
Warm	Only Non-chlorine Bleach (when needed)	Low	Drip Dry	Medium	Do Not Dry Clean
Hot	Do Not Bleach	Medium	Dry Flat	High	
CYCLE		High	Dry in the Shade	**OTHER**	
Normal		Any Heat	Do Not Dry	No Steam	
Permanent Press		**CYCLE** Normal	Do Not Wring	Do Not Iron	
Delicate/Gentle		Permanent Press			
OTHER		Delicate/Gentle			
Do Not Wash		**OTHER**			
Hand Wash		Do Not Tumble Dry			

The Soap and Detergent Association, 1500 K Street, NW, Suite 300, Washington, DC 20005
www.cleaning101.com
Developed in cooperation with the Federal Trade Commission

TIP: Scratchy care labels can be cut out and sewn into a part of the garment where they won't irritate your skin, such as in a side seam. Or, take a photo of the garment and stick it in a notebook together with the label.

— DRY CLEANING —

Air dry-cleaned garments before hanging them in your closet to ensure all the toxic chemicals used in the dry-cleaning process have dissipated. If the smell lingers for a long time, change your dry cleaner.

— CHOOSING YOUR WASHING MACHINE —

The average washing machine offers more than 15 different cycles. A survey found that 26 percent of us use three cycles; 35 percent use two; and 23 percent only ever use one cycle. Bear this in mind when you're about to spend a fortune on a fancy machine dripping in bells and whistles. Maybe a more basic model would satisfy all your laundering needs.

— WASHING MACHINE CARE —

Don't overload the machine. Clothes need room to move freely or they will not wash properly. You should be able to put your hand into the drum amongst the garments and move it around. If you can't, remove some items.

After you've taken out a wash, leave the washing machine door open to let the interior dry out and prevent smells (be sure to keep small children away).

Wipe out the soap powder and fabric conditioner compartment regularly.

Wipe the rubber door gasket where water often collects in the folds. If left, the rubber will rot.

Check your manual, and if your machine has a filter, clean it on a regular basis. If you don't, it will clog.

— WHAT DETERGENT? —

Buying a laundry detergent used to be a simple affair: you picked the one that smelled the best. These days, there's such a bewildering range and the labels are so confusing,—where do you even begin?

• Biological detergent contains enzymes that break down food stains such as protein—milk, blood, egg—and so improves cleaning. It's the best "all around," and gets clothes cleanest.

• Non-biological detergent (often shortened to non-bio) does not contain enzymes so performance on stain removal is compromised, but non-bios are environmentally friendly. The ingredients are biodegradable so when the detergent is rinsed away down the drain, chemicals are broken down by microorganisms and don't pollute rivers, causing foaming. It's also a good choice if you have sensitive skin or allergies.

Detergents come in powder, liquid, and tablet form. Liquids are handy in cold washes as they dissolve easily. If you're using powder, dissolve it in a little hot water, then add the solution to the cold water.

TIP: To get your whites whiter and your colors brighter, choose a detergent containing fluorescers; they absorb ultraviolet light, which we can't see, and re-emit it as light, which we can.

— Other Washing Products —

- Powder for colors does not contain bleaching agents, so it protects colors, but this also makes it less effective at stain removal.

- Prewash detergent is useful for presoaking heavily soiled garments prior to machine- or hand-washing.

- Hand-wash detergent is specially formulated for hand-washing delicates.

- Fabric softener adds softness and fluffiness, reducing static after washing and making ironing easier. Available in liquid, sheet, and solid form. Do not use on towels or silk.

— Stain-Buster's Essential Kit —

"I poured spot remover on my dog. Now he's gone."
—Steven Wright

Clean white cotton cloth

Scraping utensil—blunt knife or spoon

Household ammonia (not for use on wool or silk)

Laundry borax—sold as powder or salt crystals, available from the pharmacy

Glycerin—available from the pharmacy

Eucalyptus oil

Household or laundry soap (not bath soap, but a pure block of soap especially for washing clothes)

Lemon

Denatured alcohol—colorless, available from the pharmacy

White wine vinegar (brown vinegar leaves brown stains)

Paint thinner

A variety of commercial prewash stain removers

TIP: Use only the recommended amount of detergent. Adding more will not get your laundry cleaner; it will make rinsing harder and clog up your washing machine.

— The Ten Commandments —

1. *Act fast!* The sooner a stain is treated, the greater your chances of successfully removing it.

2. *Clean up before you clean off.* Scoop up surface matter before you start the stain removal process. Scrape up excess using a blunt knife, or mop with kitchen towels or a sponge, which should not be colored or you risk transferring the dye to the stained item.

3. *Be gentle.* Vigorous rubbing will cause the stain to penetrate deeper.

4. *Blot, don't scrub.* Blotting draws the stain out of the fabric; scrubbing pushes it in.

5. *Test first.* Test your stain remover on an inconspicuous area of the garment first.

6. *Work from outside in.* Start at the edge of the stain and move to the center, moving from clean to dirty.

7. *Work from back to front.* If possible, work from the reverse of the fabric to push the stain out the way it came.

8. *Don't spread the stain.* Put a cloth under the stain, reverse side up, to prevent it affecting other parts of the item.

9. *Keep cool.* Don't use hot water or heat if you're not sure what the stain is.

10. *Be patient.* Don't expect instant miracles. Allow the cleaning solution time to take effect.

— Stain Removal for Washable Fabrics —

Stain removal is not an exact science. Despite what the miracle products claim and experts promise, no product is *guaranteed* to get red wine out of your white carpet. It might; but whether it will *for sure* depends on many factors, such as how long ago it happened, the weave of the carpet, the color and acidity of the wine, who trod the grapes—well, you catch my drift. For this reason, the remedies given here should be regarded as guidelines rather than cast-iron guarantees.

Araldite/epoxy resin
Try dabbing with denatured alcohol before the glue has hardened. Once it's set, I'm afraid you're stuck with it.

Baby food/formula
So, the airplane didn't hit the mouth? Scrape excess and rinse in cold water. Presoak in biological detergent for 30 minutes, then wash immediately.

Ballpoint pen
Dab with neat denatured alcohol on a cotton wool pad, then wash as normal. Or, rub the stain gently using a pencil eraser to fade the mark.

Beer and lager
To make the stain disappear quicker than your hangover, dab on a solution of white wine vinegar and warm water (1 part vinegar to 5 parts water), then rinse, and wash in a biological detergent.

DID YOU KNOW? The ballpoint pen was invented by Laszlo Biro in 1938.

Beetroot

Save your blushes, and flush the stain from the back of the fabric, with cold running water, then wash as normal. Folk remedy: rub the stain with a ripe pear.

Bird droppings

Scrape off what you can, dab on salty water, then wash in a biological detergent.

Blood

Do NOT use hot water as it will set the stain. If the stain is fresh, flush out under cold running water. If the stain has set, soak garment in cold, salty water (1–2 tablespoons salt to 1¾ pints water) for several hours. Rub the stain briskly. Rinse and wash in cold water. Wash as normal only after the stain has gone.

Bolognese sauce

Mamma mia! Loosen the stain by dabbing with equal parts glycerine and warm water solution, then wash in a biological detergent.

Butter

Rub with household soap, then wash in a biological detergent at the hottest temperature the fabric can stand.

Candle wax

Scrape off hardened wax with a blunt knife. Sandwich the stained area between two to three layers of kitchen towels and press with a warm, dry iron. Dab residual stain with a commercial prewash grease stain remover, then wash.

Chewing gum

Place the fabric in a plastic bag in the freezer to harden the gum. When set, scrape off gum. Remove residual gum with eucalyptus oil on cotton wool. Wash as normal.

Chocolate

Scrape off excess. Add a few drops of ammonia to warm, soapy water and sponge off. Rinse with cold water, before washing in a biological detergent.

Coffee and tea

Mop up as much as you can with paper towel. Wash as soon as possible in a biological detergent containing bleach.

Cooking oil or fat

Sprinkle talcum powder over the stain. Leave for 30 minutes, then brush off. Wash as normal.

Crayons and chalk

Wash in detergent. If the stain persists, try dabbing with denatured alcohol.

Curry

Wash the garment as soon as possible in a biological detergent containing bleach, as turmeric is a fabric dye. Or learn to love yellow.

Deodorant

Soak in denatured alcohol for an hour. If the stain persists, rub the stained area with household soap and water. Soak overnight in biological detergent and warm water. Wash as normal.

Egg

Sponge with cold, salty water. Rinse, then wash in a biological detergent.

Feces

Scrape off as much deposit as you can. Rinse under cold running water. Soak and wash in a biological detergent.

Foundation

Soak in a solution of ammonia (1 teaspoon household ammonia to 18 fl. oz. of warm water). Rinse well and wash as normal.

Fruit and fruit juices

Sprinkle salt over the stain, rinse in cold water, then wash in a biological detergent which contains bleach.

TIP: Never mix bleach and ammonia.

Dried-on stains: stretch the fabric over a basin and carefully pour very hot water from a height over the stains.

Grass stains
Dab with denatured alcohol, soak in cold water, then wash in biological detergent.

Gravy
Soak in a solution of biological detergent and cold water, then wash as normal.

Ice cream
Wipe off any residue, then soak in warm biological detergent. Launder in very hot water. When dry, remove any grease marks with commercial stain remover.

Ink
Dab with neat denatured alcohol on a cotton wool pad and wash as normal. NOTE: Don't use denatured alcohol on acetate or triacetate fabrics.

Ketchup
Rinse in cold water and soak in detergent.

Lipstick
Scrape off as much as you can, then apply a prewash commercial grease stain remover. Rub the stain with a clean white towel. Wash as normal.

Nail polish
That'll teach you, painting your nails with the bottle balanced on your knee. Blot up what you can of the Passionate Pink or Ruby Red, then, on the back of the fabric, behind the spot, dab a little acetone nail polish remover. (Don't do this on acetate or triacetate fabrics.) Wash as usual.

Oil
Soak stains in a cool washing solution with a biological detergent, then wash on highest temperature possible for the fabric.

Mildew and mold
Wash recent stains in a biological detergent.

Milk
Don't cry; rinse fresh stains in warm water, blot dry, then wash in biological detergent. Soak dried-on stains in biological detergent first.

Mud
Allow the mud to dry, brush off, soak in cool water, wash as normal. A folk remedy: rub dried-on mud with a raw potato.

Paints
Emulsion: Wash with cold water while still wet. If left to dry, a skin forms which is impossible to remove.
Gloss: Immediately apply paint thinner from the reverse of the fabric.

Perfume
Dab neat ammonia on the stain. Wash in liquid detergent.

Perspiration
Sponge underarm perspiration stain with white vinegar, rinse, then wash as usual.

Pollen
Dab gently with denatured alcohol on cotton wool pad, then sponge off with warm water.

PVA glue
Soak in cold water for 15 minutes, then hand-wash using soap flakes. Avoid detergent.

Red wine
For an immediate spillage, pour plenty of white wine over the stain. If left to dry, the red stain can turn to purple, so dry by dabbing gently with paper towels. Rinse with tepid water. Drunk all the white wine? Use mineral water—or tap water, if necessary. NOTE: Some experts recommend covering the stain in salt, which in many fabrics just sets it. Don't risk it.

TIP: Use ketchup to get rid of the tarnish on your copper pots and bring out the shine.

Rust

Douse stain with salt, then pour lemon juice over stain and salt, and put outside in the sun. A small mark should fade within a few hours; a heavier mark may take days. If not, wash in a biological detergent containing bleach.

Shoe polish

Dab the stain with liquid detergent and wash as soon as possible.

Superglue

If not yet bonded, soak in warm, soapy water, the longer the better. If it's dry, try the special de-bonding solvent made by the same manufacturers of the glue.

Tar

Loosen the stain with a few drops of eucalyptus oil or glycerine, apply neat liquid detergent, then wash as usual.

Urine/vomit

Rinse in cold water and wash as soon as possible. Soak dried stains in a biological detergent with warm water.

White wine

Soak with soda water, blot up the excess, then wash.

— For Stains on Dry-Clean-Only Fabric —
Remove excess and get thee to a dry-cleaner, pronto.

— HAND-WASHING —
Check the care label on the garment to determine the correct temperature for the water. Fill a sink or basin with the water and mix the gentle hand-wash detergent in well. Immerse the garment and let it soak for about 3 minutes. Swish the suds through the fabric, gently rubbing it against itself to shift stubborn stains. Rinse by dipping in fresh cold water until the water runs clear. For a fresh smell, add fabric softener or rose water to the final rinse.

— How Hot Is Hot? —
212°F boiling—like water straight out of the kettle

203°F—just off the boil

140°F—hotter than hands can stand

122°F—as hot as hands can bear

104°F—pleasantly warm

86°F—feels cool to the touch

DID YOU KNOW? Cashmere comes from the Kashmir goat, native to the Kashmir province of India.

— Drying —

Don't wring out the garment or you'll be left with a misshapen rag. Some fabrics, such as wool, can be given a short spin in the washing machine to remove excess water. If not, lay the garment out flat on a clean white towel, then roll it up like a Swiss roll so the towel blots up the moisture.

— What Not to Soak —
Silk, wool, leather, rubber.

— How to Wash Cashmere —

Hand-wash cashmere in cool water. Use mild soap flakes or a hand-wash product. Gently swirl the garment through the water. Roll in a towel to press out moisture. Give a quick shake to remove wrinkles, and lay flat to dry. Or press inside out with the iron on a cool setting.

For drying instructions, see "Flat drying," page 28.

— Laundry SOS —

Help! I washed a pair of pink socks and now my entire wash is pink.
Remove the rogue article, place affected garments back in the machine, and rewash immediately. If your clothes still bear traces of the dye, all you can do is bleach them, then dye them back to their original color.

Help! My white socks have turned gray.
To restore whiteness, boil in water and lemon juice.
Or wash by hand with plenty of bicarbonate of soda.

Help! My denim jeans are covered with streaky lines.
Washing jeans inside out will prevent this.

Help! My cashmere/wool sweater has shrunk.
Soak the sweater in a solution of $\frac{1}{4}$ cup hair conditioner to 1 gallon of cool water. Don't wring it out; roll in a towel, then dry flat.

Help! I washed my lingerie in the machine and it's come out misshapen.
I'm afraid there's little you can do. Don't put delicate lingerie into the machine.
Wash it by hand using mild detergent.

Help! How do I wash my swimsuit?
Rinse in cold water immediately after swimming in either a chlorinated pool or the sea, then dry immediately. Never leave in a plastic bag or it will be attacked by mildew. Some bathing suits can be washed (check the care label), but don't use fabric conditioner. Avoid tumble drying or wringing.

TIP: Like wool, cashmere is a favorite of the dreaded clothes moth.
Protect your garment with suitable repellents or store in a secure environment.

— DRYING —

The more efficiently you dry a garment, the less ironing it will need.
Now if *that's* not an incentive . . .

— LINE-DRYING —

What's the ideal way to dry most clothes? As Bob Dylan said, "The answer, my friend, is blowing in the wind, the answer is blowing in the wind." Line-drying makes clothes smell and feel fresher. It's also kinder to clothes because they aren't subjected to the constant pounding of the tumble dryer. Line-drying also saves electricity. Now, if only we could rely on the weather . . .

— *Getting the Hang of It: General Tips* —

Run a damp cloth along the line before use.

Fold a couple of inches of each garment over the line.
Hanging a garment from the line by its tips can damage the fabric and ruin the shape. Clip the strongest part of the article.

If the garment is worn on the top half of the body (e.g. shirt), hang it from the bottom.

If a garment is worn on the bottom half of the body (e.g. trousers), hang them from the top.

Turn colors inside out to prevent fading.

Hang pleated, nylon, and acrylic garments on a hanger.

Line-dry whites as sunlight bleaches them even whiter.

Dry wool and silk in the shade as direct sunlight weakens the fabric.

Don't dry nylon in the sun because it will turn yellow.

Put two knots in the clothesline a little way apart and put the prop in between them so that it can't slip.

Sheet: Fold in half lengthways, couple of inches over the line, and clip the two pairs of ends to the line. Clip halfway along one side and leave the other side open. This leaves an opening for the sheet to billow out like a sail catching the wind. Who'd have thought drying your laundry could be this lyrical?

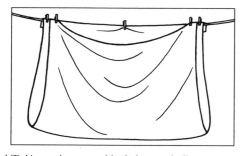

TIP: For fewest wrinkles, put dresses, shirts, and T-shirts on hangers and hook them on the line. Clip a clothespin to the hook to prevent the hanger blowing off.

Pillowcase: Fold a few inches of the open side over the line and clip either end, leaving one side to bag open to let the air inside, as for the sheet.

Shirt: Hang by the tail a few inches over the line and clip in the middle and corners. (If space on the line is limited, fold the front panels into the middle and hang as just described.)

Trousers: Fold the waistband a few inches over the line and clip at either end.

T-shirt: Fold a few inches over the line and clip from the bottom.

Dress: Straight—clip by the shoulders; full—clip by the hem.

Pleated skirt: Hang from the waistband. Clip clothespins to the bottom of each pleat to keep them
in place.

Towel: Give it a good shake so it will dry fluffy, fold a few inches over the line, and clip at each end.

Underwear: Fold the waistband a few inches over the line and clip at both ends.

Bra: Clip the end with the hook to the line.

Socks and tights: Clip by the toes.

Belt: Loop over the clothesline and fasten the buckle to avoid clip marks.

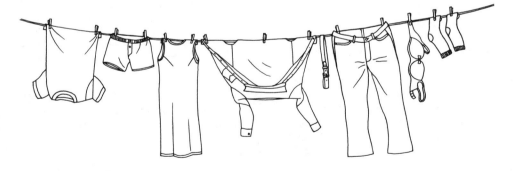

TIP: Give your clothespins a wash occasionally. There's nothing more frustrating than dirty marks on clean laundry. When clothespins start to rust or discolor, replace them.

GIVE IT A TRY: To line-dry a sweater, thread one leg of an old pair of tights through each arm and pull the waist of the tights through the neck of the sweater. Clip the tights rather than the sweater to the line, preventing stretching and peg marks.

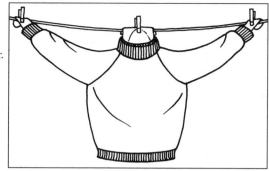

GIVE IT A TRY: During a severe frost, Victorian housemaids hung their just-laundered white linen on the clothesline and let Jack Frost work his magic. The theory was that overnight the freezing air would bleach fibers and by morning, the laundry would be sparkling white.

— FLAT DRYING —

Sometimes, after hand-washing, the weight of water left in a garment means that hanging it up would cause it to stretch. In such cases, the item should be flat dried.

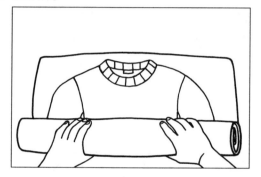

Don't wring out the garment. Roll it up like a Swiss roll, in a clean, white, dry towel on a flat surface, and press out excess moisture. Lay flat on a clean dry towel in a warm room or outside in the shade (the garment, not you). Dry away from direct heat, such as a radiator. Turn over from time to time.

— PILLING —

This is the name given to those fluffy little balls of wool that appear on knit or woven fabrics as a result of friction. I don't recommend using razors or scissors to cut them off—it's so easy to make a nick where you shouldn't. If there are just a few pills, pick them off, one by one.

If more, wind sticky tape around the back of your hand, sticky side out, and pat them off. This is also a good method for removing cat and dog hairs. You can also buy a battery-operated gadget to shave the pills off.

TIP: Hang velvet or silk garments in a steamy bathroom until creases drop out.

— TUMBLE DRYING DOS AND DON'TS —

Follow the care label on the garment and choose the correct heat setting.

Shake the garment to remove wrinkles before putting it in the dryer.

Don't overload the dryer.

Remove clothes promptly and fold or hang them.

Don't over-dry garments or they might shrink, and
bone-dry clothes are a nightmare to iron.

Don't dry white clothes with colors as they may bleed.

Don't tumble-dry wool, knit fabrics, rubber, or delicates.

— TUMBLE DRYER CARE —

"You know what I love? I love taking the lint out of the lint screen on the dryer."—Madonna

Who'd have thought a superstar would get a thrill out of such a mundane chore? Then again, it's probably the very ordinariness of the task that appeals to one for whom special treatment is the norm.

Whatever the reason, the Material Girl is doing the right thing. Lint—that soft, fluffy fuzz, builds up in your dryer over time, limiting airflow, increasing drying time—and your electricity bills. If the filter is not cleaned out regularly (i.e., after each use), it can have serious consequences. In America, each year, there are 15,000 clothes-dryer fires and 300 injuries. So, we'd all be wise to follow Madonna's example and love that lint.

TIP
*Recycle your lint! It makes ideal nest-building material for the birds, so put some outside for the birds.
If you're a camper, it also makes excellent kindling for fires.*

*DID YOU KNOW? Elizabethans laid their freshly laundered sheets over lavender or rosemary bushes
so they would dry infused with the bouquet of the herb.*

— IRONING —

You're either born with the ironing gene or you're not. For those who have it, ironing is a Zen-like experience, a ritual of deep contemplation bestowing serenity upon the spirit and giving free rein to the imagination. For those who don't, it's a pain in the neck. Whichever camp you fall into, follow these top tips to smooth your way to a wrinkle-free life.

— How To Iron —

Think of yourself as a cosmetic surgeon giving a facelift to an aging movie star. Place the patient, I mean, garment, on the operating table, I mean, ironing board. Slide the iron smoothly back and forth over the fabric, using slow, fluid movements in the direction of the thread. Don't apply any pressure—the weight of the iron will do the work. Move the garment away from you as you iron. By the end, your garment should be wrinkle-free and look 10 years younger. Oh, if only it were that easy for we humans!

Never leave an iron unattended when it is on.

Never rest the iron with the sole plate down; rest it on its heel.

— How To Press —

The words *ironing* and *pressing* are often used as if they have the same meaning, but they are actually two different techniques: ironing is about smoothing creases; pressing is more about flattening and restoring shape to garments, especially tailored clothes such as suits. NOTE: Woolens, knits, and delicate garments should be pressed, not ironed.

When pressing, the iron does not come into direct contact with the item you're pressing. You need a "pressing cloth." This can be anything so long as it's clean and colorfast—a man's cotton handkerchief, a cloth napkin, or a pillowcase would all be fine. Dampen before use.

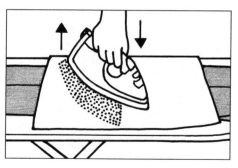

Place your damp pressing cloth on top of the garment. Press down lightly on the pressing cloth with a hot dry iron, then lift the iron and press down again in the next section. Don't glide the iron around the cloth. Just remember—lift and press, lift and press, until the cloth is dry.

TIP: Stuck somewhere without an iron? Place the garment flat under the mattress before you go to bed and by morning your body weight will have pressed it.

— STARCHING —

Starching adds crispness and body to collars, cuffs, napkins, and fabrics like cotton and linen, giving them a professionally laundered look. Starch is available in dry, liquid, and spray forms. Spray-on starch is easiest to use—and predictably, the most expensive. Apply to the right side of the fabric, before ironing.

— HOW TO MAKE SHORT WORK OF IRONING —

"I'm 18 years behind on my ironing. There's no use doing it now, it doesn't fit anyone I know." —Phyllis Diller

Catch clothes at the right stage for ironing and they'll iron twice as well and in half the time. Ideally, they should be slightly damp. Spritz dry items with water.

Iron clothes on the right side, except when you want to bring out the pattern of the fabric; e.g., embroidery is best ironed on the wrong side.

Iron hems from the wrong side of the garment.

Don't iron over zippers. Pull up the zipper, pressing its fabric flaps with the tip of the iron.

Calling all Rhinestone Cowboys! Place your sequin-studded shirt facedown on top of a thick towel. Your spangles will sink into the towel and you can iron safely over them.

Iron your tea towels! The heat from the iron will sterilize them.

Don't iron towels and other items with a pile too heavily or you'll press out all the fluffiness.

Fold large items like sheets and tablecloths double, and iron one side. Then fold in half again and iron the other two sides. This also works for smaller items like tea towels, napkins, and handkerchiefs.

Don't iron dirty clothes as the heat will simply set the stains.

After ironing, air clothes before putting them away or wearing them.

— HEAT SETTINGS —

• cool iron   acrylic, silk polyester, nylon, acetate

•• warm iron   polyester mixes, wool

••• hot iron   cotton, linen, denim

TIP: Recycle your old ironing board. It makes the ideal potting table in your garden.

— How to Iron the Perfect Shirt —

Order of ironing:
Collar
Yoke
Cuffs
Back
Sleeves
Front

REMEMBER: Start at the top and work down.

Put the shirt on a hanger immediately after washing and many of the worst creases will drop out, making it easier to iron. Iron the shirt while damp. Spritz a dry shirt with plenty of water from a plastic plant sprayer.

1. Start with the collar. Iron on the wrong side first, then the right side. Don't try to iron the collar in one long movement as this will create little puckers along the edge. Hold it taut and work from the tips of the collar toward the center, using little strokes. (figure 1)

2. Reposition the shirt over the narrow end of the ironing board to tackle the yoke (this is the fitted part of the shirt around the neck, shoulders, and chest). Iron on the wrong side, then the right side, finishing up with the shoulder seams. (figure 2)

3. Iron the cuffs, unbuttoned, the same way as the collar, wrong side then right side. (figure 3)

4. Iron the back of the shirt. If the shirt unbuttons all the way down, lay it flat on the board; if not, slide it over the narrow end of the ironing board and pull it tight. (figure 4)

5. Move on to the sleeves, front and back. Iron into the seams at the top of the arm and the gathers at the cuffs. (figure 5) A crease is optional: If you want a sharp crease, lay the sleeve flat on the board and ensure the shoulder seam is centered at the top. Give it a shot of steam if you like or a spritz of water and, starting at the top, glide the iron in one long movement to make a crisp crease from shoulder to cuff.

6. Iron the front panels of the shirt, wrong side then right side. Don't iron over the buttons on the right side as they could melt; just nose the iron carefully in and out between them. On the wrong side, the buttons can be ironed over, so long as you don't press too hard. (figure 6)

7. Give the collar a final smooth with the iron; after all, it's the most visible part of the shirt. Finally, fold down the collar with your hand and crease. Don't iron the crease.

8. Place the shirt on a hanger to air. Do up the top button to help maintain the shape.

TIP: Use the same technique for ironing blouses and dresses.

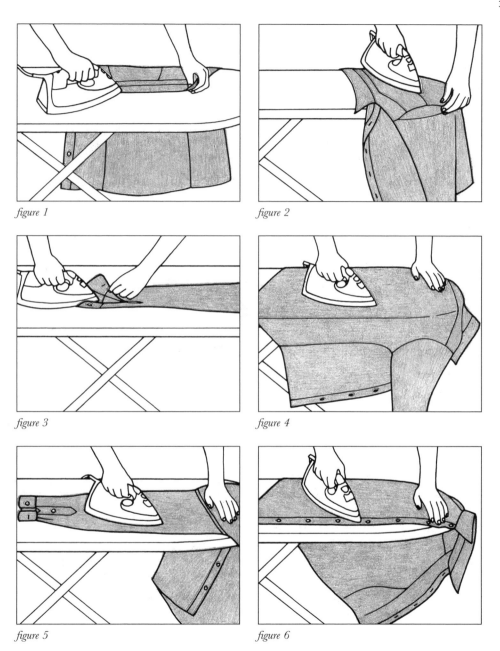

figure 1

figure 2

figure 3

figure 4

figure 5

figure 6

DID YOU KNOW? Ironing was the first use to which electricity was put in the home after lighting.

— How to Iron Trousers with a Center Crease —

"All the rudiments for success are to be found in ironing trousers." —Chris Eubank

1. Iron the pockets first. Then pull the trousers over the end of the ironing board and iron the top of the trousers.

2. Fold the trousers lengthways, so the legs are on top of each other, and the sides and seams are aligned. The seams should run down the middle and the creases should be at the outside edges. Fold back the top leg and iron the inside of the bottom leg.

3. Turn the trousers over and repeat on the other side. Finally, iron the outside of each leg. Place on a hanger.

NOTE: Don't put center creases into jeans.

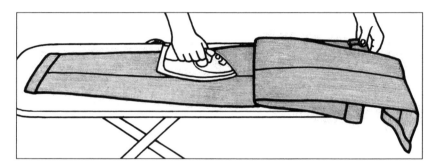

— How To Press A Pleated Skirt —

1. Keep pleats in place with bobby pins or paper clips slipped over the hem.

2. Press the entire garment, then remove the bobby pins and press the hem.

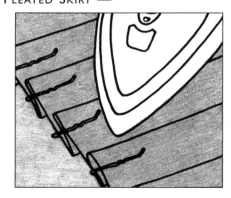

TIP: Give the crease in trousers a shot of steam as you iron and it will stay razor-sharp.

— HOW TO PRESS A TIE —

Press, don't iron. Check manufacturer's instructions.
Only press when absolutely necessary. Frequent pressing can cause it to lose its
sheen and the edges will be flattened. Minor creases are best removed by hanging
the tie in a steamy bathroom. If this doesn't do the trick, try this:

1. Take a piece of card and cut out a template the same shape as the tie
but a little smaller in size.

2. Slide the template inside the wide end of the tie. Press the tie.

This prevents the seam leaving an impression on the front of the tie.

— IRON CARE —

Use distilled water in a steam iron to prevent a buildup of deposits.

If you run out of distilled water, use water that has been boiled in a kettle.

Don't use tap water unless your iron has a special valve.

Never fill a steam iron while it is on.

If synthetic material melts on the sole plate, you need to act quickly.
Don't allow the iron to cool down because the mark will set.
Turn the iron up to hot and carefully clean off the bits of melted
material with a paper towel.

Gently rub a scratched sole plate with fine steel wool when the iron is cold.

Clean a nonstick sole plate with a sponge, warm water, and detergent.

Don't use anything abrasive as it will scratch.

Clean starch marks off the sole plate by rubbing them
with olive oil while the iron is warm.

— FOLDING —

"She's incredibly organized. She folds her underwear like origami." —Linda Barnes

Fold on a flat surface, such as a table or bed.
Preserve the natural folds at seams wherever possible.
Empty pockets of jackets, trousers, etc., and fasten zippers on trousers and skirts.

*TIP: Cheer up your ironing board with a wacky cover—a cow, a sunflower, or a pinup—whatever
you need as an incentive.*

— HOW TO FOLD A SHIRT —

If the shirt has buttons, button one at the top, middle, and bottom to keep the shirt in position while it's being folded.

1. Lay the shirt facedown on a flat surface. (figure 1)

2. Fold one side and one sleeve to the middle of the back of the shirt. (figure 2)

3. Fold the sleeve back on top of the fold. (figure 3)

4. Repeat steps 2 and 3 for the other side of the shirt. (figure 4)

5. Fold the tail (the bottom of the shirt) up just over the cuffs in order to keep them clean. (If the tail is not long enough, as is likely on women's shirts, omit this step.) (figure 5)

6. Fold the shirt over about a third of the way. (figure 6)

7. Make one more fold and turn the shirt over. (figure 7)

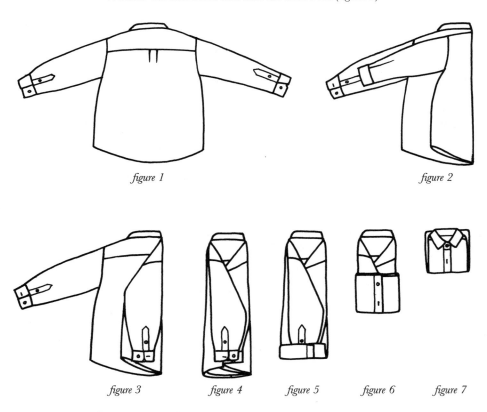

figure 1   figure 2

figure 3   figure 4   figure 5   figure 6   figure 7

TIP: Make another fold crossways if you need to save space in your closet.

— How to Fold Long-Sleeved Sweaters, T-Shirts, Blouses, Sweatshirts, Cardigans, And Casual Jackets —

Follow steps 1–4 of "How to fold a shirt" on page 36, then fold the garment in two, taking the bottom up to the top with the sleeves folded neatly between.

— How to Fold Trousers —

Align the inner and outer seams of the legs so the crease is at the front center of the legs. Fold in thirds.

— How to Fold Socks —

Sufferers from sock-separation syndrome, listen up!

1. Lay the socks flat, one on top of the other. (figure 1)

2. Beginning at the toe, roll them up nearly to the top. (figure 2)

3. Open the top of the outside sock and pull it over the roll. (figure 3)

4. You will finish up with a sock ball. Inseparable! (figure 4)

NOTE: Repeated use of this method can stretch the top of cotton socks so here's an alternative technique (admittedly, not quite so secure): Put the two socks together. Fold the top of one over the top of the other.

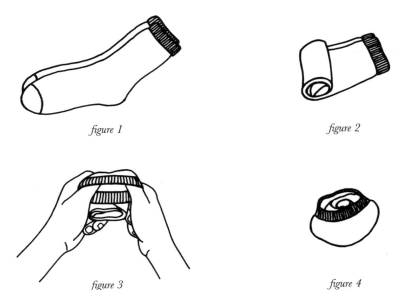

figure 1   *figure 2*

figure 3   *figure 4*

DID YOU KNOW? The reason why clothing stores fold sweaters is because they want us to unfold them. Subconsciously, we feel obliged to buy the item to overcome our embarrassment at not being able to refold it neatly.

— How to Fold a Flat Sheet —

With the right sides facing out, fold in half from top to bottom. Fold the sheet again so that the hems are in line. Fold the sheet crossways.

— How to Fold a Fitted Sheet —

This job is easier with two people. If you're folding solo, fold on a flat surface, such as the bed.

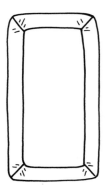

1. Neaten the corners on the sheet and ensure the elasticized ends are all facing inwards.

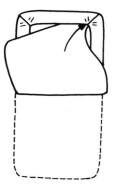

2. Fold the sheet in half from top to bottom so that the elasticized ends are together and the right sides are facing outwards. Tuck the top elasticized corners into the bottom elasticized corners so that each little seam of the contoured edge is in line.

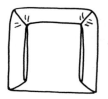

3. Arrange the corners and smooth all the edges with your hand so they lie flat. Pick up the sheet and put your hands in the elasticized corners. Give it a shake so the sheet falls into place.

TIP: Ideally, you'll have three sets of sheets for each bed: one on the bed, one in the wash, and one in the linen cupboard.

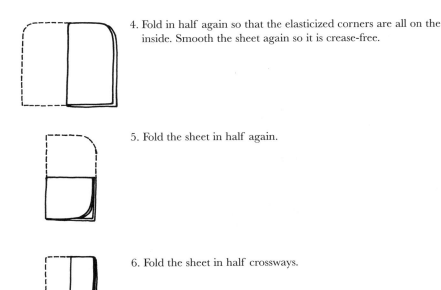

4. Fold in half again so that the elasticized corners are all on the inside. Smooth the sheet again so it is crease-free.

5. Fold the sheet in half again.

6. Fold the sheet in half crossways.

— STORING BED LINEN —

Store linen in sets (flat, fitted, and pillowcases) so when you're changing the bed, you can grab all at once.

— HOW TO FOLD A TOWEL —

1. Lay the towel out lengthways on a flat surface.

2. Take hold of the two ends nearest you (lengthways) and fold the towel lengthways just up to the center of the towel.

3. Take hold of the two ends furthest away from you (lengthways) and fold the towel in half lengthways back over itself. The towel will now be a third of its original length.

4. Take hold of the two ends (widthways) and fold into the middle.

5. Take hold of the other two ends (widthways) and fold into the middle to meet the other ends in the center.

6. Fold the towel over once more widthways.

You now have a towel with no unsightly ragged ends that is a cinch to stack and a credit to your linen cupboard.

TIP: It's recommended that you change your bed linen weekly.

— SEWING —

"If I find out the money on that horse was yours, Basil, you know what I'll do?"
"You'll have to sew 'em back on first."

—SYBIL AND BASIL FAWLTY, FAWLTY TOWERS

— SEWING KIT —

1. Magnet—
if you're a butterfingers
with pins and needles

2. Needle-threader

3. Sewing scissors

4. Thimble

5. Safety pins

6. Seam ripper

7. Tape measure

8. Assorted needles—needles are sized by
number, ranging from 1 to 24;
the higher the number, the finer the needle;
for general sewing use 7 or 8

9. Assorted hooks and eyes and snaps

10. Small, sharp scissors

11. Pins

12. Spare buttons

13. Sewing threads—variety of colors
and yarns

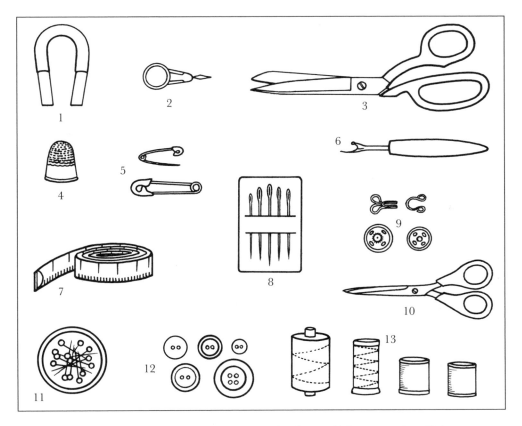

TIP: Fed up with mislaying your tape measure? Transform a table into a measuring table by applying double-sided tape to a tape measure and fixing it around the perimeter.

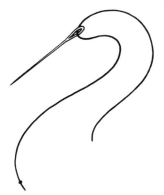

— HOW TO THREAD A NEEDLE —

Cut the thread at an angle with sharp scissors. Do not break it off, especially with your teeth, because the thread will fray and your dental bills will soar. Some people advise moistening the end of the thread with your tongue, but it's easier to lick the eye of the needle. Or you could spray the end of the thread with hair spray to stiffen it. You could also try holding a piece of white paper behind the eye of the needle.

— HOW TO DOUBLE-THREAD A NEEDLE —

Some sewing jobs call for extra strength, so you might need to double-thread the needle. Pull the thread right through the eye of the needle until it meets the other end of the thread, then tie a knot or two where both ends meet.

— HOW TO USE A NEEDLE-THREADER —

Do you have the eyesight of a bat during a power outage? A needle-threader's what you need.

1. Thread the needle-threader through the eye of the needle. (figure 1)
2. Pass the thread through the large eye of the needle-threader. (figure 2)
3. Pull the threader away from the needle, and, presto, your needle is threaded! (figure 3)

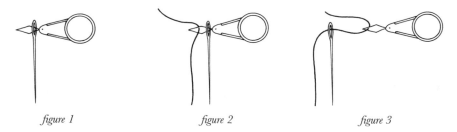

figure 1   *figure 2*   *figure 3*

*DID YOU KNOW? Victorians stuffed their pincushions with human hair.
The oil in the hair prevented the pins from rusting.*

— BASIC SEWING STITCHES —

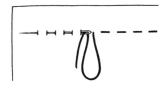

Running stitch
Use for delicate repairs.

Method: Use a single knotted thread, and work from right to left. Insert the needle in the underside of the fabric, then make small, even stitches about ⅛ inch long, by weaving the needle in and out of the fabric. Make two or three stitches before pulling the thread through.

Backstitch
Very strong, useful for repairs (e.g., zippers).

Method: Use a single knotted thread, and work from right to left. Insert the needle in the wrong side of the fabric and bring it up ⅛ inch further along the stitching line.
Then take the needle backwards to the point where the last stitch ended. Make another stitch and continue in the same way, making evenly spaced stitches.

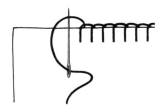

Blanket stitch
Use to edge heavy fabric (such as a blanket) and prevent fabric fraying.

Method: Sew this stitch with the edge of the fabric facing away from you. Insert the needle ⅛ inch from the edge. Bring it over the edge of the fabric and insert it ⅛ inch away from the last stitch, but before you pull the needle through, take it through the loop of its thread to form a chain edge.

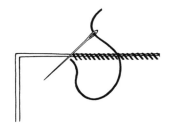

Whipstitch
Use to sew two edges together.

Method: Make small, slanting stitches very close together.

TIP: For most stitches, work from right to left.

— HOW TO SEW ON A BUTTON TO STAY PUT —

To ensure a button stays put when you sew it on, what it needs is a shank or a "neck."
A shank is simply a short stem of thread that is made as you sew the button on.

1. Select a thread to match either the thread color used on the other buttons, or the color of the button, or the color of your garment. General-purpose sewing thread should be fine most of the time; heavy-duty button thread is useful for coats and heavy items. Cut off about 24 inches. If you make your thread too long, it's likely to tangle.

2. Choose the right gauge needle for your fabric. A silk shirt will need a finer needle than say, a tweed coat.

3. Thread the needle. If the button is on a coat, you might want to double-thread it. (See page 42.)

4. Position the button on the garment, making sure it is aligned with the buttonhole. Now's the time to make the shank. Lay a matchstick, needle, or toothpick across the top of the button. This will create the slack necessary to make the shank.

5. Start sewing! From the wrong side of the fabric, push the needle up through one of the holes in the button. Pull the thread taut till the knotted end meets the fabric.

6. Bring the needle down through the hole beside it, and back through to the wrong side of the fabric.

7. Repeat steps 5 and 6, pushing the needle up and back through the material, going over the matchstick. (figure 1) For four-hole buttons, you can crisscross the thread to form an X on top of the button or you can go straight across to make two lines. Follow the same pattern as the other buttons on the garment.

8. When you've made between six and ten stitches, push the needle back between the fabric and the button. Remove the matchstick, pull the button taut, and wind the thread tightly around the slack thread three or four times to complete the shank.

9. Pass the needle back and forth through the shank several times to reinforce it. (figure 2)

10. Push the needle through to the wrong side of the fabric and finish up by making a small stitch, passing the needle through the loop and pulling tight. Repeat to anchor it really well. Or you can just cut the thread and tie a knot.

11. The finished button and shank. (figure 3)

NOTE: Some buttons are made with a shank. If there's a metal loop on the back of the button, there's no need to create a shank.

TIP: Apply a little clear nail polish to the threads of buttons on new garments and they're less likely to come off. To secure buttons on children's clothes, use dental floss as thread.

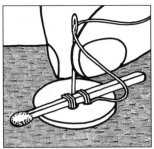

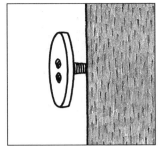

figure 1   *figure 2*   *figure 3*

GIVE IT A TRY: If you prick your finger while sewing a natural fabric like cotton or silk, and you get blood on the fabric, the best way to remove the stain is to dab on your own saliva. Note: Your saliva will only work on your own blood.

TIPS

If you lose a button on a conspicuous part of your garment and don't have one to match, remove a button from a less noticeable position and sew it in the spot that is more visible. Sew the button that doesn't match in its place.

New garments often come with an extra button. Sew the button on in an inconspicuous place on the garment, such as in the hem, and if you lose a button, a replacement will be right there. Just don't forget that you did so. That would be soooo annoying.

— SEWING ON A BUTTON IN A HURRY —

Buttons do have a habit of flying off at the most inopportune moments. You're just about to set out for the evening when—ping! Where'd the little devil go? Rolled right under the sofa, knowing your luck. But try not to panic. Retrieve the button and reach for your trusty sewing kit.

If you keep a needle pre-threaded in your sewing kit, you're already ahead of the game. If not, get it threaded.

Follow steps 1–7 of "How to sew on a button to stay put" on page 44, but omit the matchstick. Simply pass the needle back and forth through the material until the button feels secure, but don't make it so tight that you can't fasten the garment.

Push the needle through to the wrong side of the fabric and tie a knot.

Job done. Now, off you go and enjoy your evening—oops, don't forget to cut the thread!

TIP: You could sew only two holes of a four-hole button on at a time. Finish sewing two holes, tie a knot. Use a new thread to sew the other two holes. If one set of stitches comes loose, you have a backup set to keep it secure.

— HOW TO REPAIR A HEM —

Many of the fashion garments we buy today just aren't finished as well as we might have hoped. After only a couple of wearings, the hem's already hanging loose. Act now! You know what they say about a stitch in time . . .

1. Turn the garment inside out. Find where the stitching has come loose and start your repair about ½ inch before that.

2. Use a single knotted thread in a color that most closely matches that in the hem.

3. Insert the needle into the hem, below the seam, but only pierce through the folded inner edge of the fabric. Don't pass it through to the right side of the fabric. Pull the knot taut with the fabric.

4. Now, start hemming. The stitch to use is called the hemstitch, spookily enough. The idea is that you secure the hem so that no stitches are visible on the right side. Use the needle to catch up a thread of the main fabric. Any more and your stitch will show through on the right side. Then pick up a thread of the hem edge before pulling the needle through.

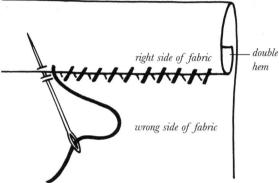

right side of fabric

double hem

wrong side of fabric

5. Continue hemming until you have gone about ½ inch beyond the end of the loose stitching. As you sew, don't pull the thread too tight or the material will pucker.

6. Finish up with another knot.

TIP FOR EMERGENCIES: If you are without your emergency sewing kit when your hem comes loose, use clear sticky tape to keep it up until you can sew it properly.

— HOW TO MEND A HOLE IN YOUR FAVORITE SWEATER —

Darning is a simple technique used for repairing small holes and thin patches so no one will ever know they were there. Use it for a hole in your favorite sweater or designer jeans. It's particularly useful if you buy secondhand or vintage clothes, as it means you can easily repair garments even though they may have a frayed area or thin patch.

TIP: The hemstitch is also a handy stitch to use for edging fabrics that fray.

— GENERAL DARNING TIPS —

Darn like with like: cotton with cotton, wool with wool, and match the thread as closely as you can to the original.

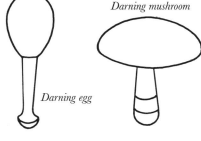

Darning mushroom

The hole will be easier to darn if the fabric is spread taut over a curved surface such as a darning mushroom or a darning egg (shown at right). In a pinch, you could use a lightbulb, but take care not to press too hard.

Darning egg

If you are using thick wool and finding it hard to thread the needle, fold the wool around the eye of the needle, pinch it together tightly, slip it off the needle, and thread the loop through the eye.

Use a proper darning needle with a round end so you won't damage any threads in the garment.

— DARNING TECHNIQUE —
Work on the wrong side of the fabric.

The darn should be bigger than the hole, so start by making a frame of small running stitches around the hole about 1 inch from the edge. This will strengthen the edges. Always make a circular darn because it puts the strain on fewer threads.

Darning is basically a weaving technique: Run the thread in and out of the material in a straight line and then back again, parallel with and close to the last line. Leave a small loop at the end of each row, so it has some give in it when the garment is worn. (figure 1)

When the hole is filled, "weave" across these stitches at right angles, using the same little running stitches. (figure 2) And that is that. Doesn't it make you feel like a big grown-up sewer?

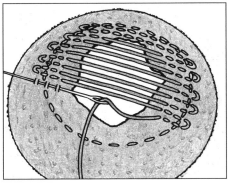

figure 1

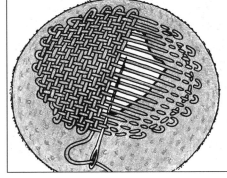

figure 2

TIP: If you're repairing the hem on a flimsy garment such as a silk skirt, sew a small coin into the hem to stop your skirt flying up in a high wind.

— ZIPPER REPAIRS —

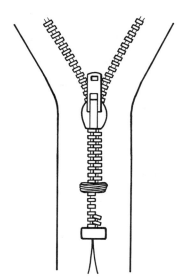

If one of the teeth breaks off at the bottom of the zipper, repair it above the break. Make several stitches horizontally over the teeth just above the gap. This makes a new stop, preventing the zipper from being pulled down any further than that.

To get a stuck zipper moving smoothly again, rub both sides of the teeth with the edge of a bar of soap or a candle. You can also use a pencil (preferably a No. 2), as the graphite in the lead acts as a lubricant.

If the lining of your jacket/skirt/garment gets stuck in the zipper, stop zipping. Gently ease the caught material away from the zip. Pull sideways, not up or down. Don't try to pull the zipper, or the jam will worsen.

DID YOU KNOW? When Swedish engineer, Gideon Sundback, designed the zipper fastener in 1914, it was used mainly as a fastener on boots and tobacco pouches. It took another 20 years to persuade the fashion industry of its benefits.

— PANTIES! HOW TO REPLACE ELASTIC —

If the elastic snaps in an elasticized waistband (e.g., panties, pyjamas), don't panic—here's what to do.

1. Open up just as much seam as you need to in order to pull out the old elastic.

2. Cut the new elastic to size, less 1¼ inches.

3. Attach a small safety pin to one end of the elastic and push it through the opening.

4. Pin a large safety pin to the other end of the elastic so you don't pull it through by mistake.

5. Overlap the two ends of the elastic and stitch them together.

6. Finish by stitching the seam you opened back into place.

TIP: To avoid jams, align the two rows of teeth in a zipper as closely as possible before you start to zip.

— NO-SEW PATCHING —

Glue-on fabric patches are not just for kids' jeans. A patch is a quick and easy fix for a small tear in your own jeans, shirt, or even a sheet.

1. Trim the edges of the hole so they're not ragged.

2. Cut the patch about 1 inch bigger than the hole.

3. Turn the garment inside out. Put a piece of plastic under the hole so you don't get glue on the right side. Apply glue carefully around the hole.

4. Glue the patch in the same way.

5. After about 15 minutes, when the glue is tacky, stick the patch onto the hole.

— TIGHT SPOT —

To stop a ladder from running, dab clear nail polish at the top of the run. If none is available, use the edge of a bar of soap.

To extend the life of tights or stockings, rinse them in water when you first buy them, then put them in a plastic bag and freeze them for 24 hours. Remove and dry.

TIP: When moving, wrap crockery inside old clean tights to avoid those hard-to-clean newsprint marks.

— CLEANING —

"If your house is really a mess and a stranger comes to the door, greet them with, 'Who could have done this? We have no enemies.'"

—PHYLLIS DILLER

— CLEANING KIT —

Vacuum cleaner

Broom: soft broom for wood, tiles, and vinyl; hard broom for concrete.

Sponge mop: one with a sponge that you can wring out is best.

Dustpan and brush

Rubber gloves

Dusters: undyed if possible. If they're colored, wash them first to remove the dye. Old T-shirts are excellent so long as they are lint-free.

Chamois leather: for glass and windows

Feather duster

Squeegee (rubber blade on a handle for cleaning windows)

Scrubbing brush

Clean soft cloths

Old toothbrushes: for crevice work

Scouring pads

Lavatory brush: one for each toilet

Buckets: rectangular buckets are easier to use with mops.

— RUBBER GLOVE TIPS —

Buy a size larger than you need.

Buy several pairs—keep one in the kitchen and one in the bathroom.

Sprinkle talcum powder in your rubber gloves before you put them on.

If you have a problem getting your gloves off, run your hands under cold water.

Turn them inside out to dry.

Clean your cleaning equipment after each use.

DID YOU KNOW? American Susan Hibbard invented the feather duster in 1876. She had to fight her husband in the patent court when he tried to claim the invention as his own.

— CLEANING PRODUCTS —

Dishwashing liquid

Furniture polish

Household ammonia

Commercial nonabrasive cleaner—for cleaning floors and work surfaces

Commercial abrasive cleaner—usually a cream, for ceramic sinks and baths

Bleach—the thicker the better.
Bleach makes things white but isn't a cleaner per se; use very sparingly.

Borax—a mild bleach in granule form

Rubbing alcohol (isopropyl alcohol)

Denatured alcohol

Turpentine

Paint thinner

Commercial metal cleaners—cream or liquid

WARNING: Never mix bleach and ammonia as the chemical reaction releases toxic gases.

Keep a supply of cleaning equipment upstairs and down so you're not constantly running up and downstairs—unless you want to turn cleaning into your keep-fit session.
Or carry a supply around with you in a holdall.

— CLEANING GREEN —

Traditional cleaning methods and natural cleaning products are enjoying a resurgence of popularity. Deservedly so, for they are kinder, safer, cheaper, and sometimes more effective than commercial products, even if you do often have to make repeated applications to remove a stain.
Lemon is wonderful because it not only cleans well but smells fresh too.
Vinegar also works well on stains, but if you're worried it will make your house smell, there are a few tips to prevent this.

TIP: Store brushes upside down to keep the bristles from bending (and to save space).
To make a simple hanger: nail two wooden dowel rods to a wall and hang the head of the brush on it.

Ensure the room is well ventilated. Open the windows during and after use.

Rinse off the vinegar thoroughly after use.

Add a few drops of essential oil to the vinegar and water solution
(unless you're cleaning an item of kitchen equipment like the inside of a kettle).
Choose a fresh-smelling oil such as lemon, lime, vanilla, peppermint, or pine.

— CLEAN-GREEN PRODUCTS —

Bicarbonate of soda (also known as baking soda and sodium bicarbonate)

Salt

Lemon juice

Washing soda crystals

White vinegar

Often, there's no substitute for hot, soapy water and elbow grease.

— VACUUM CLEANERS —

"I got the wife implants for Christmas. She didn't want 'em. She wanted a Dyson."
—*Roger Kavanagh, The Royle Family*

A vacuum cleaner with a high wattage doesn't necessarily mean better cleaning power.
How much dust a vacuum picks up also depends less on the power of the motor than
on airflow. Look for the suction power rating (given in air watts) as a guide to efficiency.

ALLERGY SUFFERERS

A good option is a vacuum with a HEPA (high-efficiency particulate air) or ULPA (ultra-low-penetration air) filter. These filter smaller particles than traditional vacuum cleaner filters.

BAG OR BAGLESS?

Bagless saves on buying replacement bags and trying to remember where you stored the spares.
The downside is you have to empty the dust container.

*TIP: Greenpeace's website has details of brands of cleaners it considers most harmful.
Visit the site on www.greenpeace.org.*

— VACUUM CLEANER ATTACHMENTS —

Do you recall those peculiar-shaped brushes, nozzles, and swivelly things that came with your vacuum cleaner when you bought it? You know, the ones you pushed to the back of the cupboard never to be thought of again. Weird they may be, but the right nozzle attached to your vacuum cleaner vastly improves performance, saving you time, effort, and backache. Who wouldn't want that?

CREVICE TOOL

Angled to reach the parts other tools cannot reach, like carpet edges, stair treads, skirting boards, nooks and crannies. Sucks creepy crawlies without contact. And zaps house-dust mites in mattresses. Also cleans refrigerator grilles.

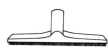

UPHOLSTERY NOZZLE

Cleans soft surfaces like sofas, cushions, curtains, and mattresses.

DUSTING BRUSH

The circular swivel action cleans picture rails, dado rails, banisters and carved wood, tops of doors. Also good for cobwebs, lampshades, curtains, floorboards, curved and carved surfaces.

SMOOTH FLOOR BRUSH

Two rows of bristles shine up hardwood floors, tile, stone, or linoleum, but not carpets.

COMBINATION FLOOR TOOL

This straight suction tool can be adjusted to smooth flooring or carpeted surfaces simply by flicking the switch on it.

RADIATOR NOZZLE

Usually fits onto the end of the crevice tool. Does what it says on the tin, but can also be used to dust narrow shelves and crannies.

TIP: Place a ball of cotton wool doused in a favorite perfume or aromatic oil in your vacuum cleaner bag and it will scent your room as you clean.

How to find a lost contact lens/earring/screw, etc.: Cut the foot from a pair of tights (ensure there are no holes) and fix it onto the vacuum hose with an elastic band. When you turn on the vacuum cleaner, the missing item will be sucked against the tights so you can remove it.

How to unclog a blocked vacuum hose: If suction is weak, the most likely cause is a blockage in the vacuum hose. To remove, straighten a wire coat hanger and use the "hook" to free up the obstruction.

If your vacuum is the kind that blows as well as sucks, switch to blow and that might do the trick.

— VACUUMING TIPS —

Before vacuuming, pick up loose hairs by blotting them up wearing a damp rubber glove or wrapping a strip of wide sticky tape around your palm. This will prevent hairs becoming tangled in the roller or hose.

Never use the vacuum to try to pick up lighted cigarette ends, hot cinders, or sharp objects such as pins.

Tape a small bag to the vacuum cleaner so you can pick up larger items such as bobby pins as you are vacuuming.

On carpets and rugs, use a gentle action, moving in the direction of the pile. Perfectionists will be delighted to know that the professionals recommend you go over each area of carpet at least 8 times.

GIVE IT A TRY: In Scandinavia, snow is often used to clean rugs and carpets. They are laid outside on a winter's day, and covered with snow. This is then brushed off, taking with it the dust and dirt. It adds a whole new meaning to the phrase "carpet of snow."

— ORDER IN WHICH TO CLEAN THE HOUSE —

Start at the top of the house and work your way down (i.e., bedrooms, bathroom, landing, stairs and hall, family room, kitchen).

Start at the top of a room and work down to the bottom i.e. ceilings, walls, floors.

Start at the front of a room and work your way to the back.

Clean wet before dry (e.g., wash windows before dusting and sweeping the room).

Dust or polish furniture from the top down.

Vacuum last of all.

TIP: Never vacuum when the hamster's loose.

— Cleaning Tips —

Secure ornaments in place with Blu-Tack if you're inclined to be over-zealous with the duster.

Give yourself plenty of coffee breaks in between cleaning rooms. Play your favorite music or listen to the radio. Show tunes always put a spring in your step.

— How to Cut Down Cleaning Time —

Don't try to clean the entire house in one go. Concentrate on one room and give it a thorough going-over.

Put a sturdy doormat outside every external door.

Do as the Japanese do, and take off your shoes before entering the house. Keep sets of indoor and outdoor shoes.

Designate one room as your dining room and do all your eating in there.

Share the cleaning chores with the rest of the family. Choose your favorite—or least unfavorite!

Put a large wastebasket in every room and empty it regularly.

Air rooms daily by throwing open the windows.

Make a list to suit your personal schedule of cleaning tasks to be done daily, weekly, monthly, occasionally, and annually.

— CLEANING WOOD —

Dust before you polish. Get right into any nooks with a soft toothbrush.

— Waxed Wood —

Silicone and aerosol products are best avoided because they don't allow the wood to breathe. Why not try making your own polish?

HOW TO MAKE BEESWAX FURNITURE POLISH
2 oz. beeswax
5 fl. oz. turpentine

Coarsely grate the beeswax into a bowl and add the turpentine. Melt the mixture gently over a saucepan of warm water. Take care because turpentine is flammable. Remove from the heat and pour the mixture into a screw-top jar. Put on the lid and shake until well mixed. Allow to cool. The finished polish should be the consistency of double cream.

TIP: Beeswax smells lovely, but if you want a different scent,
add a few drops of an essential oil such as lavender or lemon to the mixture in the jar just before it hardens.

TO USE: Put a tiny amount on a cloth and rub well into the wood, using plenty of elbow grease. Buff with a clean soft cloth to prevent sticky residue.

NOTE: Polishing wood once or twice a year is enough.

Water rings on wood
White rings on waxed furniture should be treated as soon as possible: Apply a small amount of white toothpaste on a clean cloth and rub the stain in the direction of the grain. Prevention is better than cure: use coasters and placemats!

Wooden and laminate floors
Sweep and vacuum regularly; clean with a well-wrung-out mop. Avoid excess water on the wood. Never use abrasive detergents.

Grease spots on wooden floors
Apply ice cubes to harden, then carefully scrape off with a blunt knife.

Heel marks on wooden floors
Rub with a pencil eraser.

Painted / distressed wood
Treat as if they are painted walls, not wood. Dust, then wipe over with a solution of dishwashing liquid.

— A–Z OF CLEANING —

Acrylic plastic
Clean with metal polish or a solution of dishwashing liquid.

Alabaster
Never wash alabaster as it is porous. Use a solution of dishwashing liquid on a clean cloth. Don't put fresh flower arrangements in an alabaster vase as the water will leach into the alabaster and leak. Save it for dried arrangements.

Baking tins
That rarity—the less you wash them, the better they are! Wipe with a paper towel.

Bath
Plastic—clean with automatic dishwasher liquid on a cloth.

Acrylic—clean with dishwashing liquid, especially if you have used bubble bath, as this leaves a film on the surface.

Fiberglass—don't use harsh abrasive cleaners or metal polish, as you could rub off the color. Clean with dishwashing liquid.

TIP: When cleaning wood, clean with the grain, not against it. If the grain is horizontal, dust horizontally. If it's vertical, dust vertically.

Enameled—use only products suitable for enamels. Avoid abrasives. Clean heavy stains with "paint thinner or turpentine".

Bath mats and shower mats (plastic)

Scrub with a brush and solution of dishwashing liquid. Rinse thoroughly. Hang bath mats and shower mats on a trouser hanger to allow both sides to dry. Candlewick bath mat: treat according to label. Don't tumble-dry or the backing will melt.

Binoculars/telescope

Dust the outside of the lens with a lint-free cloth. Dust the lens itself with a specialist lens-cleaning fluid available from photography shops.

Books

Take one book at a time, blow off the dust, dust along the top of the book with a soft cloth, keeping the book closed so that dust doesn't fall between the pages. For a water spillage, act quickly: Blot up as much as possible with a paper towel then dry with a hair dryer to prevent the paper from buckling.

Bookshelves

Use the crevice tool of the vacuum cleaner to clean along shelves and between books. To treat bookworm: Clean the shelves using an insecticide spray.

Camera

Best tackled by an expert. Take it to a photography shop.

Candlestick

Silver or metal—carefully chip off dried wax. Pour hot water over to melt the wax.
Wooden or plastic—use a hair dryer to melt wax.

CDs

Use a special cleaning pack from CD stores. Store them in their cases when not in use.

Ceiling or desk fan

The blades are notorious dust collectors. Dust with a feather duster to get right between those blades. Keep a cover on your desk fan when not in use.

Chandelier

If it's a priceless family heirloom, leave it to the experts. If not, use a stepladder to clean each piece with a dry chamois. Or, turn off the electricity, remove glass lusters one by one, and wash in a solution of dishwashing liquid, drain on a lint-free cloth, then buff with a chamois leather.

Coins

Dip them in fizzy cola for a few moments (see the effect it has; now think what it's doing to your teeth . . .).

Computer

See "Computer care" on page 236.

TIP: A traditional remedy for cleaning dirt off books is to rub them with breadcrumbs.

Crayon on walls
Rub with ammonia or toothpaste on a clean cloth.

Decanter
Rinse as soon as possible after use to prevent staining.

Earphones/headphones
Clean with a cloth dampened with rubbing alcohol.

Flowers (dried and artificial)
Dust with a hair dryer on a low setting near an open window.

Freezer
Exterior—Use a solution of dishwashing liquid. *Interior*—Use neat bicarbonate of soda on a damp cloth.

Glasses (spectacles)
Use one of those special cloths from the opticians. (Many opticians will also clean your specs for free using an autosonic system.) Greasy marks can be removed with denatured alcohol.

Glass-top table
Use a commercial window cleaner.
CLEAN GREEN: Rub with lemon juice and dry with a paper towel. Polish with newspaper.

Hat (straw)
Brush off dust. If it's dirty, scrub with lemon juice and let dry in the sun.

Houseplants
Need to be kept clean to breathe. Dust shiny-leaved plants with a soft cloth, then sponge with tepid water. Large plants can be put in the bath and given a very gentle shower with lukewarm water.

Iron
See Iron care on page 35.

Ivory
Never immerse in water as it may crack. Dust with a soft cloth.

Kettle
In hard-water areas, mineral deposits will fur up the element and slow down the heating, costing you more. Remove furry deposits using a commercial descaler.
CLEAN GREEN
Method 1: Fill the kettle with equal amounts of water and white vinegar. Boil, switch off, and let cool. Rinse thoroughly with clean water. Boil the kettle several times to eradicate any vinegary smell.

TIP: The safest place to keep your hat is on your head.

Method 2: Dissolve a denture tablet in water and leave for 12 hours.
Place a clean marble in the bottom of the kettle to prevent the buildup of lime scale.

Lampshade

Up to 30 percent of light can be lost through dusty shades. If your lightbulb is also dusty, that's nearly half the light you're losing. Blow off the dust using a hair dryer on a low setting, or use the vacuum upholstery attachment.

Leather

Furniture—Dust frequently. Clean with a barely damp cloth. Protect with a stainproofing product suitable for leather (check with the manufacturer of the furniture and test it on a small area first).

Black—Touch up scuffs on shoes or handbags by brushing on Indian ink, then polishing with shoe polish.

Handbags—Follow instructions for "How to polish leather shoes" page 203. Ensure all polish is removed so that it doesn't transfer to your clothes.

Patent—Rub with white vinegar on a clean cloth.

Lightbulb

A dusty lightbulb robs you of at least 20 percent of light—light that you're paying for. Switch off the light and remove the bulb. Allow it to cool, then run a barely damp cloth over the glass. Dry carefully and thoroughly with a soft cloth. Clean fluorescent light tubes the same way.

Locks

Don't be overzealous with the polish or you could gum up the lock. If the key sticks, insert a sharp lead pencil into the keyhole; the graphite will ease the mechanism.

Marble

Wipe with a cloth using water and mild detergent. Don't soak it. Wipe dry and polish with a soft cloth.

Microwave

Interior—Wipe up spills immediately with a damp cloth. Clean the walls with a damp cloth. Remove the glass shelf and wash in hot, soapy water. Don't forget to clean the inside of the door too. *Exterior*—Use a cream cleaner.
CLEAN GREEN: Place an uncovered bowl of water and lemon juice in the microwave and heat on high for three minutes; the condensation will loosen any dirt so you can wipe it away with a paper towel.

Mirror

Use a commercial glass cleaner or rubbing alcohol on a lint-free cloth. Never use water to clean a mirror as it can get between the glass and the silvering and cause staining.
CLEAN GREEN: Use a solution of two tablespoons of white vinegar to $\frac{1}{2}$ cup water on a lint-free cloth.

TIP: Give an old lampshade a new look by putting a different-colored bulb inside.

Ornaments

Dust can be blown off robust knickknacks with a hair dryer on a low setting. Clean with a paste mix of powdered whiting (no, not the fish, but a chalk available from art shops) and warm water. Rub on with a soft cloth, wash in warm, soapy water, then rinse and dry.

Oven

Clean according to manufacturer's instructions. Wipe with a damp cloth after cooking and mop up any spills immediately. Line the bottom with a sheet of aluminum foil to catch spills and dispose of when necessary.

Paintings

If it's precious to you, don't even risk a once-over with a soft cloth. Take it to a professional.

Piano

Dust the ivory keys, then wipe gently with a chamois leather wrung out in a solution of warm water with a teeny amount of white vinegar. NEVER let water seep through between the keys. The black keys should just be dusted.

Plasma screen

Wipe gently with a wrung-out damp soft cloth. Avoid abrasive cleaners as they can damage the glass.

Plastic container

To prevent stains like tomato, coat the inside with a protective thin layer of vegetable oil before placing the food inside. Try using a pastry brush.

Playing cards

If sticky marks on your plastic-coated cards are ruining your poker game, clean them off with a baby wipe or fabric conditioner sheet.

Plugs (rubber)

Clean with turpentine or paint thinner.

Radiator (behind)

Use the radiator nozzle on your vacuum cleaner or improvise with a duster tied onto a wire coat hanger.

Refrigerator

Exterior—Wipe with a damp cloth and warm, soapy water. *Interior*—When turned off and empty, wash the interior walls and shelves with warm, soapy water. Clean crumbs and dust in the seals on the door with a clean, soft toothbrush. Take care not to damage the seal.

Shower curtain (mildew)

Remove from the rod and soak in a solution of bleach (one part bleach to four parts water). Rinse thoroughly, then machine-wash. If just the bottom is soiled, leave the curtain on the rod and hang it in a bucket of water with a few squirts of bleach. To prevent mildew: After

TIP: Keep the piano lid open on sunny days to prevent keys yellowing.

showering, pull the curtain all the way along the rod to dry so damp doesn't hang inside it. CLEAN GREEN: Scrub the shower curtain with a paste of lemon juice mixed with bicarbonate of soda.

Sink

Stainless steel—Clean with a dab of white vinegar on a cloth. Never use abrasive cleaners on stainless steel sinks. To get rid of rust marks, rub with lighter fluid.

Ceramic—Whiten by laying a paper towel over the bottom of the sink and soaking with bleach. Leave for half an hour and rinse off.

Stove

Wipe off spills with commercial cleaner. Clean with a damp cloth after each use. Wash the grill pan by hand or in the dishwasher. Line the tray with aluminum foil each time you cook, then dispose of it, and you'll keep the grill pan clean. Follow manufacturer's instructions for ceramic or halogen cooktops.

Telephone

Dust with a small brush. Use a cotton bud dipped in a mild detergent to clean into the nooks and crannies but don't let any liquid fall inside.

Television screen

Clean with window cleaner or a tiny amount of dishwashing liquid on a dampened a paper towel, then dry with more paper towels. Antistatic wipes also do the job. Never spray the screen itself as you can't control where the particles fly and they might find their way into the inner workings. Clean the remote control with baby wipes. Do not get the remote control wet.

Tiles (ceramic)

Use commercial tile cleaner. CLEAN GREEN: rub with a solution of white vinegar (one part vinegar to four parts water), rinse and dry. Clean grubby grouting with an old toothbrush dipped in a solution of bleach (one part bleach to four parts water). Dust with the dusting brush attachment on the vacuum.

Toaster

Follow manufacturer's instructions. Never try to remove crumbs with a knife even when the toaster is switched off.

Toilet

See "How to clean the toilet" on page 196.

Tray

Trays are notorious germ carriers. Dirt accumulates in the corners. On plastic, use a damp cloth and detergent. With antique trays, seek professional advice.

Umbrella

That dank smell you get when you open an umbrella comes from not drying it properly.

TIP: Soak a new or newly cleaned shower curtain in salted water for a few hours, then allow to dry before rehanging. This will protect against mildew.

Stand a wet umbrella on its side, fully opened in a warm room but not close to a fire. The covering can be cleaned with dishwashing liquid on a clean cloth.

Vase

See "How to clean a glass vase" on page 254.

Venetian blinds

Notorious as dust gatherers, but they're no problem if you slip an oven glove on your hand, dip it in a solution of 1 tsp. ammonia per 2 pints water, and run it along the slats.

Wastebaskets (household)

Empty as soon as they smell and clean weekly with a solution of bleach. Never put rubbish directly into the bin, line with a plastic bag. Recycle plastic supermarket bags for small wastebaskets.

Wicker, Cane, and Bamboo

Remove dust using the upholstery attachment on your vacuum.

Windows

See "How to clean windows perfectly" below.

— HOW TO CLEAN WINDOWS PERFECTLY —

Cleaning kit
Squeegee—a rubber blade on a handle
Soft, cotton cloth
Chamois leather

Cleaning solution
$\frac{1}{2}$ cup white vinegar
$\frac{1}{2}$ cup household ammonia
$8\frac{1}{2}$ pints hot water

1. Clean the dirt from around the window frame before you clean the window.

2. Clean any dirt or dust on the window with a soft cloth or vacuum.

3. Use a sponge to apply the cleaning mixture all over the glass.

4. Drag the squeegee just once down the entire window from top to bottom. Wipe the rubber blade on a clean cloth and drag it down again, starting from a dry spot. Don't go over the same spot as this is what causes streaks. Repeat over the entire window.

5. Buff up with a chamois leather.

TIP: To help the squeegee glide down the window, add a little dishwashing liquid to the cleaning solution.
TIP: Choose a dull day to clean windows as sunlight dries them too rapidly, leaving streaks.

CLEAN GREEN: Mix a solution of one part white vinegar and nine parts water in a plant sprayer. Apply to windows with a clean cloth. Dry with another lint-free cloth. For added sparkle, buff with crumpled newspaper. The ink adds shine to your windows. NOTE: If you use tabloids, wear a pair of rubber gloves as the ink will rub off on your hands.

— HOW TO REMOVE STICKY LABELS . . . —

. . . From china and glass
Immerse item in warm water and leave to soak, ensuring the label is covered.
The label should disintegrate, but if any sticky residue remains, dry the item and rub with methylated spirit or furniture polish on a dry cloth.

. . . From fabric
Place aluminum foil over the label and iron it with the iron on warm to soften the glue.
Peel off while the label is still warm. Alternatively, use a commercial stain remover for glue.

. . . From plastic containers
Soak in hot water and label should peel off.

. . . From metal
Rub with nail polish remover on a cloth.

. . . From walls
Peel off the label parallel to the wall, then remove any residue with a ball of Blu-Tack.

All-purpose label remover
Peel off as much as you can of the top paper layer of the label. Saturate with spray lubricant (WD-40), let it soak in for a few seconds, then wipe off with a paper towel.

— HOW TO CLEAN METALS —

Metals need to be cleaned regularly or many will tarnish—that's when gases and moisture in the air react with the surface of the metal. Metals like copper and brass will stain and form a greenish residue called verdigris.

— GENERAL TIPS —

Keep items well dusted and they'll need less cleaning.

Tarnishing is caused by humidity and temperature, so keep metals in dry conditions.

Don't overpolish. Rub the hallmark too hard and it could wear off, devaluing the piece.
Often the charm of antique pieces lies in the patina of age they have acquired.

Don't use commercial cleaners on any other metal than the one specified (i.e., don't use silver cleaner to polish gold unless the instructions say you can).

TIP: A traditional remedy to clean pewter is to rub with a cabbage leaf dipped in cigarette ash.

Wear cotton gloves when cleaning, as the acid on your hands can tarnish the metal.

Don't leave polish on the object you are cleaning as this encourages it to tarnish.

HOW TO POLISH: Polish is usually applied with a clean soft cloth. Work it into the metal in little circular movements, round and round, all over the object. The metal is then buffed; that is, brought to a shine using a clean soft cloth in a back-and-forth movement.

THE GOLDEN RULE: If your item is precious, don't risk any cleaning yourself. Take it to an expert.

— LACQUERING —

Metals like brass, copper, and bronze can be lacquered to help them keep their shine and prevent tarnish. To apply, clean the metal and apply two coats of transparent metal lacquer with a brush. Lacquer is also available in spray form. Clean a lacquered piece by simply wiping with a soft cloth.

— Metals —

TARNISH	DON'T TARNISH
Silver	Gold
Brass	Bronze
Copper	Chrome
Iron	Platinum
	Pewter
	Aluminum
	Stainless steel

— CLEANING SILVER —

Polish silver at the first sign of tarnishing.

Use a commercial silver polish and work it into the silver.

Wash silver dishes and cutlery as soon as possible after use, as certain foods—such as salt, fish, eggs, and broccoli—cause tarnishing.

Never wash silver and stainless steel cutlery together in a dishwasher, as the silver could transfer to the steel.

Treat silver plate as if it were solid silver, but take even greater care as the coating could come off.

Never polish silver gilt or the gold may rub off. Keep well dusted instead.

TIP: Silver benefits from handling so if you use your silver it will only need the occasional dip in very hot water and dishwashing liquid.

Once clean, wrap the silver item in acid-free tissue paper and special tarnish-proof bags (available from jewelers). Don't wrap silver in plastic bags or plastic wraps as this will cause condensation, leading to tarnishing.

CLEAN GREEN: To clean a lot of silver cutlery (except silver-plated) together, lay aluminum foil, shiny side up, at the bottom of a plastic washing-up bowl, and lay the cutlery on top. Pour over enough boiling water to cover the cutlery, and add one of the following: 3 tablespoons of baking soda or, a tablespoon of Calgon water softener. Allow the cutlery to soak for 15 minutes, turning them over from time to time.
Rinse in hot water and buff.

— CLEANING OTHER METALS —
GOLD
Wash in warm, soapy water or dishwashing liquid solution.
Rinse and dry, then buff with a chamois leather to bring out the shine.
Low-carat gold: Use silver polish.

PLATINUM
Clean with detergent, or a solution of soap and water, then pat dry.

CHROME
Wipe marks with dishwashing liquid on a damp soft cloth.

CLEAN GREEN: Use white vinegar on a soft cloth, then dry thoroughly.
Avoid abrasive cleaners such as salt, which will scratch the plating.
Polish taps with cider apple vinegar on a cloth.

STAINLESS STEEL
Wash in hot soapy water and dry immediately, or the salts in the water will stain it.
Do not use silver polish on stainless steel.

CLEAN GREEN: Shine up a stainless steel pan using flour on a clean cloth.
Remove marks with lemon juice on a cloth.

BRASS
Polish with a commercial brass cleaner for a high shine.
Don't polish the inside of a brass saucepan with polish, as it could contaminate it.

CLEAN GREEN: For minor stains, clean with a paste made from lemon juice and salt, then rinse off. For bad staining, a non-precious piece can be boiled in a solution of 2 cups water, 1 tablespoon salt, 1 tablespoon white vinegar.

TIP: Steer well clear of the knight in shining armor. He'll only want you to polish it.

COPPER

When copper tarnishes it develops a green coating called verdigris.
To remove: Put on rubber gloves and rub with a solution of household ammonia
and salt, then rinse and dry. Commercial verdigris cleaner may also be used.

CLEAN GREEN: Rub tarnish with half a lemon dipped in salt. Rinse and dry.

PEWTER

Pewter should have a mellow sheen, not a high shine, so it doesn't need polishing
like, say, silver; indeed, antique pewter can lose its value if polished to a high shine.
But in damp conditions, pewter forms a gray coating called a "hume."
Clean with commercial pewter polish or wash in soapy water and buff.

CLEAN GREEN: Rub the surface with raw cabbage leaves. Rinse and dry well.

BRONZE

Bronze should not be washed; dust with a soft cloth. Use turpentine or paraffin
on a soft cloth to remove any stubborn marks. Remove any verdigris with a toothbrush.
Never use abrasives as they will damage the surface.
Have antique bronzes cleaned professionally.

LEAD

Scrub with paint thinner or turpentine.

CLEAN GREEN: For a very dirty object: Place in a solution of one part white
vinegar to nine parts water, with a pinch of bicarbonate of soda. Rinse in distilled water.

IRON

To remove rust, rub with wire wool dipped in paraffin.
Clean the surface with paint thinner.

CAST IRON

Wash and dry a cast-iron pan, then rub with vegetable oil to "season" it.

WROUGHT IRON

Dust off the dirt. Clean with dishwashing liquid on a soft cloth.
Remove rust with a solution of water and white vinegar.

TIP: Pewter absorbs smells, so beware polishing the inside of your favorite drinking goblet!

— HOUSEHOLD PEST CONTROL —

Sharing your home with a bunch of little critters that carry disease, destroy your belongings, aren't house-trained, eat garbage, and don't pay a cent in rent can be extremely aggravating. Unfortunately, you're stuck with your kids. Not so those other little nuisances that take up board and residence uninvited. Identify and evict your unwanted guests—before they take up squatters' rights.

Pest	The Lowdown	Controls
ANTS	Most ants are harmless and can even be beneficial, preying on fleas, silverfish, etc. If they enter the house, they're probably in search of food, the sweeter the better.	Sprinkle peppermint, cloves, or curry powder around points of entry. Destroy nest with boiling water. Place feet of picnic table in bowls of water.
BEES	Attracted by bright colors and flowery fragrances, so avoid Christian Lacroix and Chanel No. 5.	Never swat a bee. They emit an alarm signal that brings out reinforcements. Lure a bee out of the house by offering up a long-stemmed flower. When the bee lands on the flower, take it outside.
BOOK LICE	Love Shakespeare, Dickens or, more accurately, the glue that binds old books. Thrive in damp conditions.	Put infested books in freezer bags and store in freezer 3–4 days. Keep book-storage areas ventilated. The leaves of the herb costmary used as a bookmark work so well that it's nicknamed Bible Leaf.
CLOTHES MOTHS	The larvae, not the moths, wreak havoc on woolens, furs, and other natural fabrics. Telltale signs are ragged holes in garments.	Put mothballs in the pockets of at-risk garments. To make sweeter-smelling repellent: Fill clean nylon stockings with dried lavender, bay leaves, or cedar chips. Hang in closets and tuck in drawers between clothes.
COCKROACHES	Carry diseases like food poisoning. Lurk in damp, dark areas, e.g., under sinks, behind fridges. Eat anything from pet food to photographic film. It's said that a cockroach can survive 6 months on the glue on the back of a postage stamp.	Dust hiding places with boric acid (but keep away from children and pets). A kinder method is to place a bowl of cheap wine under the sink. After a tipple, roaches tipple drunkenly in and drown. Salted herrings in their path also work.
DUST MITES	Bedding, towels, carpets, and stuffed toys are all havens. Feed on dead skin. Dust mite allergens are believed to be a factor in asthma and eczema.	Use mattress protector. Wash bedding at 140°F. Tumble dry soft toys on hot for 20 minutes to kill mites. Vacuuming can aggravate allergies, so choose a cleaner with good filtering system.

Pest	The Lowdown	Controls
FLEAS	Feed on blood; can cause tapeworm. Animal fleas will bite humans. Flea pupa live in carpets and crevices and can lie dormant for months until disturbed by vibrations of a living being.	Treat pets with flea powder. Destroy infested bedding. Fumigate a place you're moving into that has had animals living there.
HOUSEFLIES	Carry more than 100 different diseases. Attracted by animal feces, food, and garbage. Lay eggs in bins, rubbish heaps, and decaying matter.	Cover all food. Spray inside bins with insecticide and keep lids on. Keep a pot of basil on your windowsill. Zap a fly with firm-hold hair spray, which stiffens its wings (works on any flying insect).
MICE	Carry food poisoning. Their bladders have no sphincter so they're urinating all the time; their front teeth never stop growing so they gnaw constantly. Can squeeze through a gap the size of a pen.	Plug cracks and crevices with steel wool or metal scouring pad. Bait traps with fruit and nut chocolate or peanut butter. Plug-in sonic devices are good. But most effective of all: get a cat.
MOSQUITOES	Feed on human blood; attracted by body odor. Partial to people who eat sugar. Breed in stagnant water.	Eat less sugar! Clean out areas of standing water, e.g., gutters, birdbaths. Repellents include citronella and camomile. Air-conditioning or electric fans also work. If bitten, soap or hemorrhoid cream relieve itching.
SILVERFISH	Wingless, fast-moving creatures with silver scales; favor warm areas with high humidity, e.g., bathrooms. Also damage books.	Eliminate condensation, leaks, and rising damp. Trap insects by laying double-sided tape where they run (works for other small, crawling pests). Lay down slices of lemon in their hiding places.
SPIDERS	Hide in dark nooks. Most house spiders are helpful, not harmful; they eat disease carriers like flies and mosquitoes. Make friends with a spider! He may eat that bug that was going to sting you!	Invert a glass over the spider, slide a piece of card underneath, and carry outside. Phobics, if you must, suck him up with a vacuum cleaner. Rub soap on windowsills, plugholes, and spouts—spiders hate the smell.
WASPS	Love sugary substances, which is why they're often found trying to share your cola drink. Other attractions include ripe fruit, honey, and jam.	Cover food and drinks. If a wasp lands on you, keep still and it will fly off. Never swat a wasp (see under "Bees"). Make a trap by putting a little diluted jam in a jar. Wasps' nest? Call in the professionals.

– INTERIOR DESIGN –

*"I'm no interior decorator, but I just have a feeling that plastic plants in
the bathroom . . . not a good idea."*

—KYAN DOUGLAS

— CREATING A FABULOUS ROOM —

Despite what those inferior desecrators would have us believe, there's really no mystery to creating fabulous rooms. It's simply a question of tying together elements of color, style, pattern, and texture into a harmonious design. This is best done by breaking the process down into simple steps . . .

Finding inspiration: To kick-start the creative process, you need a hook on which you can hang your design scheme. Your inspiration could come from anywhere—a favorite painting, a piece of furniture, a bedspread, or a found object, such as a shell or even a wrapper. It could be as large as a sofa or as small as a bottle. It might even be a place you love—Provence . . . Paris . . . Peoria—any place or any thing that evokes a mood and resonates with you to get those creative juices flowing.

Make a moodboard: Interior designers wouldn't dream of decorating a room without first making a moodboard. It couldn't be easier to make and it's worthwhile because it firms up all the ideas that are whizzing around in your head . . .

1. Taking your cue from whatever inspired you, start gathering any images and samples that chime with it in terms of color, style, texture, and pattern. Tear pictures out of magazines, find paint and fabric samples, anything that helps you translate your look into these key elements: color, furniture, fabric, flooring, lighting, and accessories.

2. Fix all your images onto a piece of thick card or pin them to a memo board. The swatches should be roughly in the proportions they will occupy in the room, so, for example, the flooring swatch will be larger than the lighting swatch.

3. Prop the board up in the room you're decorating and leave it there for a few days so you can view it under natural and artificial lights. Play around with the swatches, adding to and rejecting images, until you find a combination you're happy with.

Planning the layout: A scale plan of your room will help you visualize how features and furniture work together so you can create the best layout. No need for architect's plans; you can draw your own simple plan. Here's how:

1. Measure the area of the room and mark the outline on a large sheet of graph paper.

2. Next, measure the position of objects and features in the room including doors, windows, fireplace, radiators, light switches, and built-in cupboards. Sketch these on your plan.

3. On a separate sheet of graph paper, draw scale-model templates of your sofa, table, chairs, TV, etc. Glue them onto cards and cut them out.

4. Arrange the furniture shapes in various positions around the room. Place large items such as sofa or bed first, as there are likely to be fewer places these will fit and other furniture will have to fit around them. Play around with the plan until you find a combination you are happy with.

TIP: Take advantage of the free design advice often offered by paint and wallpaper companies.

— INTERIOR DESIGN: GENERAL TIPS —

Plan ahead to avoid costly mistakes.
Set a budget and add an extra 15 percent for those inevitable unexpected extras.

Think about the sort of atmosphere you want to create—
warm and welcoming for a living area, calm and relaxing for a bedroom . . .

Consider the way a room will be used and how the design
will work with other spaces in the house.

Think about the direction the room faces.
A north-facing room that never sees the sun, needs warm colors;
a south-facing room can tolerate cooler colors.

Work with existing features in the room.
If there is a Victorian fireplace and picture rail,
don't impose a modernist all-chrome look on the room. It will jar.

Identify any problems to be overcome, e.g., too dark, too small.

Identify the best features to be highlighted.

Design your room to suit your lifestyle.
Is that white carpet a practical choice with three kids under five?

Don't follow fashion fads. Nothing dates like fashion.
Choose a timeless look, incorporating smaller statement pieces to keep right up-to-date.

Steer clear of wacky designs and garish colors if you're planning on moving soon.

Don't forget comfort in the design equation.
What's the use of a stylish sofa so uncomfortable no one wants to sit on it!

Don't overlook the finishing touches like cushions, vases, linen, etc.
Every detail counts to create that final impact.

Pay attention to dull yet practical concerns like storage, heating systems, boilers, etc..

GIVE IT A TRY: Hire an interior designer. Not all of them want to put a Buddha on the sideboard and a concert-sized harp in the corner.

IF YOU REMEMBER JUST ONE THING:
The simpler you keep your design, the more striking and successful it's likely to be.

DID YOU KNOW? There's a cushion in Windsor Castle embroidered with the motto, "A man's home is his castle . . . until the Queen arrives."

— Color —

Don't buy your color from a paint chart. Buy a small sample pot (better still, two) and paint up a piece of card at least 12 inches square. Display it in the room.

— Tone —

Striking the right tonal balance in a room is vital. Pale colors make a room seem larger; dark colors make a room look smaller. Tone dramatically changes our sense of a space and, artfully used, can disguise a whole range of design flaws in a room.

Now you have the overall picture and know that all your chosen elements tie in together, you can start decorating with confidence.

— FLOOR COVERINGS —

Floor covering occupies more space than any other design element in the home and is likely to be your greatest expense, but it is often overlooked in the grand design scheme of things. Because it's underfoot, there's a sense that it's not that important. In fact, floor coverings should be the first thing you think about when planning a room, before wallcoverings, paint, and furniture. Not only because it is the most expensive item, but also because it's easier to match fabrics to flooring than vice versa.

— Choosing a Floor Covering: General Tips —

Think about the purpose of the room; e.g., in a bathroom you need something that will cope with a soaking but also be kind to bare feet.

Is the room a main route through the house? If so, choose a low-maintenance covering that will tolerate traffic without showing all the dirt.

To give a feeling of continuity and an illusion of space, use the same carpet (in a neutral tone) throughout the house.

In a multipurpose room, define the space by using a different floor treatment; e.g., in a living/dining room, the sitting area could be carpeted, and the dining area could be hardwood.

Color: Light colors give a feeling of space, but is it practical for your lifestyle?

Texture: Choose something that will give a good grip on smooth floors.

Pattern is practical, good at disguising wear and tear, but can make the room look smaller.

Are you planning on moving anytime soon? Many carpets are hard to get up once laid.

Choose foam-backed carpet if you want to change it often, and keep up with trends.

TIP: Always get a large sample of floor covering to try in your own home.

Budget for underlayment. A good quality carpet can be ruined by a cheap underlayment. A good quality underlayment will prolong the life of a carpet and improve a carpet's heat- and sound-insulating properties.

Do you really need a new covering? That dirty carpet may be concealing a beautiful hardwood floor. Some carpets can be dyed. Floors can be painted.

— FLOOR COVERING CHOICES —

Vinyl
Bright, cheerful, practical, but tears easily.

Rubber
Wears well, absorbs noise, good choice of colors and patterns.

Natural fibers
Grasses and other natural materials add texture but not much softness.
Sisal, coir (made from coconuts), rush—rough texture holds pet hair.

Woods and laminates
Stylish and practical but can also be draughty, noisy,
and don't always react well to moisture in kitchens and bathrooms.
Scratch marks can be difficult to repair. You can now buy laminate flooring that
has underlayment specifically designed to reduce the amount of sound produced
when someone is walking around, or drops something on it.

Linoleum
More durable than vinyl but not as easy to lay. Will break if mishandled.
Not waterproof. Tiles are easier to handle.

Ceramic tiles
Tough and long-lasting, practical solution for "wet" areas like bathrooms and
kitchens, but can be cold on bare feet! Ensure the subfloor is
moisture-proof before laying.

— CHOOSING CARPET —

Carpet has been out of fashion for a while but there are signs it's on the way back. Not surprising, really, because for comfort and warmth, it's hard to beat.

Carpets can be natural fibers or synthetic, or a combination of both. They are either woven, tufted, or bonded. Most carpets sold today are synthetic. Many are treated with stain repellent, which can be a boon if you're accident-prone but a health hazard if you suffer from allergies, as the chemicals used can be quite toxic. Wool carpets are the most durable, lustrous, and static-resistant. They're also the most expensive.

*TIP: Carpets stretch over time. If yours has developed unsightly bumps and bulges,
call your carpet fitter to restretch it.*

Checking the quality of a carpet: The denser the weave, the better the carpet will wear. Hold the carpet sample faceup and bend it around your wrist. The less backing you see, the better. Now test for durability: Press your hand on the pile and see how long it takes to bounce back into shape—the faster the better.

— Measuring for Carpet —

ROOM: Measure the length and width of the room at its longest and widest points and allow some extra where the carpet passes underneath the door to the threshold strip.

STAIRS: Use a piece of string to measure the length.

— The Subfloor —

To lay a carpet on an unprepared surface is as fatal as putting up wallpaper on an unprepared wall. Ensure the subfloor is dry, level, and bump-free before laying floor covering.

— RUGS —

A nest needs feathers to give a warm and welcoming atmosphere.
Rugs are the ideal way to soften hard floors and create the perfect comfort zone.
If you're wondering about the difference between carpets and rugs,
well, the two terms are pretty much interchangeable, although some experts
use *rug* to refer to anything 4 feet by 6 feet or less,
and *carpet* for anything larger than that.

Rugs are versatile and decorative. Choose bold ethnic rugs such as kilims and durries,
or modern synthetic.

Rugs look good in both traditional and contemporary settings.

Lay a rug on top of a carpet for added luxury. In a multifunctional room,
a rug can define the space, e.g., the sitting or dining area.

A luxurious shag rug beside your bed might just be enough to tempt you
out of bed on a cold morning . . . sink your toes into those soft, warm tufts; how soft
does that feel? Wait a sec, that's no rug—that's Fluffy! *Meowwwwwwww.*

TIP: To level an uneven concrete subfloor: Use a ready-mixed self-leveling compound or screed, about ⅛ inch thick.

— How to Buy an Antique Oriental Rug from an Armenian Rug Salesman —

Baffled in the bazaar? Stymied in the souk? Here's how to get the best deal with your salesman—let's call him Ali . . .

"Handmade!" Check the reverse of the rug: the design should be clearly visible on the back as well as the front. Part the pile. If you see loops rather than knots, it's machine-made.

"Finest craftsmanship!" How fine are the knots used to attach the warp and weft? The more knots per square inch, the finer the rug.

"Best quality material!" Rugs are usually wool or cotton. Top-quality wool is fine, soft, and has a unique luster. Poor-quality wool is coarse and has no shine.

"Natural dyes!" Color speaks volumes about the quality of a rug: rich, deep reds and subtle blues indicate natural vegetable and insect dyes; chemical dyes are brash and the color range is much wider. The rug should have developed an attractive patina with age.

"Border control!" Check that the borders are intact and that the rug has not been cut and repaired.

Great, you've made your choice. That was the easy part. Now comes the negotiation over the price. Time to haggle . . .

Even if you badly want the rug, don't show your interest. Keep a poker face. Ali will know you're sold on it and be unlikely to reduce the price.

Unless you're very confident in your bargaining skills, don't be the first person to make an offer. Ask Ali the price of the rug. If he says 100, offer 25, and settle for 50.

If Ali insists you make the first offer, suggest a low price to start but not so low that it's an insult. Never suggest a price you're not willing to pay.

Always be polite. Uttering a phrase or two of the vendor's language, no matter how faltering, will dispose him more favorably toward you.

On expensive purchases, it's customary to offer the purchaser tea: accept graciously.

Over tea, chat about everything but the rug. Don't try to rush the sale. Try to build a rapport with Ali. Think of it as a love affair. A brief encounter. And do drink the tea; it's considered rude not to.

If Ali's final price is still more than you're willing to pay, thank him, bid him good-bye, and start to walk away deliberately but slowly. Ali will more than likely catch you up and accept your lower offer. If he doesn't, don't fret, it's nothing personal; this romance wasn't meant to be, and you'll probably find the same rug a couple of stalls down—or at Pier 1 when you get home. At half the price.

DID YOU KNOW? Cleopatra, Queen of Egypt, had herself rolled in a carpet, which was then unfurled in front of Julius Caesar. Her dramatic entrance captivated the Roman emperor.

— Caring for Carpets and Rugs —

Use nonslip rug underlayment or special tape to secure a rug to a polished floor, or it's a banana-skin routine waiting to happen.

Protect your carpet by placing castors under heavy furniture.

If the pile of your wool carpet has been flattened by a heavy piece of furniture, put an ice cube on the dent, let it melt, and allow to dry before vacuuming.

New carpets should not be vacuumed for a month after they are laid so that the pile has time to bed down.

Vacuum carpets and rugs at least once a week. Have them professionally cleaned maybe once every year. Don't do it too often, as shampooing and steam-cleaning can cause them to shrink.

— PAINTING WITH LIGHT —

Lighting literally alters the way we see things. Think about how light is used in the theater, where the look of the stage can be transformed in an instant. Light can be used creatively in the home too. Think of light as paint for defining shape and building mood and atmosphere.

— LIGHTING TYPES —

Just as there are specific paints for the job, so there are different types of lighting:

Natural light
Daylight entering through a window.

General lighting (aka ambient or background)
Used for the general illumination and visibility in a living space,
usually provided by a ceiling light and wall lights.

Task lighting (aka local)
Used to focus light in a particular space for a specific job such as reading, cooking, or sewing.

Accent lighting (aka display / directional lighting)
Used to highlight certain features or objects in a room, such as a painting.

Decorative lighting
Includes oil lamps, fairy lights—anything that adds visual interest and atmosphere.

A well-lit house uses a combination of all of these.

DID YOU KNOW? According to a survey, home buyers rank dark houses one of the biggest turnoffs.

— MAKING THE MOST OF NATURAL LIGHT —

You don't have to be Turner to appreciate the glories of natural light, though we do tend to take it for granted. A bright, airy room with plenty of natural light will look larger than a dim room with little natural light. Here are some simple measures to make the most of the natural light in your home . . .

Paint walls white or pale colors that reflect light.

Remove heavy curtains and valances and replace with sheer fabrics such as voile, which diffuses light.

Prune back trees and shrubs that might be hanging over windows and obscuring the light.

Place mirrors directly opposite windows to reflect the light back into a room.

Don't place furniture in front of windows.

Replace interior doors with clear or stained glass.

Use metallic wallpaper or shiny surfaces to reflect light.

Install a skylight.

— LIGHTING SPECIFIC ROOMS —

Plan your lighting early in your design scheme so power points and switches can be installed before decorating. Assess the room in daylight and at night.

Hallway

There's nothing worse than a dingy hallway, so make it cheerful and welcoming with general lighting. A central pendant light will make a hall look narrower, so go for sconces to create a warmer tone. Put your main overhead light at the top of the stairs to illuminate your path upstairs. Recessed spotlights above each stair will not only provide illumination but also an original decorative feature.

Living room

You'll need a combination of general, task, and decorative lighting.

In interior design circles, the humble central pendant light is frowned upon. It's a relic from the Victorian days of oil lamps and gives a bland, flat effect, casting shadows in the room. But if you fit a dimmer switch you can control the intensity of the light, and with a suitable shade, it can be a good source of light. Lamps can be scattered strategically around the room for a more intimate, homier atmosphere.

TIP: Sometimes letting in the light can be as simple as cleaning the windows!

In a multipurpose room, such as a living/dining room, fit a couple of different lighting circuits. This enables you to keep one area in darkness when not in use.

Kitchen

Bright task lighting is needed for food preparation and cooking. Position them so that you're not standing in your own shadow when you're at the sink, stove, or counter. Downlighters or strip lighting under wall cupboards direct light onto a work surface. In the ceiling, recessed lights, track lights, or spotlights work well.

Bedroom

General, task, and decorative lighting can all play a role here. You'll need a table lamp or clip-on spotlight to read by. Make sure the switch is accessible from the bed; there's nothing worse than having to get out of bed to switch off the light! Ceiling lights can be recessed spots or a pendant light. Fairy lights are not just for Christmas: Highlight specific areas of the room, such as around the headboard, with twinkling lights for a warm and cosy glow, perfect to lull you off to dreamland.

Bathroom

Task lighting is essential: an eye-level mirror surrounded by low-wattage lights (like the kind you see in theater dressing rooms) will give shadow-free light ideal for applying makeup or for shaving. Overhead, recessed lights are a better choice than a pendant light or fluorescent strip that might be affected by the humid atmosphere.

Lighting plants

With a few strategically placed lights you can create a dramatic living sculpture. Check that the plant will not be adversely affected by having a bright light shone on it at night. Use low-wattage bulbs or the heat might scorch the leaves. For a large palm, place an uplighter on the floor behind the plant. For smaller plants, buy battery-powered fairy lights and wind them around the stems.

— KNOW YOUR BULBS —

Tungsten or incandescent: regular household bulb.
Comes in a variety of shapes, sizes, and brightnesses (wattages), from 8 to 200 watts.
A clear bulb gives a cold, harsh light and a white bulb is more diffused. A bulb with
a silver coating on the glass gives a narrow beam of light.
Average life span is about 1,000 hours.

Tungsten halogen: produce a very bright, pure, white light.
Unflattering on human skin but useful in the kitchen and home office or in spotlights.
Also effective to light a painting or design feature.
Gives out a lot of heat, so use only in suitable fixtures.
More expensive than incandescent bulbs but last up to three times as long.

Fluorescent tubes: light can be cool or warm according to the coating on the glass.
Cost more than ordinary bulbs but last longer and use less electricity.

Energy-saving: lighting accounts for 10 percent of the average electricity bill.
There are big savings to be made simply by switching to energy-saving bulbs.
They are more expensive than ordinary bulbs but last up to six years and save electricity.
A 20W energy-saving bulb is equivalent to an ordinary 100W bulb.
Use in the light fittings that get the most use, e.g., in the living room.

— WINDOW TREATMENTS —

"If it wasn't for Venetian blinds, it would be curtains for all of us."
—Anonymous

When we come home after a long day at work and draw the curtains, we are shutting out the world and making ourselves feel safe, cocooned in our own private space. When we wake the next morning and throw back the curtains, we are welcoming the world anew. Curtains and blinds are both our shields and security blankets. Most of us could not live without them. Whether you're the damask-drapes-with-swags-and-rails-and-frilly-pink-tails type or the pared-down-bamboo-blind type, there are a few things to consider before you hit the store.

— WINDOW TREATMENT DOS AND DON'TS —

Consider the style and shape of the window when choosing the type and style of covering.

Think about the way the window opens. For example, French windows need curtains that pull clear on either side so that the doors can open easily.

If the room is dark, go for longer curtain rods so you can open the drapes fully.

Place something outside the window to create a focal point and give a sense of perspective to the room.

If you have nosy neighbors, you might prefer to have sheers or blinds during the day, as well as curtains at night.

To insulate drafty windows, choose heavy fabric or add a lining. Heavy fabric will also help muffle sounds outside the window.

Throw open your windows and breathe in the fresh air whenever possible— you'll feel so much better for it.

Don't skimp on fabric quantities. Better a less-expensive fabric with lots of fullness than an expensive fabric in sparse quantities. For a full effect, curtains should be at least twice as wide as the window they conceal. (See "Estimating the amount of fabric for curtains" on page 82.)

Always request large fabric samples so you can see them against walls and furniture at home. The color, pattern, and texture are likely to look very different when hanging.

TIP: Add a piece of jewelry to your curtains to add glamour and sparkle.
A diamante brooch pinned onto velvet becomes rich and sumptuous.

— Lining Curtains —

Lining is not essential, but it will improve the look of your curtains, making them drape better and seem fuller. Bear in mind that lined curtains will have to be dry-cleaned, even if both inner and outer fabric are made of cotton, as they're liable to shrink at different rates.

You can save money by using old curtains as a lining for your new curtains. It's easy and requires no sewing. Enclose the old in the new, then secure around the edges with "fusible web"—an interfacing that becomes sticky when you apply heat from an iron.

To block out light completely, line curtains or blinds with blackout fabric.

TIEBACKS/HOLDBACKS

The function of tiebacks is to hold back curtains to allow the light in. Tiebacks also add a finishing touch to window treatments. They are usually positioned about one-third of the way up the wall, but you can change the appearance of the window by trying tiebacks at different heights. To make your window seem longer, position the tieback higher. Leave plenty of fabric draped in the center of the window if you want to soften the effect.

SHEER DELIGHT

Net curtains are often seen as a necessary evil either to provide privacy or to disguise an unpleasing view. But with so many beautiful, floaty sheer and semi-sheer fabrics available, they can be a desirable choice in their own right. The fabric should be hung right against the window without actually touching the glass in case of condensation. Be aware that when you turn on the light in the room at night, the curtains become see-through.

— Curtain Lengths —

Curtain length will depend on the size and shape of the window, as well as the height of the window on the wall. There are four main lengths:

A: Curtains hang just above the windowsill.

B: Curtains hang just below the windowsill.

C: Curtains hang just above the floor.

D: Curtains "puddle" on the floor.

There are no hard-and-fast rules, but, generally, curtains for tall windows fall to the floor while small windows look better with a simple treatment. Go for a longer length if you want to retain more warmth in the room.

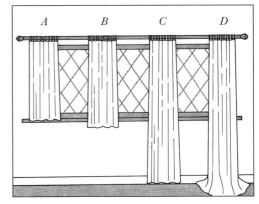

DID YOU KNOW? Queen Elizabeth, the Queen Mother, never drew a pair of curtains in her life.

— ESTIMATING THE AMOUNT OF FABRIC FOR CURTAINS —

Always fix the track or rod to the wall before you measure for curtains, as this will affect the amount of material required.

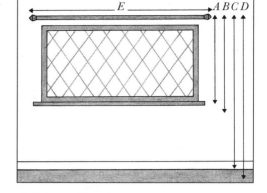

Calculating the width: Measure the full width of the track or rod (E), not just the width of the window. Now you have to decide how full you want your curtains: multiply the figure by 1½ to 2 for a reasonably full look. The total tells you how many widths of fabric are needed for each curtain.

Calculating the length: Measure lengths A/B/C/D according to the length you want and multiply by the number of widths to find the total length.

Remember, if you choose a fabric with a large design, you will need extra fabric to match the pattern.

DID YOU KNOW? It could soon be curtains for curtains. Revolutionary advances in glass technology have produced the "smart window." At the flick of a switch, it can change from clear to totally dark, or any level of tint in between. Smart windows are already available commercially, but because the technology is so new, they're still prohibitively expensive. Me, I'm waiting for the self-cleaning window—at any price!

— BLINDS —

The clean-lined simplicity of blinds makes them a popular choice for contemporary living spaces. The have a number of advantages: You can control light, ensure privacy, and they're often cheaper than lined curtains. They are available in numerous different materials, including bamboo, wood, metal, and paper. You can even have them custom-made to match the fabric of your curtains. Blinds are particularly good for small rooms.

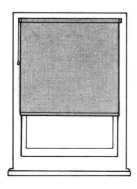

Roller blinds
The simplest type of blind. A flat piece of fabric or vinyl is operated by a simple spring-loaded roller. You can soften the look with a scalloped bottom edge.

TIP: Take the measurements of each window for curtains, especially in older properties. Windows may look the same, but they can vary considerably.

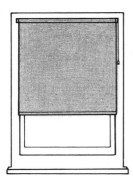

Roman blinds
Look like roller blinds when down but when pulled up they form pleats like a concertina, creating a simple, architectural look ideal for a modern interior.

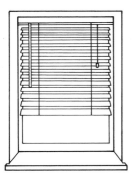

Venetian blinds
Horizontal slats may be opened or closed to create different moods with light and shade. They are usually made of wood, plastic, or aluminum.

TIP: If your Venetian blinds are looking a bit worse for wear, clean them and then spray with aerosol paint. (To clean, see page 63 of "A-Z of cleaning.")

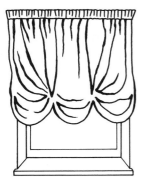

Austrian or festoon blinds
Drapes like a curtain, but is operated like a blind.
Is frilly and flouncy.

— SHUTTERS —

Timeless and clean-lined, shutters allow the architectural structure of a window to speak for itself. They also offer increased security. Scour flea markets for traditional shutters made of solid wood, then cut to size. Go for louvred plantation shutters that fold back on hinges and filter light—very *Gone With the Wind*.

TIP: On larger windows, use two or more blinds rather than one large one. This will give you more control over the light.

— PAINTING &
DECORATING —

"I went to the hardware store and bought some used paint.
It was in the shape of a house."

—STEVEN WRIGHT

— HOW TO PAINT —

Painting is the quickest and easiest way to give a room a facelift, so why not banish the blues and paint the room red—or lilac, or whatever mood you're in. Here's how to brush up on the basics and paint like a pro.

— PAINTING KIT —

1. Paint bucket

2. Paintbrushes, variety of sizes

3. Ladders

4. Roller and tray

5. Paint

6. Knife to open paint can

TIP: Keep plenty of plastic bags handy to slip your hands into if you need to answer the door or the phone.

— OTHER USEFUL STUFF —

Plastic bags

Old newspapers

Drop cloths

Painter's tape—A tape made of paper and special adhesive, used to mask off areas that you don't want to paint, such as window frames and -panes. The length of time painter's tape can be left on varies from tape to tape. It's always best to remove it as soon as possible after the paint has dried.

Cutting-in brush—An angled brush for painting window frames. You can make your own by cutting off a regular paintbrush at a 45-degree angle.

— CHOOSING PAINT —

There are an incredible variety of interior paints to choose from, but they all boil down to two main types:

Water-based paints: Quick-drying, easy to apply; pleasant to work with as they don't give off strong odors and, glory of glories, the brushes are washable in water. On the downside, they're less durable than solvent-based paints. Emulsion is the most versatile and popular, an excellent choice for walls and ceilings. Gloss is suitable for woodwork.

Solvent-based paints: aka oil or oil-based, these include gloss and lacquers. They are tougher and more durable than water-based paints, so are the recommended choice for woodwork and metal. But they're slow-drying, give off pungent fumes, and are merciless in showing up any faults in the surface (and the painter!). The biggest pain is that the brushes cannot be washed in water. Paint thinner should be used.

Common types of paint you might encounter are:

Nondrip gloss: Has a gel-like consistency, which makes it easy to apply, but it is less shiny than standard-gloss paint.

Solid emulsion: Ideal if you're inclined to be a bit drippy or are a beginner. The consistency is a bit like cream cheese (but doesn't taste nearly so good on a cracker) and it comes in a tray ready to be applied with a roller. The main drawbacks are the limited color range and the cost.

Anticondensation paint: Perfect for steamy rooms like kitchens, bathrooms—and maybe your bedroom?

Enamel paint: Ideal for tiles and glass.

TIP: Cheap paints are false economy. They have a higher water content, lower pigment content, and less binder than quality paints, so they won't give as good coverage, the colors won't be as good, and they won't last as long.

— PAINT FINISHES —

Vinyl matt: Absorbs light, giving a smooth, flat finish.
Has no shine, so will hide minor imperfections on the walls,
but it's the least-durable finish. Good choice for walls and ceilings.

Vinyl silk or satin: Reflects light, giving a soft sheen.
More durable than matt but not so good at disguising imperfections.
Works well on smooth surfaces or paneled walls.

Gloss: Gives a very high, lustrous shine.
Most durable finish but not good at hiding imperfections.

Eggshell: Has just a hint of a shine.
Water-based eggshell looks a little more matt than solvent-based eggshell.
Works well on surfaces that need to be wiped clean.

THINK GREEN! No, I'm not suggesting a lime color scheme, but a consideration of the type of paint products you use. Paints and varnishes release chemicals called *volatile organic compounds*. VOCs are air pollutants; they contribute to climate change and have been linked to asthma. If you want paint that is kinder to you and the planet, choose one low in VOCs.

PAINTING OVER TILES: If you can't face the upheaval and cost of ripping out old tiles, you *can* paint directly over them. First, paint tiles and grout with two coats of tile primer to provide a good base for the paint and prevent flaking. After it's dried, apply either a special tile gloss paint or, if you want to match your walls, apply a couple of coats of emulsion paint, leaving it to dry between coats. Finally, waterproof with two coats of a good-quality clear varnish.

— HOW MUCH PAINT WILL I NEED? —

Paint coverage depends on several factors, including the brand of paint and how porous the surface you're painting is.

Wall: To calculate the surface area of your wall, measure the length of the room and multiply it by the height from ceiling to floor. This will give you the number of square feet.

Ceiling: Use the length of the perimeter of the floor.

As a general rule of thumb, 2 pints of emulsion covers about 150 square feet. Five pints should be adequate to cover the walls of an average room with one coat of paint.

For satin or gloss paint, 2 pints covers about 172 square feet.

TIP: To get the best idea of how the paint will look on your walls, paint the inside of a cardboard box.

— PREPARING TO PAINT —

Any professional painter will tell you, the secret of perfect painting is in the prepping. Not what you wanted to hear when you're champing at the bit to start slapping paint on. Tempting as it is to skip this stuff, resist. It will make all the difference *and* save you time in the long run, because you'll only have to go back and rectify any shortcuts you take.

SAFETY FIRST
Make sure the room is well ventilated, especially if you're using solvent-based paints. Don't smoke or use naked flames. Keep pets and children out of the room.

PREPARING WALLS
Clear walls of all mirrors, Picassos, etc. Sponge walls with a mild detergent solution to clean, then allow to dry.

DEALING WITH WALLPAPER
It is possible to paint directly over wallpaper, but any embossed pattern is likely to show through, and several coats will be needed to cover a patterned paper. Some papers, like vinyl, should simply peel off, leaving the lining paper in place to provide you with a base for your new covering. To paint directly over vinyl paper, apply a water-based primer. For the most professional finish, the old wallpaper is best removed.

How to strip wallpaper
Soak the walls thoroughly with a solution of warm water and a little household detergent or a commercial wallpaper stripper. Remove the old paper with a wallpaper scraper, working from the bottom up. Try not to dig into the plaster, causing gashes and holes, and take care around electrical outlets. If it's a washable paper, score the surface (make lines across it with a knife) before wetting to allow the water to penetrate and ease stripping. Some papers, like vinyl, should peel off, leaving behind the backing paper, which can be used as a lining paper if it is not damaged.

If you're faced with many layers of old paper it would be worth your while to rent a steam stripper. This machine uses steam to loosen the paper right down to the plaster. Perhaps you can rope in a few friends to give you a hand. Lure them around with the promise of "getting steamy with a stripper."

GIVE IT A TRY: Practically the first thing people do when they move into a new place is to strip off all the wallpaper. Whoaa! Hold your horses. Don't you know that a feature wall of vintage paper adds character and individuality? Some original papers still look contemporary today, so think before you strip! Oh dear, that bad, eh?

TIP: If you do intend to paint over wallpaper, test a small, inconspicuous area to ensure that the wallpaper won't bubble.

DEALING WITH MOLD ON WALLS

Painting over moisture is pointless. Mold spores hang around in the air, so, like the Terminator, they'll be back. Strip off contaminated wallpaper. Wash off the mold with a solution of 1 part household bleach to 4 parts water and leave on the wall for four days. Rinse off with water and then let the wall dry out. Treat the wall with a fungicidal sealer before painting. Be sure to deal with the moisture or condensation, the likely causes of the mold.

Paint highlights rather than hides flaws, so any small cracks and holes in the walls need to be filled in. (See "How to fill in cracks and holes in plaster" on page 138.)

NOTE: New plaster is very porous and should be left for four weeks before painting with regular paint. If you're in a hurry because you have Auntie Annie coming to stay, you can use microporous paints (available from DIY stores). Follow the instructions on the can.

— PREPARING THE ROOM —

Clear the room
Remove or cover furniture and carpets. Take down curtains.
Cover door handles and wall fixtures with plastic bags, remove wall lights,
and cap ends of loose wires with insulating tape. Put painter's tape over light switches.
Push large items of furniture into the middle of the room and protect with a drop cloth.
TIP: Old sheets and old shower curtains make excellent drop cloths.

Clean the room
Dust and vacuum the room, paying particular attention to the tops of the doors
and picture rails. Use a lint-free cloth and turpentine on horizontal surfaces.

What to wear
Dress for comfort in something baggy. Avoid woolly sweaters, as loose fibers
could be shed on the paint. Slip an old pair of nonslip socks over your shoes to
prevent them from being spattered with paint. Tie your hair back and remove jewelery.
Especially when painting a ceiling, unless you're using nondrip paint,
wear a shower cap to protect your locks from paint splashes.
Pray your date doesn't show up unexpectedly.

— HOW TO REMOVE PAINT ODORS —

Method 1: Cut an onion in half and place it cut side up on a dish in the room.

Method 2: Add a tablespoon of ammonia to a large dish
of water and leave it in the room with the doors closed, for a few hours or overnight.

Method 3: Add a few drops of vanilla essence to the paint before use.

TIP: If you're worried about your privacy while you're without curtains, frost your windows: Mix 1 cup of beer with 4 tablespoons of Epsom salts and paint the solution on the windows. Wash off once the decorating is over.

— PAINTING TOOLS —

— Paintbrushes —

A good-quality brush will last; a poor-quality brush will drive you to distraction because you'll spend most of your time picking stray bristles out of your otherwise perfect paintwork— soul-destroying.

Choose nylon or polyester bristles for water-based paints; natural bristles are suitable for all paints.

Match the brush to the surface: A 4 in. brush is good for walls and ceilings; 3 in. or 2 in. is good for corners and edges, baseboards, and doors.

To test the quality of a brush: Brush the bristles over the back of your hand. They should have plenty of bounce and not fan out too much. The length of the bristles should vary, as this means the paintbrush can hold more paint.

How to hold a paintbrush: Hold a small brush like a pen. Hold a large brush like a Ping-Pong paddle.

— How to Apply Emulsion Paint with a Paintbrush —

With a well-loaded brush, lay on the paint horizontally, brushing outwards.
Then, with a lightly loaded brush, make upward strokes to make a crisscross pattern.

— How to Apply Gloss Paint with a Paintbrush —

This technique will ensure an even finish and is suitable for painting most flat surfaces with undercoats and topcoat.

1. Paint several vertical stripes about 12 inches in length. Reload the brush for each stroke. (figure 1)

2. Without reloading, spread the paint using horizontal strokes in a crisscross fashion. (figure 2)

3. Without reloading, gently brush the area vertically to remove any blobs and to create an even finish. (figure 3)

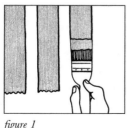
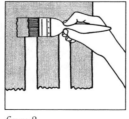

figure 1   *figure 2*   *figure 3*

TIP: Never dip more than one-third of your brush into the paint.
An overloaded brush will drip, and you'll have paint dripping down your arm.

— Rollers —

Rollers are unbeatable when you have large expanses of wall to paint.
They cover surfaces faster and more efficiently than paintbrushes.

Choosing a roller

The smoother the surface you're painting, the shorter the pile on the
roller should be. Lamb's wool pile is ideal for ceilings. Avoid cheap foam rollers.
They're spongy and leave air pockets so your paintwork ends up looking like the
surface of the moon—full of craters.

Attach an extension handle to the roller to reach the tops of walls and ceilings.

Rollers are not good at reaching into corners and edges so before starting to
roll on a wall, use a small brush to paint a strip about 2 inches wide to get
right into those edges and corners. Feather out the paint from the edge
(i.e., paint loose, diagonal strokes, so you're not left with a hard edge).

— Paint Tray Tips —

TIP: Use an old soup ladle to transfer paint from the can to the tray without dribbles.

*TIP: Turn a supermarket plastic bag inside out and slip it over the paint tray before you pour in the paint.
When the job's done, remove the bag and you'll have a spotless tray.*

— How to Apply Emulsion Paint with a Roller —

Pour paint into the reservoir at the bottom of the tray up as far as the edge of the slope.
Dip the roller in the paint reservoir and roll it gently up and down to load it with paint.
Run the roller over the ribbed part of the tray to remove excess paint and ensure it is
evenly coated. Don't overload it, or you'll splash paint everywhere.

Apply the paint in random, crisscross strokes, ensuring even coverage, then go over it again in
one direction for a neat finish.

— Paint Pads —

Paint pads are fast, use less paint, and spatter less than rollers, but the best thing about them is
that they're easy to clean—so long as you use water-based paints. Oil-based paints, such as
gloss, are best avoided, as the solvents used to clean such paints off the pad can damage it.
Various-sized pads are available. The larger the pad, the more surface you can cover.

How to use: Pour some paint into the speed tray, which comes with the roller. Load the paint pad
by running it back and forth in the speed tray. Do not overload. Start near a corner and use the
same technique as a roller.

*TIP: You can speed up painting considerably by using a battery-powered
brush or roller, as they eliminate the need for reloading.*

— Paint Can Tips —

To painting novices, it may seem pedantic to devote an entire page to the paint can, of all things, but anyone who's ever picked up a brush will tell you that the actual painting is a dance around the maypole compared to coping with a messy, encrusted paint can. Follow these tips to keep your paint can pristine and your sanity intact.

Don't use a screwdriver to open the paint can. Not only will you damage your screwdriver, but you'll also damage the can and make resealing tricky. Use the side of a knife blade or a special paint-can opener to lever it open.

Before you pour the paint from the can, put painter's tape on top of the rim all the way around. Remove the tape when you've finished pouring. Result: a clean rim, and your lid will fit perfectly. You can also smear petroleum jelly around the rim before replacing the lid so that the seal will be tight.

Never paint straight from the can. The reason for this is that the solvents in the paint will evaporate, dirt will get in the paint, and a skin will form on top. Decant the paint into a container; any old can or plastic bucket with a handle will do . Fill it about one-third full of paint.

Line your bucket with aluminum foil; you can dispose of it when you've finished painting, and you won't have to clean the bucket.

Use a clean, wooden stick to stir the paint. Stir in several different directions so it is thoroughly mixed. If your paint is lumpy, pour it through an old sieve or a pair of tights.
NOTE: Don't stir nondrip paint.

Don't wipe surplus paint on the edge of the can. Stretch a straight piece of wire or string tautly across the opening of the can so you can wipe off excess paint and avoid drips.

To prevent a skin forming on the paint, store the can upside down. If a skin does form, trim around it with a knife and remove in one piece.

Brush a dab of paint on the bottom of the paint can so that you can instantly identify the color.

In order to keep a check on how much paint you have, place a large elastic band over the can and keep it level with the amount of paint in the can.

GIVE IT A TRY: Waiter, waiter, there's a fly in my paint! Add a few drops of citronella oil to your paint to keep away blackflies and mosquitoes.

TIP: When painting baseboards,
apply wide masking tape around the edges of the carpet to protect it from drips.

— PAINTING A ROOM —

Work methodically from top to bottom:
1. ceiling
2. walls
3. doors
4. window frames
5. radiators
6. baseboards

If you're right-handed, paint from right to left, and start from a top corner.

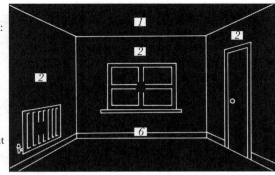

— PAINTING A WALL —

Start painting in the corner nearest a window, working away from the light.

Start at the top of the wall.

Never start painting from the bottom of the wall.

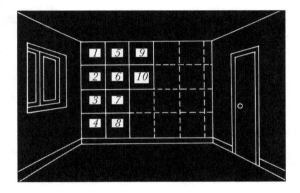

— PAINTING A CEILING —

Paint in strips of about 12 inches wide, parallel to the window, working away from the light.
Feather around the edges where the ceiling meets the wall.
To stop drips down your brush, push your paintbrush through the middle of a small disposable paper plate or cut out a circular shape from a piece of card. Secure the brush with sticky tape.

— PAINTING DOORS —

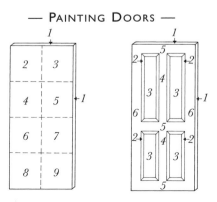

TIP: If you need to take a break, wrap your roller/brushes loosely in plastic wrap to prevent them from drying out.

— PAINTING WINDOWS —

Clean out dirt from the corners of the window using an old toothbrush. Wipe down the frame with a lint-free cloth and turpentine to remove dust.

Apply painter's tape all around the window between the frame and the glass. This may be time-consuming, but it will save you scraping paint off the glass afterward. It also makes painting easier and gives a better finish.
NOTE: A gadget called a metal shield is also available. You hold it against the window as you paint the frames.

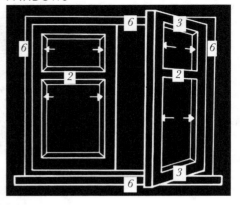

— PAINTING WOOD —
Preparing wood for painting
In order for the new paint to adhere, you need to provide a "key".
Do this by sanding the woodwork with dry abrasive paper.
Strip away blistering or flaking paint using a hot air gun or paint stripper if necessary. Then apply a primer sealer to prevent old finishes showing through the new paint.

New wood has to be primed to give it a good base for painting.
If you don't prime the wood first, you'll need lots of topcoats.
Apply white wood primer on softwoods or hardwood.

Painting wood
Solvent-based gloss is the usual choice as it gives good protection.
Paint the wood in the same direction as the grain.

NOTE: Medium Density Fiberboard is more porous than wood,
so some experts prefer to use a special MDF primer.

— PAINTING TRICKS —

PAINTING STAIRS
The problem with painting stairs is that the moment you start to paint, you remember something you need urgently from upstairs. The solution is simple: Paint every other step on one day, and the remaining steps the day after.

PAINTING FURNITURE
Slide jar lids under the legs of tables or chairs to catch any drips.

TIP: A short blast with a hair dryer should loosen painter's tape that sticks to the window, so you can peel it off cleanly.

PAINTING CUPBOARDS
Paint the inside of cupboards a pale color to reflect light back when the door is open, enabling you to see the contents better.

PAINTING A DRAWER KNOB
Unscrew it from the drawer and place in the neck of an empty bottle.
Use a brush or spray paint.

PAINTING PIPES
Paint pipes when cold and allow to dry before turning on the heating.

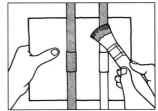

Painting pipes that are close to a wall can be tricky. A simple solution is to hold a piece of cardboard behind the pipes to protect the wall from splashes. Move the card as you paint.

— CARING FOR PAINTING EQUIPMENT —
Rinse away water-based paints with cold water and then wash in warm water with a little detergent.

Remove solvent-based paints with paint thinner, then wash in warm water with a little detergent.

Use ordinary vegetable oil or baby oil to remove paint from your hands— it's gentler than chemical solvents but equally effective.

PAINT DISPOSAL: Never pour paint down sinks or drains as it can cause pollution and contaminate water. Dispose of it with household waste.
Or why not decant it into a jam jar and use it to touch up scuffs or scratches?

— Painting SOS —
Help! There are drip marks down my walls.
Don't overload your brush;
allow paint to dry, then sand down and touch up the over-affected area.

Help! The brush marks are visible.
Don't overload the brush or use too-thick paint; sand and recoat.

Help! The dried paint is splitting and cracking.
Usually caused by applying a second coat
before the first has dried. Leave to dry, rub down and repaint.

Help! The paint looks patchy on the walls.
Load paintbrush with sufficient paint; apply enough coats for good coverage.

TIP: Wear a pair of disposable latex gloves when painting and you'll save yourself no end of scrubbing and chapped hands.

Help! The old paint is showing through the new.
Don't paint emulsion over gloss paint; ensure paint is properly stirred.
If emulsion, apply another topcoat; if gloss, apply another
undercoat and topcoat.

Help! My wood has blistered.
Usually caused because the wood was damp when painted.
Let the paint dry, then prick the blister with a pin.
If there is wet paint inside, you'll have to strip back and start again.

Help! The stain on the ceiling keeps bleeding through the emulsion.
Try cleaning off the stain, then applying a coat of aluminum primer sealer to the stain.
When dry, repaint.

— WALLPAPERING —

"It takes only four men to wallpaper a house, but you have to slice them thinly."
—Jo Brand

Wallpaper does for a room what a great outfit does for a person—adds instant color, pattern, and texture, as well as hiding any unsightly lumps or bumps that might be lurking beneath (not that you have any unsightly lumps or bumps). Like an outfit, wallpaper can make a bold statement or blend into the background. Whatever style you go for, follow a few basic rules and you'll soon get the hang of it.

— CHOOSING WALL COVERINGS —

Before you get carried away by the sheer wonder of wall coverings, a word of caution to all you novice hangers: master the basics before tackling more difficult wall coverings like flock-papers or foil papers. One of the trickiest types of paper to hang is cheap wallpaper, as it tends to crease and tear easily. Large patterns are also best avoided if you're a total beginner, as matching patterns across a join can be tricky.

DARE TO BE DIFFERENT: For a themed room, log onto eBay (www.ebay.com) and search for original vintage wallpapers, often with bargain price tags. You'll find everything from psychedelic flowers to *Star Wars* and authentic 1970s OpArt. Groovy, baby.

GIVE IT A TRY: A friend of mine, who works in the city, has his downstairs bathroom wallpapered in old copies of the *Financial Times*. Try the same technique in your own bathroom using old copies of your favorite newspaper (tabloids may be used, but they're double the work, as are comics or magazines). Choose the most eye-catching headlines, paste the pages up neatly, then varnish.

TIP: Pasting is one of the biggest pains about wallpapering, so if you choose a pre-pasted paper, the job will be easier.

— WALLPAPER TIPS —

Holding up heavy sample books to the wall or sticking up a small scrap of wallpaper is not good enough to make a decision on a wallpaper. Some companies will let you have a 91 cm (3 ft) sample for a small charge—a sound investment.

Stick your sample on the wall it's intended for. Live with it. Look at it in different lights. See if you still like it after a few days. Check how easy it is to clean by giving it a wipe with a damp cloth. Check how easily it tears; if it tears easily, it's likely to be tricky to hang.

— ESTIMATING HOW MUCH PAPER —

Standard rolls of wallpaper come in rolls about 11 yards x 21 inches.
Measure the distance around the room and check this chart to estimate how many rolls you require (based on an average wall height of 8 feet).

Distance Around the Room	Number of Rolls Required
30 feet	5
38 feet	6
46 feet	7
54 feet	9
62 feet	10
70 feet	11
78 feet	12

Buy all the paper you need at the same time from the same batch, as shades vary slightly between batches.

If your paper has a large pattern, you'll need extra rolls to allow for wastage.

Buy a few extra rolls anyway—just in case.

A PERSONAL PLEA: Do *not* wallpaper with your partner. Those photos you see in glossy magazines of impossibly jolly couples sharing the delights of decorating together are lies, damned lies. At best, it'll end in tears; at worst, it'll end in the divorce courts.

TIP: Make a feature of just one wall using a dramatic, luxurious wallpaper. This is a good compromise if the paper you've fallen in love with is expensive.

— DECORATING EQUIPMENT —

1. Ladders

2. Plastic bucket

3. Pasting brush

4. Paperhanger's brush

5. Wallpaper paste

6. Wallpaper scraper

7. Plumb line

8. Sponge

9. Seam roller

10. Tack to hang plumb line

11. Pencil

12. Pasting table

13. Scissors

14. Measuring tape

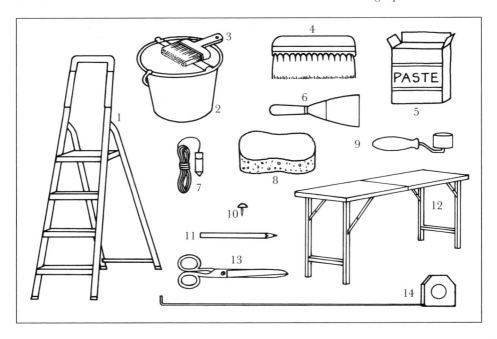

A good place to start decorating is adjacent to a window. This will save you cutting full lengths of paper around the window; however, if you're using paper with a large pattern, start at the focal point of the room, like the fireplace if you have one.

Before you start papering, it's a good idea to put bits of matchsticks into the plugs in the walls where pictures and other fittings need to be put back. Allow them to stick out just enough for you to feel them underneath the paper.

TIP: Invest in a proper pasting table. Your dining table or kitchen table won't do.

To wallpaper over painted walls, wash the surface with a mild detergent and allow to dry. If the wall is rough, the experts would recommend hanging lining paper.

What is lining paper?
Lining paper is cheap plain paper that provides a good base if your walls are in poor condition. You do need patience, though, because, you're essentially wallpapering twice. Lining paper is traditionally hung horizontally, across the wall, in the opposite direction to the wallpaper so you don't have two layers of vertical joins. But if you have long walls, this can mean you need very long lengths. So long as you use a thick lining paper, it's fine to hang it vertically; that is, in the same direction as the wallpaper. You need to ensure that the seams of the two papers do not fall in the same place. Don't overlap the joins, and allow at least a day before wallpapering on top.

— MEASURING YOUR FIRST LENGTH —

Let's assume you're starting by a window. Begin by taking a measurement equal to the width of the wallpaper away from the window minus 1 inch, so that will give you a little to trim to make a neat join with the window frame.

In order to know exactly where to hang your first length you'll need to establish an exact straight line, or "find a true vertical" as it's known in the trade. Few homes are blessed with perfectly straight walls, so if you start papering without first doing this, chances are that each piece of paper you hang will list more and more and your decorating scheme will end up as a two-dimensional version of the Leaning Tower of Pisa. Not a good look—unless you're after the Romanesque style. To find a true vertical, you need a plumb line or plumb bob.

— How to Use a Plumb Line —

Suspend the plumb line from as high up the wall as possible and secure it in place with a pin. (figure 1) Allow the weight to stop swinging, then press the line against the wall and make pencil marks down the wall following the line. (figure 2) Your first piece of paper will be hung to the left of this line.

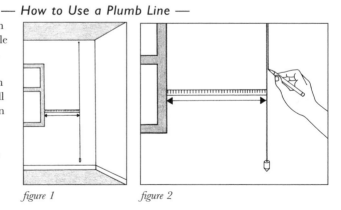

figure 1   *figure 2*

TIP: Plumb lines are so low-tech that you can make your own: simply tie a heavy weight to a length of string.

— CUTTING AND PASTING WALLPAPER —

Wallpaper paste is best mixed in a plastic bucket so it can stand while you cut the paper. Tie a string across the rim of the bucket, secured around the handles, so you have somewhere to rest your brush when not in use.

Measure the height of the wall and cut the paper, allowing an extra 2 inches top and bottom for trimming. Cut several strips at a time, matching any pattern.

Number each strip on the back so you know which order to hang them, and put a "T" for "top" so they won't be hung upside down (there speaks the voice of experience).

REMEMBER THE OLD ADAGE: Measure twice and cut once.

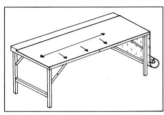

1. Lay the strip of paper on a pasting table, design-side facing down, with one end overhanging the end of the table, and one edge fractionally overlapping the edge of the table. So that you don't get paste on the front side of the paper, this is the way to paste: Apply a good amount of paste down the center of the strip, then start pasting from the center outward, spreading the paste smoothly, right up to the edge that overlaps the table.

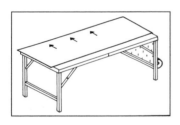

2. Pull the paper over to the other side of the table so that it slightly overhangs it again, and coat the remaining edges of the paper without getting paste on the table.

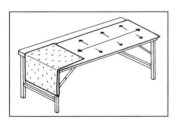

3. Fold the pasted end of the paper over, with the pasted sides together, but don't crease the folds. Pull the folded section along the table, so it hangs over the edge. Paste the other half of the strip as described in steps 1 and 2.

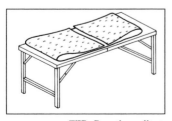

4. Once the entire strip is pasted, fold the rest of the paper in half so that it nearly meets the first. Again, don't crease the folds.

TIP: Pour the wallpaper paste into a roller tray and use a roller to spread the paste.

— HANGING THE FIRST PIECE —

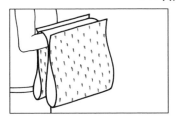

1. Drape the paper over your arm to carry it to the wall.

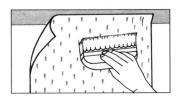

2. You will know exactly which spot on the wall to hang the paper, because you took the trouble to find a true vertical (see "How to use a plumb line" on page 99). Position the pasted paper about 2 inches above the wall to allow for trimming both above and below the paper. Line up the right edge of the paper perfectly against the pencil line on the wall.

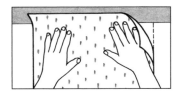

3. Use a paperhanger's brush to smooth the paper into position, brushing downward, from top to bottom, then from the middle outward, to remove any air bubbles or creases. If the paper wrinkles, unpeel and brush back into place.

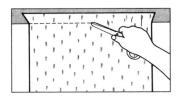

4. Use the brush to push the edges of the paper into the angle between the wall and the ceiling. Mark the line by running the back of a scissor blade over the angle so you can see the crease.

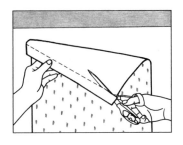

5. Carefully peel the paper away from the wall and cut along the crease, then brush the paper back on the wall.

TIP: You may find long lengths of paper easier to handle if you fold it concertina-style.

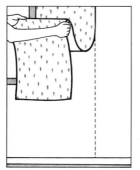

6. Open out the bottom fold of the paper. Smooth the paper into place, brushing downward with the brush. Don't smooth the very bottom of the paper. Leave it resting against the baseboard. Trim off the excess on the bottom of the paper against the baseboard in the same way as you did at the top against the ceiling, described in steps 3 and 4 (see page 101).

7. Paste the next strip of paper in the same way and hang it to the right of the first piece, matching up any pattern, and aligning the seams so there are no overlaps or gaps. To smooth joins, go over them with a seamroller (not to be confused with a steamroller), except on embossed paper.

— PAPERING THE DIFFICULT PARTS —

— Papering around an Internal Corner —

Don't try to turn an internal corner with a full width of paper. It won't hang straight and you'll be left with unsightly bulges. The best approach is to cut one length of paper into two long strips. Here's how:

1. Measure the distance from the edge of the last full length you put on the wall to the corner. Take the measurement, top, middle, and bottom, and add ½ inch to the largest figure. The extra length is for the turn around the corner. (figure 1) Cut a length of paper to this exact size, but make sure you save the offcut because you'll be needing it in a moment.

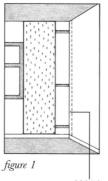

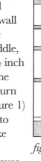

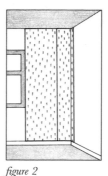

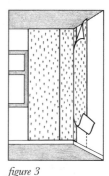

figure 1   figure 2   figure 3

add ½ inch

2. Paste and hang the cut piece next to the last length you hung, brushing the cut edge well into the corner with the ½ inch turning around the corner onto the adjoining wall. (figure 2)

TIP: Wipe surplus paste off the wallpaper and pasting table before they dry hard.

3. Measure the width of the offcut. Suspend a plumb line this distance from the corner on the new wall, and mark the line with a pencil. Paste and hang the offcut using the vertical pencil line as a marker for the far edge of the paper. There will be a slight overlap with the previous strip but it won't be noticeable in the corner. (figure 3, below left)

— Papering around an External Corner —

1. Don't try to turn an external corner with a full width of paper. Paper the wall until there is less than one full width to the corner. Now you're going to cut one length of paper into two long strips: first, cut a narrow width of paper to turn 1 inch around the corner. Hang the paper and fold the spare 1 inch around the corner onto the new wall. Smooth it into place with the paper-hanger's brush.

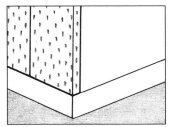

2. Hang the reserved offcut next to the paper on the new wall, matching any pattern if necessary and butting the joins, pushing them right up together. NOTE: If the walls are very "out of true" (not straight), it might be better to overlap rather than butt the joins. Subtract 1 inch from the width of the offcut, mark a straight line on the new wall with your plumb line, and hang the paper overlapping the piece turned around the corner.

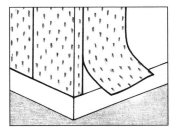

— Papering around a Light Switch —

Turn off the electricity at the mains (it's a good idea to do this job in daylight hours).

1. Remove the retaining screws and lift the fitting away from the wall a little.

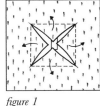

figure 1   *figure 2*   *figure 3*

2. Press the wallpaper gently against the fitting, then make four diagonal cuts from the center with scissors. (figure 1)

3. Slip the light fitting through to the front, and trim away excess paper. (figure 2)

4. Brush the edges of the paper onto the wall behind the fitting to give a neat finish. (figure 3)

NOTE: Don't fit foil (metallic) wallpaper behind a light switch; paper around the light fitting and trim off excess paper.

TIP: Don't cut all your paper in one go unless you're absolutely sure of all your measurements. Better to cut a few pieces at a time, to be on the safe side.

— *Papering around a Non-recessed Door* —

Hang a full width of wallpaper so it overlaps the door. If there is a lot of excess, cut it off, leaving about 2 inches all around. Crease the paper into place with the back of the scissors. Peel it back and trim off the excess, then brush back into place.

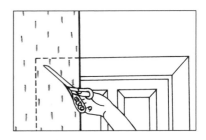

NOTE: Use the same technique around a nonrecessed window.

— *Papering around a Recessed Window* —

1. Hang a full length of paper over the window, allowing it to overlap the recess. (figure 1)

2. Slit the paper along the top of the window horizontally so it is exactly level with the front edge of the reveal (you may find this easier to do with a sharp craft knife), allowing the middle part of the length of wallpaper to wrap around the side wall. Don't stick the paper around the wall just yet though.

3. Make another horizontal cut level with the surface of the windowsill. Trim to fit the paper around the end of the sill.

4. Now you can press the paper around the wall and up against the window frame. Trim off the excess around the window frame and brush into place. (figure 2)

5. You will see that you are left with a gap on the top inside corner of the recess. This has to be patched. Cut a strip of paper to fit, adding 1 inch all around. The part that will be tucked under at the top of the window should be torn to make a ragged edge, which will be less visible under the paper than a sharp cut.

6. Lift the paper above the recess and tuck under the patch with the torn edge. Smooth the paper over the patch and trim the other edges of the patch. (figure 3)

7. Repeat this process on the other side of the reveal.

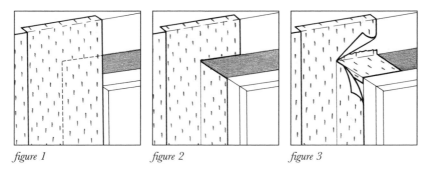

figure 1   *figure 2*   *figure 3*

TIP: Use the same technique around a recessed door.

— Papering behind a Radiator —

Method 1

Hang a full length of paper, allowing it to hang down in front of the radiator.
Use a pencil to make a little mark on the wallpaper where the supporting brackets of
the radiator come (they're the fixtures located behind the radiator). Starting at the bottom,
cut up to the pencil marks in line with the brackets and then across the paper so you've
cut out a rectangle. Smooth the excess paper behind the radiator on each side of the
brackets to give the impression of a full length. Trim the paper at the baseboard.
Wipe off any paste on the radiator.

Method 2 (the easier option)

Turn off the radiator and allow it to cool. You might also need to clean out any dust
that might have accumulated behind. (See page 62 for how to clean behind a radiator.)
Cut a length of paper so that it hangs down behind the top of the radiator by about
6 inches. Then cut another length of paper to cover the gap at the bottom
of the radiator.

— Papering Ceilings —

Are you mad? Don't even go there. If painting was good enough for Michelangelo
(Sistine Chapel, remember?), surely it's good enough for you.

— WALLPAPER SOS —

Help! The seams between the pieces of wallpaper have not joined.
This happens if you haven't butted up (pushed together) the lengths properly.
Color in the seams with a felt-tipped pen which matches the background color.

Help! I've torn the wallpaper!
Put a little PVA glue underneath the tear and stick down.
If it's very conspicuous, hang a picture over it!

Help! There are air bubbles all over my wallpaper.
These should disappear as the glue under the wallpaper dries. If they're still there after
24 hours, slit the paper with a razor blade, add a little glue, and stick the paper down.

Help! The wallpaper's peeling off.
Did you glue the paper right up to the edges? If not, re-paste. If the paper still peels,
you could a have problem with damp. (See "Dealing with moisture" on pages 141–142.)

Help! There are shiny patches on the wallpaper.
This is likely to be paste drying on the surface. Remove with a damp sponge.

TIP: If you have any leftover bits of wallpaper, keep them and use for lining drawers.

– HOME MATTERS –

"Oh, Auntie Em—there's no place like home!"

—*DOROTHY,* THE WIZARD OF OZ

— PICTURES AND PHOTOGRAPHS —

— CHOOSING A FRAME —

A good frame enhances a picture; a bad one can wreck it.
Put as much thought into choosing a frame as you do your artwork.

Don't choose a frame that dominates the picture. Proportion is crucial.
If in doubt, take your picture to a professional framer.
They will advise you on depth of frame, size, color of mounts, etc.

Wallpapered walls with bold patterns need special consideration.
Choose a plain frame in a color picked out of the wallpaper
and use a wide mount so the wallpaper won't overwhelm the picture.

GIVE IT A TRY: Frame a fragment of embroidery or fabric such
as antique lace to create a beautiful 3-D artwork.

— PICTURE HANGING —

The most common mistake people make is hanging pictures too high. You shouldn't get a crick in your neck looking up at them. As a rule, hang pictures so that the focal point is at eye level or below.

Think about where you will be when the picture is viewed. For example, in a living room, where you spend most of your time sitting down, try hanging the pictures at your eye level when you are seated. This applies particularly to small pictures. On a staircase, remember the pictures will be viewed sideways.

If you are hanging a picture above a piece of furniture, like a sofa or above a fireplace, don't leave too big a gap between the two or the picture will look disconnected—like it's floating in space. The furniture will anchor the picture to the ground.

Match a picture to the proportions of a wall. A large, bare wall suits a large painting or several medium-sized pictures. Small pictures would be lost on a large wall unless they're part of a group. Small pictures look good in narrow spaces such as stairways.

If you are filling a whole wall with pictures, find the center and work out evenly from that point.

Generally speaking, delicately toned pictures, like pastels and watercolors, suit light-colored walls, in light-colored frames and mounts. Bolder prints, like oil paintings in ornate frames, are best displayed on dark walls.

TIP: If the first thing you notice about a painting is the frame, you have the wrong frame.

Think about lighting. This would be the first consideration of a curator organizing an exhibition in an art gallery. Use a proper picture light or a directional spotlight to throw a dramatic light on an individual picture. But beware of aiming it directly at your valuable painting—heat created may damage it.

If windows or lights reflect off the glass, reposition the picture or use nonglare glass in the frame.

Avoid exposing pictures to direct sunlight, humidity, temperature extremes, and smoke.

If you've had the same picture hanging in the same spot for years, reposition it in the room or elsewhere in the house. You'll look at it with fresh eyes.

— HOW TO GROUP PICTURES —

Spread your pictures on the floor under the wall on which they're going to hang.
Shuffle them around on the floor, trying out different arrangements.
You can choose a formal or informal grouping; let the art dictate.
For a neat look, keep the same distance between pictures.

Pictures in a group have more unity if they share a common theme.
This could be subject matter (e.g., all seascapes, all portraits) or visual tone
(e.g., all black and white, all pastels). Giving all the pictures matching frames
and mounts also helps coordinate a mixed selection.

To get an idea of what your grouping would look like on the wall,
cut out a sheet of paper the size of each picture to be hung.
Stick the sheets on the wall using low-tack masking tape or Blue-Tack
and keep shuffling them around until you find the most pleasing arrangement.
Keep stepping back for an overall view. Trust your eye. Mark the final
position for each picture by making a little mark on the wall with a pencil.
Make a quick sketch of your final arrangement so you have a plan to work to.

TIP: Use the paper templates in frames to mark the position of the hook on the wall for the actual picture.

NOTE: Smaller pictures look best grouped close together. Don't leave big gaps between them.

REMEMBER: Pictures don't have to be hung on walls. They can look just as effective on shelves, bookcases, freestanding easels, etc.

GIVE IT A TRY: A steamy bathroom is not the ideal place to hang pictures, but have you thought of using designer tiles? They're waterproof, and some of them are as pretty as a picture. Choose something to match your design and fix it to the wall using tile adhesive.

TIP: Modern art usually looks better unframed.

— Picture Hanging Arrangements —

Imagine a cross shape and arrange the pictures around it. Group smaller pictures above and larger pictures below.

Hang a large picture (or mirror) in the middle of the wall and group smaller pictures evenly around it for a symmetrical arrangement.

Group square and/or rectangular pictures in two rows, some hanging below one imaginary line, others sitting on top of a second imaginary line. Make sure the outside edges of the rows are even to give the effect of one large picture.

Hang pictures of equal size in a formal, symmetrical arrangement, with even spaces between them.

Group mixed-shaped pictures in an imaginary framework. Hang the largest pictures at each corner and fill in the gaps with smaller pictures.

TIP: To give a gold picture frame an antique look, rub it with brown shoe polish.

— How to Hang a Picture —

Choose a picture hook suitable to bear the weight of the picture. Proper picture wire is the most secure way of hanging pictures. Thread the wire through the eyelet on each side of the frame. Use pliers to twist the wire so that it's tight.

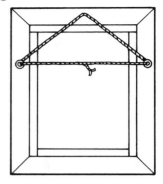

To fix a picture hook to the wall, see "How to drill" on page 137.

— REMOVING ODORS —

DID YOU KNOW? The human nose can distinguish more than 10,000 different smells.

The secret of removing a bad odor is not to disguise it, but to locate the source and eliminate that. Often it's a simple case of sniffing the air and following your nose to the rotting cabbage in your vegetable rack. Commercial air fresheners are expensive, fill the air with chemicals, and can often be as irritating to your nose as the smell itself. Fortunately, there are a number of excellent alternative home deodorizers:

Activated charcoal

Bicarbonate of soda (aka sodium bicarbonate or baking soda)

Cat litter

Coffee grounds

— A–Z of Odor Removal —

Bathroom smells

See "How to get rid of bathroom smells" on page 196.

Book

Place bicarbonate of soda in a muslin bag, tie it up, then pop it in a plastic bag with the book for 7–10 days.

Cabbage and cauliflower cooking

Place a slice of bread on top of the vegetables, or add a whole walnut to the cooking water.

TIP: Deodorize your waste disposal unit by putting orange and lemon rinds through and rinsing with water.

Chopping board (wooden)
Scrub with a paste of lemon juice and salt.

Cigarette smoke (on clothes)
Laundering is best in the long term, but for a quick fix, if the garment is not delicate, you can put it in the dryer with a couple of dryer sheets for about 10 minutes on "cool." In a room: Open all windows, place small bowls of vinegar around the room. Best solution: Quit smoking!

Cutlery
Remove strong smells like fish or onion by rubbing with lemon juice and rinsing immediately.

Dishwasher
Use a commercial dishwasher cleaner and run an empty cycle. Keep the door open when not in use to allow air to circulate.

Doormat (sisal or coir)
Beat with a brush outdoors.

Freezer
Put a tray of cat litter in there—but keep the cat out!

Hands
If you've been preparing fish, don't wash your hands straight away, as this will seal in the smell. First, rub lemon juice between your palms. To rid your hands of the smell of garlic, rub coffee grounds between your palms.

Luggage
Wrap several sugar lumps in muslin and put in the case before storing to prevent musty odors.

Microwave
Slice a couple of lemons and put them in a bowl of water in the oven. Heat on high power for 2–3 minutes, or until the water boils.

Musty smell in a room
Sounds like mildew or moisture—see "Dealing with moisture" on page 141.

Plastic container (food smells)
Method 1: Fill with a solution of bicarbonate of soda and water and leave for 24 hours. Rinse thoroughly.
Method 2: Freeze for several hours.
Method 3: Place a couple of lemon wedges in the box, close it, and leave for several days. Wash.

TIP: To remove onion odor from your hands, rinse them with mouthwash.

Plates

Remove strong odors like fish or onion by adding a few drops of vinegar to the final rinse when washing dishes by hand.

Refrigerator

See "How to eliminate refrigerator odors" on page 157.

Saucepans

Boil a panful of water containing 2 tablespoons of white vinegar. Fish smells—fill with cold tea, leave for an hour, and wash thoroughly.

Sneakers

See "How to refresh smelly sneakers" on page 203.

Thermos

Fill the thermos with a solution of hot water and 1 tablespoon of bicarbonate of soda. Do not immerse in water as the thermos will be damaged. Store with the top off and a couple of sugar lumps inside to keep it fresh.

TIP: Sometimes the best solutions are the simplest: Throw open the windows in your rooms each morning and let you and your house feel the benefits of fresh air for a few hours. You and your home will both feel better for it.

— SCENTING YOUR HOME —

Light a scented candle in a room to get rid of an unwanted smell such as tobacco.

Carpets absorb smells from cooking, pets, and cigarettes. To restore freshness, sprinkle with bicarbonate of soda, leave for 20 minutes, then vacuum.

Throw pinecones or dried citrus peel onto an open fire and they will scent the whole room.

Dab a tiny amount of perfume on a cold lightbulb. As the bulb heats up, the scent is diffused throughout the room.

Put empty soap cartons in drawers to scent your underwear.

Bake brown sugar and cinnamon in the oven on the lowest heat for at least an hour to make the whole house smell warm and welcoming.

Fill a plant sprayer with a mixture of water and 8–10 drops of your favorite essential oil. Keep it on hand to use as an air freshener.

DID YOU KNOW? Polar bears can smell a human 20 miles away.

— CANDLES —

"There isn't enough darkness in the world to snuff out the light of one little candle."
—*Siddhartha Gautama*

Whether for celebration, contemplation, or relaxation, here's how to shine a light on your life . . .

— CANDLE TIPS —

Keep a range of different candle shapes—ball candles, square candles, pyramid candles, multiwick candles, metallic-finish, jelly candles.

Build up a variety of candleholders so you can change them often. Secondhand shops and yard sales are good sources.

If you have children or pets, you don't have to be without candles: create a chandelier or wall sconces with candles.

Arrange same-color candles but different shapes together to create visual impact. An odd number is more effective than an even—try 3 or 5.

Add interest to your floral arrangements by including candles, but be sure to extinguish them before they burn down close to the flowers and foliage.

Brighten up an unused fireplace. A profusion of candles creates the glow of a real fire.

Transform old glass tumblers into tea light holders: glue cinnamon sticks, bamboo, or preserved leaves to the outside of the glass using a hot glue gun, tie with cord, and insert a tea light.

Don't pay more money for so-called "floating candles": wax floats, so any candle that is wider than it is tall should float. Be sure to use a suitable container to float your candles in. Steer clear of fragile glass because it is unlikely to bear the weight of the water.

Punch a pattern of holes in an old tin can, string a wire through it, place a candle inside, and you have a glowing lantern.

Candles can look wonderful even when they aren't lit. Customize a fat pillar candle by sticking colored pins (or sequins and beads threaded onto pins) into it in interesting patterns.

Use unwanted CDs as candleholders—they reflect back the light beautifully.

If a candle is scratched or marked, polish with your hand in the foot of a nylon stocking until smooth.

If your candle won't fit your candlestick, dip the bottom in very hot water. The wax will soften enough for you to shape it to fit the holder.

DID YOU KNOW? Beeswax makes top-grade candles. To produce 1 pound of beeswax, a bee must eat about 10 pounds of honey.

Light up someone's life: a beautiful candle and candleholder make a welcome gift.

Relax in a candlelit bath. Cluster tea lights all around the bathroom, fill the tub with your favorite bubble bath, switch off the electric lights and the worries of the world, and submerge yourself in a sea of dreams.

— How to Make a Votive (Tea Light) Candleholder —
Make your own candleholders out of fruit and vegetables.
Sounds silly, but they're really effective, especially if you group a few together.

1. Choose an apple that doesn't wobble or cut the base off one so it is stable.
Remove the stalk.

2. Place a tea light on top of the apple and draw around it.

3. Cut around the circle using a knife,
and scoop out just enough flesh so the candle will fit securely.

4. Place the candle inside so it is flush with the top.

Variation on a theme: Substitute miniature pumpkins and gourds for a spooky Halloween display. If the fruit is very large, insert a piece of florist's foam and sink the candle into that.

— Storing Candles —
Store candles in a cool, dark, dry place, such as a drawer or cupboard.

Tapers should be stored flat to prevent warping.

Refrigeration is not recommended as candles might crack.

— Candle Care and Safety —
Always keep a lighted candle in your sight. Extinguish all candles before leaving the room or going to bed.

Place candles on a flat, heat-resistant surface. Never put a candle on top of electrical equipment such as the television or on window ledges where curtains may catch on fire.

Don't place candles in a draft, as this will cause the flame to smoke.

Keep candles out of reach of children and pets.

Trim wicks down to $\frac{1}{4}$ inch before lighting or relighting to prevent smoking and flickering.

TIP: Never put candles or tea lights directly on the side of a plastic bath. The heat will melt the plastic and could cause a fire.

If a candle starts smoking, blow it out, trim the wick, and relight.

If the flame is off center, the candle will burn unevenly. To rectify, extinguish the candle and, while the wax is still soft, move the wick back to the center using the handle of a metal spoon.

Always extinguish a candle before moving it.

The safest way to extinguish a candle is with a snuffer. If you don't have one, cup your hand behind the flame and blow gently. Never use water to extinguish the flame.

— WAX REMOVAL —

Glass
If the wax has hardened, soften it using a hair dryer. Ease off wax with a razor blade.

Glass candleholder
Place in the freezer overnight. The wax will shrink and should come off quite easily.

Carpet
Scrape off hardened wax with a blunt knife. Place a few layers of kitchen towel or brown paper over the stain and press with a warm, dry iron until the paper absorbs the wax.

Wooden floor
Apply an ice cube to the spilled wax to harden it, then scrape it off carefully with a blunt knife. Apply floor polish and clean with a lint-free cloth.

Fabric
See "Stain removal for washable fabrics" on page 22.

— HOW TO MAKE A RENTED PROPERTY FEEL LIKE HOME —

Renting a flat or a house doesn't mean it's not your home. It's where you eat, drink, sleep, and hang out, so it's not surprising you want to make it *feel* like home.

Trouble is, most rental properties are deliberately designed to be as bland-looking as possible to maximize appeal, and they also have restrictions on what you can and can't do in terms of decoration; moreover, you won't want to spend a fortune transforming a place you might not be living in for very long. So, the design challenge is how to personalize a space without breaking the lease—or the bank.

First off, find out what you can and can't do. Leases vary considerably. Some landlords allow you free rein to do whatever you like; others will fling you out for knocking a solitary nail in the wall. Any restrictions should be stated in your lease. Check with your landlord before you do anything if you don't want to lose your deposit.

A lick of paint will make the biggest difference for the smallest outlay.

TIP: Do an inventory when you move in. Be thorough. Take photographs of any damaged items, e.g., scratched tables, stained sofas, etc., so you won't have to take the rap for them.

Painting verboten? Use rugs as wall hangings to add color and texture to plain walls. Put up a decorative screen, or create panels of color by draping swathes of colorful fabric over wooden rods attached to the wall to hang down like banners.

Brighten up featureless walls with pictures and posters. Remove creases by pressing the poster under a dry clean cloth using a cool iron. Don't use Blu-Tack to fix it to the wall. Buy a cheap frame and mount (or pick one up from a flea market) to show off your art to best advantage.

Rearrange the furniture until you find an arrangement that suits you. There's no reason why you shouldn't take a chest of drawers out of the bedroom and put it in the living room if it would be more useful to you there. So long as everything is put back in its original position when you leave, the landlord can hardly object.

If the space is small, double it with a huge mirror—you can take it with you when you leave. And don't think that because it's a small room, you have to have small furniture. Just the opposite is true: Small furniture will make a small room even smaller. Choose a piece of furniture such as a dresser to act as a focal point and distract the eye from the size.

Threadbare carpets in ghastly floral prints won't make you want to frolic barefoot. A new fitted carpet would not be a wise investment. Go for one room-size rug or use rugs to define different areas in a multiuse space.

TIP: Did you know a carpet remnant can be "edge-bound" to make a rug?
Simply sew a strip of binding over the edge of the carpet to prevent it from unraveling.
(No-sew alternative: Use thick masking tape in a contrasting color or painted with emulsion.)

Landlord permitting, you could rip out the carpet if the floorboards beneath are sound. If there's paraticle board under the carpet, it can be painted or varnished and look quite good in its own right.

Hideous curtains? Take them down carefully and store them somewhere safe so you can reinstall them when you move. Made-to-measure curtains are a no-no. Use cheap muslin nailed to the top of the window frame. Or buy a cheap roller blind kit and customize it with stencils. Think beyond ready-made curtain fabrics—saris, calico, sheets, recycled wedding veils . . . most fabrics can be used for window dressing.

Sofa seen better days? Drape a throw, an Indian sari, or Japanese obi over it.

If the property is unfurnished and space is tight, go for a sofa bed or a futon, which can double as a sofa.

Good lighting can instantly transform a dingy and depressing place. It may be as simple as changing to higher-wattage lightbulbs. Inexpensive shades will make you view the place in a whole new light. Buy freestanding lamps so you can take them with you when you go. Fit colored bulbs in the fixtures to warm up white, sterile-looking walls.

TIP: Get rental insurance to protect your personal belongings. Your landlord's insurance is unlikely to cover it.

It may seem like a small detail, but changing old-fashioned knobs on drawers and units in the kitchen and bathroom can bring a place right up-to-date. Landlord obliging, spray a rusty fridge with enamel paint for a new lease on life.

Details make the difference, especially if the room is in neutral shades. Colorful cushions and throws, and small accessories like candles, vases, photographs, and knickknacks are the personal touches that create a feeling of home.

Bring the place to life with plants and flowers. (See "How to choose the perfect houseplant" on pages 251–252.)

And so to bed: Even if bed linen is provided, you'll sleep better if you feel your own sheets next to your skin. If you're on a budget, it's simple to make your own duvet cover: take two flat sheets, put the right sides together, and sew around all sides (but leave the top open). Insert a Velcro fastening at the open end and turn the right side out.

— BEDS FROM A TO Zzzzzzz —

We spend a third of our lives in bed but most of us put more thought into buying a TV than a bed. Since a good night's sleep is vital to how we feel and function, it's worth putting a little effort into your purchase.

— HOW TO BUY THE PERFECT BED —

Think about the area the bed will occupy. Lay a string where the bed will go and walk around the space. Jot down the dimensions and take them with you when you go bed-hopping—I mean, bed-shopping.

Buying a bed is one decision you should take lying down. You wouldn't buy a car without taking it for spin, so test-drive your bed! Don't be shy. Slip off your shoes and coat, ask the salesperson for a pillow, and lie down on the bed for at least 10 minutes. If a double bed is being purchased, you should both test it together. Ignore any amused looks from other shoppers; after all, you're never going to see them again—oh, hang on, isn't that your boss and his wife?

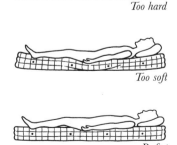

Too hard

Too soft

How to test the firmness of a bed
Lie on your back and slide the flat of your hand into the hollow of your back. If there's a distinct gap, the bed is too hard. If your hand won't budge, the bed is too soft. Roll over onto your side. If you have trouble turning, the bed's too soft; if you feel pressure on your shoulders and hips, the bed's too hard. The ideal bed will mold to the contours of your body. There is no industry standard grading the firmness of a mattress, so one manufacturer's "firm" rating could be another's "medium."

Perfect

DID YOU KNOW? Despite manufacturers' claims, orthopedic beds will not cure a bad back. Usually, they're just firmer than average. A new bed may be all that's needed to ease your aching back.

How to check the size of the bed
Is the bed long enough? It should be at least 6 inches longer than your height.
On average, we toss and turn more than 70 times a night, so ensure it's wide enough, too.

How to test the width of a bed
Lie flat with your hands linked behind your head. If your elbows stick out over the side,
the bed is too narrow. If a double bed is being purchased, both people should lie flat next
to each other with their hands behind their heads. If one person's elbows touch the other
person or the sides of the bed, it's not big enough. If you do opt for a larger size, ensure
it will fit through your bedroom door.

TIP: Don't shop for beds when you're tired; chances are they'll all feel comfortable!

— Mattress Tips —

The mattress will feel different depending on which type of box spring it is on, so choose a
mattress and box spring that are designed to go together. In other words, don't put a foam
mattress on a box spring intended for a sprung mattress and vice versa.

Preserve your mattress with a mattress pad. A cotton one is best, as those made from man-made
fibers rustle so much that it can sound like you're sleeping on a bag of potatoe chips.

Turn a sprung mattress over end to end and side to side regularly to vary the pressure points. If
you do it each time the seasons change, you won't forget.

Vacuum the mattress and box spring of the bed regularly to keep dust mites at bay.

— Bed Linen —

Hold the sheet up to the light to check density. The tighter the weave, the better.

DID YOU KNOW? Jackie Kennedy had her bed linen changed twice a day:
each morning and then again each afternoon following her nap.

— Duvets —

Duvets work differently than bedclothes: whereas bedclothes create a tent around the body,
a duvet drapes around it so it does not feel restrictive.

The filling inside a duvet acts like insulation, keeping the body warm in
cold weather and cool in all but the hottest, most humid conditions.

Another advantage is that you can make the bed very quickly.

Duvets are often given a warmth or weight rating, such as "summer," "fall," "winter," or "Arctic."

TIP: Duvets are more dust-free than blankets, so a good choice for allergy sufferers.

— How to Put a Cover on a Duvet —

METHOD ONE

1. Turn the duvet cover inside out.

2. Reach through the opening of the cover and grasp, in each hand, the two inside far corners of the cover. At this point the material will be gathered over your arms.

3. Keep your hands in those inside corners and pick up the two top corners of the duvet through the cover.

4. Lift your arms high in a sort of "Mexican wave" movement, then shake the whole thing so that the duvet cover turns the right way round and rolls down over the duvet.

5. Pull the bottom corners of the duvet into line with the bottom corners of the duvet corner and close the cover.

METHOD TWO

1. Fold the duvet cover in half, then in half again, keeping the opening on top.

2. Fold the duvet in half, then in half again.

3. Slip the duvet into the opening of the duvet cover and line up the top of the duvet with the top of the duvet cover.

4. Hold the top of the duvet and duvet cover and shake them so that the cover falls neatly over the duvet.

DID YOU KNOW? The word "tog" comes from the British slang word for "clothes."

— Duvet Fillings —
As any pie eater will tell you, it's all about the filling . . .

DUVET FILLING	QUALITIES
Goose down	Warm, lightweight, durable, molds to your shape—top of the range
Duck down	slightly heavier than goose down; still warm
Duck down and feather	51:49 mix—light, warm; good value
Duck feather and down	85:15 mix—feels heavier than down
Synthetic/fiber	usually polyester fibers. Nonallergenic, but tend to be less durable and cozy than down or feather-filled.

TIP: Beware low-quality duvets containing chicken feathers: they can feel scratchy.

DID YOU KNOW? Down is the undercoat of waterfowl, such as swans and geese.
The birds use their feathers for flying, but they use down to trap air at high altitudes and low temperature.

— HOW TO TEST IF YOU NEED A NEW PILLOW —
For a down or feather pillow:
Lay the pillow on a hard surface.
Fold it in half and squeeze out the air.
When you let go, the pillow should resume its shape.

For a synthetic pillow:
Put a clean sneaker on the pillow.
The pillow should spring the shoe off and return to normal shape.

— HOW TO STUFF A PILLOWCASE —
Even the plumpest pillow will soon lose its shape if constantly forced into a narrow pillowcase. Instead of stuffing it in, give the pillow a gentle karate chop lengthways down the middle to create a dent, then hold the folded pillow together. Pinch the ends and push it into the end of the pillowcase down to the corners. Plump it up.

DID YOU KNOW? To ensure a good night's sleep, you should make your bedroom as dark as possible.
A gland in the brain called the pineal gland secretes melatonin, the hormone that brings on sleep,
and this is stimulated by darkness. Wear a sleeping mask, or buy inexpensive blackout curtains.
These are made of a material that light cannot penetrate and fit under your regular curtains.
Ideal for shift workers or for coaxing kids to bed on a light summer's evening.

DID YOU KNOW? A man is twice as likely to fall out of a hospital bed as a woman.

— HOW TO MAKE THE PERFECT BED —

1. If you have one, throw the dust ruffle over the box spring.
Place your mattress on top.

2. Put the bottom sheet on the mattress. If it's a fitted sheet (i.e., the sheet is
elasticized with the corners sewn-in), the work is done for you.
Fix it in place in one corner and work your way around the bed
until all corners are snugly in place.

3. If it's a flat sheet (i.e., no sewn-in corners), you can make "hospital corners."
(See "How to make hospital corners" on pages 122–123.) Make hospital corners on all four
corners of the bed. Smooth the sheet so there are no lumps or wrinkles.

4. Now, you have several options:
(a) Put on the duvet—don't tuck it in at the sides of the bed (go to step 7);
(b) Put on top sheet and blanket/bedspread.

5. Option (b): At the head of the bed, line up the top sheet with the top
of the bottom sheet. The top sheet should go on wrong side up so that when
you fold it back over the blanket, the right side will be uppermost.
Here's another opportunity to practice those hospital corners, but this time
only at the foot of the bed. If you like to be snug as a bug in a
rug, tuck it in; if not, leave the sides untucked.

6. Put the blanket or bedspread on now. At the head of the bed, fold the top
sheet back over the blanket, pulling the sheet back to a depth just larger than
the width of your pillows. Tuck in the side flaps.

7. Place the pillows (in pillowcases) at the head of the bed.
Lay them flat or prop them up.
(If you're using a duvet, you're done!)

8. Next fold the sheet and blanket/bedspread back over the pillows,
making sure that the blanket/bedspread is tucked slightly under the pillows at the front.

9. Smooth out any wrinkles in the bedspread.

Phew, after all that, you deserve a rest.
No, don't get into bed—you just got it looking perfect!

GIVE IT A TRY: Does your newly made bed pass the U.S Army's coin-bounce test?
On a properly made bed, a small coin will bounce.
If not, do 40 push-ups and report to the sergeant major on the double!

TIP: For extra warmth in bed, add a blanket under the bottom sheet.

— HOW TO MAKE HOSPITAL CORNERS —

"Some are born with cold feet, some acquire cold feet, and others have cold feet thrust upon them."
—Anonymous

Making hospital corners may seem like a drag, but your bed will be comfier and cozier, and easier to make in the morning. Once you've mastered the technique, it will become second nature and it won't take you any longer than putting on a fitted sheet.

1. Spread the sheet evenly over the bed, leaving enough overhang to tuck under the mattress on all four sides.

2. Tuck the sheet tightly under the head of the bed and again under the foot of the bed. To make the hospital corner, stand near the middle of the bed and pick up a side hem at point A.

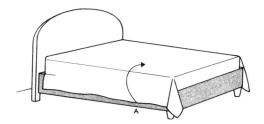

3. Lift up the sheet and pull it taut toward you so that it forms a diagonal crease from where you are holding it at A to the corner of the bed (B).

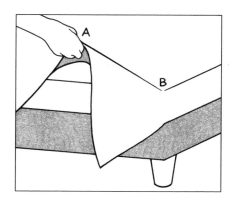

TIP: Throw back the bedcovers each morning for 20 minutes to air your mattress. Dust mites thrive in warm, humid conditions.

4. Lay the diagonal fold flat on top of the mattress. Then tuck that part of the diagonal fold that is still hanging over the bed (C) under the mattress.

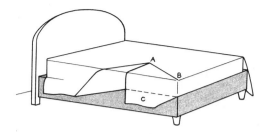

5. Now pick up the diagonal fold that you laid on the mattress and bring it back down to hang over the side of the bed.

6. Tuck all the overhanging sheet under the mattress, as indicated by the dotted line.

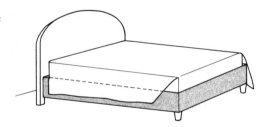

7. What you end up with is a neat diagonal fold of 45 degrees on the side of the bed, guaranteed to keep your tootsies toasty at four in the morning!

TIP: Tests prove that people sleep better in their own space. Twin beds, darling?

— HOW TO SAVE ENERGY —

Saving energy isn't all about installing solar panels and insulation. There are many simple measures you can take which all help save you money—and the planet, too.

— All Over the House —

Get into the habit of switching off lights when you leave a room.

Change to low-energy lightbulbs. They do cost more, but they last up to 12 times longer than standard bulbs and use less energy.

Draft-proof doors and windows.

Install double glazing.

Switch off your television, stereo, and other electronic equipment rather leave them on standby. Some appliances consume up to 50 percent of full power even in standby mode.

Move sofas and other furniture away from the front of radiators so that warm air can circulate.

Put reflector foil behind radiators on external walls, to reflect heat back into the room.

Turn the thermostat down by 1 degree. This will reduce your fuel bill by up to 8 percent.

— In the Bathroom —

Take a shower instead of a bath. A 5-minute shower uses only a third as much water as a bath. However, a power shower uses as much water as a bath.

Don't leave the tap running while brushing your teeth. A tap left running will fill a bath in 5 minutes.

Flushing the toilet requires lots of water. Reduce the water used by putting a simple water-saving device in the tank. NOTE: If you are in a low-pressure area, or have an older model of toilet, you may find this reduces the efficiency of the flush too much to be viable.

Check that your hot-water tank is properly insulated. Also, ensure that the hot-water pipes leading from the tank to the taps are insulated so they will remain hotter for longer.

Ensure the hot-water pipes under the floorboards are insulated.

TIP: Pull the curtains right back and let the sunshine in. Solar energy is free. Close the curtains at sundown to keep the insulation in.

— In the Kitchen —

If you are making a cup of tea, fill the kettle with only as much water as is needed.

Kettles usually boil faster than saucepans. Boil the water for your rice and pasta in the kettle.

Use the microwave, especially for reheating food. It uses up to 70 percent less energy to heat than a regular oven.

Make toast in a toaster rather than turning on a large grill on the stove.

Wait until you have a full load before running your washing machine or dishwasher.

Modern detergents mean that results are just as good if you wash clothes on a cooler cycle. A wash cycle of 100°F uses a third less electricity than a wash at 140°F.

Give the energy-hungry dryer a rest. Dry and air clothes naturally whenever possible.

Shut the fridge door promptly. For each minute the door is left open, it takes 3 minutes to return to the correct temperature.

— Energy Costs —

Have you any idea how much your washing machine or hair dryer cost you to use? Here's how to work out what's watt . . .

Look at your electricity bill. You pay for electricity by the unit. A unit is equivalent to 1,000 watts of electricity used for a period of 1 hour (this is usually called a kilowatt-hour, or shortened to kWh).

The power of an appliance should be marked on it in either watts (W) or kilowatts (kW). So, here's how to make the calculation:

1 kwH (1000W) electric fire x 1 hour of use = 1 unit used

2 kwH (2000W) fan heater x 1 hour of use = 2 units used

100 watt lightbulb x 10 hours of use = 1,000 watt hours = 1 kilowatt = 1 unit used

When you know how many units an appliance uses, you simply multiply by the cost per unit (your bill will tell you this), and you'll be able to work out the running cost for that length of time.

TIP: Put your computer to sleep! Enable the "sleep mode" when you aren't using it and you'll save energy and prolong the life of your computer.

This chart estimates the length of time an appliance can be used per unit of electricity:

APPLIANCE	TIME PER UNIT OF ELECTRICITY	APPLIANCE	TIME PER UNIT OF ELECTRICITY
Tumble dryer	40 mins	Fridge	10 hours
Iron	2½ hours	Freezer	10 hours
Lightbulb (100w)	10 hours	Oven	20 mins
Lightbulb (40w)	25 hours	Extractor fan	13 hours
Color TV	3 hours	Vacuum cleaner	3½ hours
Kettle	30 mins	Fan heater (2kw)	30 mins
Washing machine	20 mins	Hair dryer	3 hours
Immersion heater	20 mins	Drill	4 hours

REMEMBER: An appliance that produces heat requires a lot more power.

— HOW TO GET SOME PEACE AND QUIET —

"There are two things we can all live without—hemorrhoids and neighbors."
—Spike Milligan

According to a report by the World Health Organization, what is the number-one threat to health and welfare today? Avian flu? Pollution? Obesity? The answer is noise.

Noise affects us physically, psychologically, and emotionally. Blood pressure rises, sleeping and eating patterns are disrupted. In severe cases, noise has driven people to suicide or murder. So, what can you do to bring peace and tranquility to your life?

Here's the thing: Noise is much easier to control at its source. In other words, if noisy neighbors are the problem, it is easier to prevent noise leaving *their* house than it is for you to prevent their noise entering *your* house. What it comes down to is being a good neighbor.

TIP: Love your neighbor but don't cut down your hedge.

— How to Be a Good Neighbor —

— About the House —

Don't clatter around in noisy heels if you live in an apartment and have neighbors living below—particularly if you have hardwood floors.

Close doors quietly. There is no need to slam them.

Site noisy appliances such as fridges, freezers, and washing machines away from party walls. Set them on level surfaces and place a rubber mat or carpet under those that vibrate, like the tumble dryer.

Site bookshelves against a shared wall to act as a shock absorber for noise.

In a bedroom, position built-in closets on a shared wall so the clothes will absorb some of the noise.

Midnight vacuuming or dawn mowing may be convenient for you, but consider your close neighbors; they may need more beauty sleep than you.

Forewarn neighbors if you're doing DIY using power tools or knocking against a party wall. Don't carry out such work during unsociable hours. And don't let it drag on for months.

Ensure a key holder can be contacted if your house alarm goes off while you're away.

— Stereos and Televisions —

Site televisions and speakers away from party walls. Raise them above floor level.

Listen to music at a volume that will not disturb others. Set the bass control at a low level as it is this that creates the persistent throbbing sound, which upsets so many people.

Use headphones when you want to listen to loud music.
Cordless, infrared headphones allow unrestricted movement.

— Dogs —

Train your dog not to bark unnecessarily.
If your dog doesn't respond to training, try an ultrasonic collar to change its behavior.

Don't leave your dog unattended in the house or garden for long periods. If you are at work, leave it with a friend or family member.

— Parties —

Warn your neighbors of any forthcoming party or barbecue, or better still, invite them, and they're likely to be more tolerant. Inform them exactly what time the music will stop and keep to that time. Keep merrymakers under control.

DID YOU KNOW? After an intruder broke into the Queen's bedroom in Buckingham Palace in 1982, Her Majesty remarked: "I realized immediately that it wasn't a servant because they don't slam doors."

— Cars and Motorcycles—

Don't rev the engine excessively.

Honk your car horn Only in an emergency.
Honking to say hello or good-bye when arriving or departing
does NOT constitute an emergency.

Carry out repair work in the garage, not in the driveway or the street.

Keep the car windows closed when playing your car stereo in a residential area.

— TAKING MATTERS INTO YOUR OWN HANDS —

Unfortunately, neighborliness is something we can rely on less and less these days. If you work from home, if you're a shift worker, or if you simply crave a bit of peace and quiet, how can you take matters into your hands?

Acoustics made simple

Acoustics is a complex science, but, at its simplest, sound travels in two ways: There's impact sound, such as the sound of footsteps on stairs and objects dropping on a floor. Then there's airborne sound, which is the noise that travels through the air from sources such as stereos, televisions, and people's raised voices. Whatever measures you take, accept that for both types of noise, it's going to be damage limitation rather than complete cure.

Soundproofing

The word *soundproof* is a misnomer, since the plain truth is that there is no way to completely soundproof a room. The closest you can get is to create "a room within a room," like a professional recording studio, but even then, a certain amount of outside noise leaks in, and it's not usually practical in the average residential dwelling.

Sealing gaps

Sealing around doors, windows, baseboards, floorboards, and shared walls will reduce airborne noise. Noise can seep through the teeniest of cracks.

Secondary glazing

Helps to dampen outside noise, like traffic, car alarms, and barking dogs. This should not be confused with double glazing. In secondary glazing the air gap between the two panes of glass is much bigger. It needs to be at least 4 inches, and better still, 7¾ inches to make any noticeable difference. The larger the gap between the panes, the better the noise reduction. It also helps to use glass of a different thickness to the panes. Of course, when you open the window, any benefit is lost.

Acoustic blinds

Look like regular shades but are reinforced with fiberglass or foam to reduce outside noise.

Earplugs

Earplugs are one of the most basic methods of reducing noise and, worn correctly, are one of the most effective. They limit everyday noises such as traffic, DIY enthusiasts, and snorers. Earplugs are made of various materials. Beeswax earplugs will not reduce noise as well as foam earplugs or the latest silicone earplugs, which mold to the contours of your ears. Whichever type you choose, a proper seal is critical to performance. They need to be inserted deep into the ear canal.

Partition wall

If the noise is coming through a shared wall, you could build what is known as a partition

TIP: To close a door discreetly: Open the door, keep your hand on the handle until you are through the door, then, without releasing the catch, grasp the handle with your other hand. Close the door and slowly release the catch.

wall. This is another wall built at a distance from the existing wall using timber batten and plaster. The cavity between is filled with a sound-insulation material, such as a glass-fiber blanket. Don't expect miracles. You'll be lucky if you get a 20 percent improvement in noise level from this kind of construction. There will be no reduction at all in impact sound, like footsteps, and airborne sound, like the throbbing bass of a sound system.

New floor

Uncarpeted wooden floors are very popular but they permit sound to travel through them. The noise of heels clattering across the floorboards can be a living hell if you're the unlucky neighbor living in the apartment below. Unfortunately, the best solution to the problem lies in the apartment with the heel-clatterers. Their floor and your ceiling need to be separated by a new floor, with joists between but not touching, the ceiling joists below. All you can do from downstairs is have a false ceiling fitted or fit acoustic tiles, but the effect will be minimal; in fact, you'll be preventing sound from leaving your room more than preventing it entering, thereby doing your upstairs neighbors a favor! You could always buy your noisy neighbors upstairs a pair of slippers each for Christmas and tuck a copy of the *Manifesto for How to be a Good Neighbor* inside their Christmas card, and see if they take the hint!

Move out!

But beware of jumping out of the noisy frying pan into the noisier fire. Never take the word of the real estate agent or vendor when they assure you it's "a nice, quiet area." Get yourself a trench coat and make like a private dick. Do a recce of the area, case the joint thoroughly, and do so at different times of day. A peaceful haven by day may turn into the *Nightmare on Elm Street* by night. Suss out the neighbors, too. Don't think that the more exclusive the area, the quieter it will be. It doesn't work like that. There are no class barriers when it comes to noise nuisance.

White noise machine

Replicates natural soothing sounds like ocean waves, falling rain, or a babbling brook to mask disturbing environmental noise such as traffic, slamming doors, and loud voices. Manufacturers also claim it can soothe babies to sleep and offer relief to tinnitus sufferers. The machine resembles a radio alarm and it can be switched to a timer to turn itself off after a set time. You have to persevere with it. At first, crashing waves may sound even more irritating than the noise you're trying to cover, but after a few days you get used to it.

White noise CDs

These work on the same principle as a white noise machine, but they can be played in a regular CD player.

File a complaint

If the noise nuisance is persistent, make a formal complaint to your town's environmental health authority or launch your own action through the courts.

If all else fails

Move to Switzerland! The Swiss take their tranquility as seriously as their chocolate. If you live in an apartment, it is against the law to flush the toilet after 10 P.M. in case the noise wakens your neighbors. It's also illegal to use your lawn mower on a Sunday. Yeah, but what about all those cuckoo clocks and cowbells?

Find out more about coping with noise by visiting the website of the Noise Abatement Society, www.noiseabatementsociety.com.

TIP: Choose from a variety of earplugs, white noise machines, and CDs at www.earplugstore.com.
The CD replicating the sound of an electric fan is particularly recommended.

– DIY –

"Does that screwdriver really belong to Phillip?"

—GEORGE CARLIN

— TOOL KIT —

1. Pliers: For gripping, twisting and cutting. Go for a pair with PVC-insulated handles as the grip will be more comfortable and less likely to slip. Or wrap tape around the handles.

2. Backsaw: For general joinery—cuts wood and manufactured boards like MDF. Ideal for a beginner or if you don't do a lot of woodwork, as the teeth don't blunt as fast as a regular "panel" saw. The more teeth, the sharper the cut.
NOTE: On a Backsaw the teeth cannot be sharpened, so when the edge becomes blunt, the saw will need to be replaced.

3. Adjustable wrench: What else would you use to grip your nuts?

4. Level: Used to find a vertical or horizontal line. The glass tube is filled with liquid in which floats an air bubble. Position the bubble between two lines on the tube to find the exact level. Choose a 3 ft. size.

5. Putty knife

6. Awl: Used to make small starter holes in wood and walls before inserting a screw to prevent timber splitting or the drill slipping.

7/8. Hammers: You need two: a 16-in. claw hammer (7) and a pin hammer (8)—a lightweight hammer ideal for small jobs such as tapping in tacks.

9. Chisel: Choose a robust one that you can hit with a hammer.

10. Steel tape measure: A retractable measure is best as its end catches onto an edge to make measuring easier. Choose one that is at least 16 feet long. Digital tape measures, with an electronic display, are also available.

11. Craft knife: For general-purpose cutting. The blades are often stored in the handle. Choose one with a retractable blade.

12/13. Screwdrivers: You need two: a flat-head screwdriver (12) 8 in.; and a 6 in. Phillips or "cross-head" screwdriver (13).

14. Try square: For establishing right angles. Buy the largest.

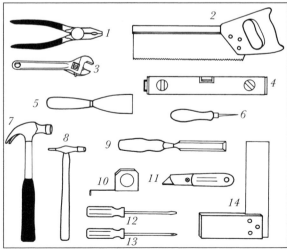

DID YOU KNOW? In 1934, Henry F. Phillips, an Oregon businessman, invented both the screw and the screwdriver that bear his name.

— OTHER USEFUL ITEMS —

Hot glue gun
Ideal for decorative crafts projects or when precise dabs of glue are needed.
Solid sticks of glue are inserted into the back of the gun; plug it in, let it heat up,
then ready, aim, and fire! The glue becomes molten, so watch your fingers.
Cold glue guns are also available but are not as effective.

Staple gun
Use for a variety of purposes from putting up posters to covering chairs with fabric.

Sandpaper
From coarse to fine, use for finishing surfaces and rubbing down paintwork.

Small screwdriver
For fiddly jobs like opening the backs of children's toys to change the batteries.

— SAFETY FIRST —

Dust mask: protects you from wood or plaster dust.
Essential when cutting MDF.

Protective gloves

Safety goggles: for cutting or sawing

Earplugs

— FIXINGS —

"Fixings" is the word for items such as nails, tacks, staples, etc.,
used for so many DIY jobs from repairing a dripping tap to putting up a shelf.

— POWER TOOLS —

ELECTRIC DRILL: If you can buy only one power tool, choose this. It makes light work of
drilling holes in wood and plaster.

JIGSAW: Cuts curvy edges and decorative cutouts in timber, metal, plastic, and ceramic.

ELECTRIC SCREWDRIVER: Takes the slog out of many DIY jobs. Invaluable when
assembling furniture.

SANDER: Takes the sweat out of removing old paint from wood.

*TIP: If you use a variety of power tools, an extension cord is essential. Buy one of a suitable ampage.
Uncoil fully before use.*

TIP: If "hunt for the screwdriver" is not your idea of fun, get a toolbox to keep everything together.

— NAIL IT —

A claw hammer is suitable for most nails: one side knocks the nails in; the other side pulls
'em out. Also flattens bent metal. The split end or "claw" is used to lever out nails.

Nails come in all shapes and sizes, from small "panel pins" to "tacks." Choose the right one for
the job.

— HAMMERING A NAIL INTO WOOD —

1. Tap the nail gently to start it off in the wood.

2. Hold the hammer near the base, and keep your gaze fixed on the nail.

3. Now, strike the nail by swinging the hammer, pivoting your arm from the elbow,
   to make a good, clean blow.

NOTE: Nails driven in at a slight angle are more resistant to pulling out.

*TIP: If you're hammering in a small nail, put the nail into a thin piece of card first, and use that to hold it.
Simply pull off when the nail is secure.*

— REMOVING A NAIL —

A bent nail, like a rotten
tooth, needs pulling out. If
you've ever dreamed of being
a dentist (does *anyone* ever
dream of being a dentist?),
now's your chance . . .

Use the reverse side of the
claw hammer known as the
claw. Hook the claw into the
nail head and use it as a lever
to pull on the nail. (figure 1)

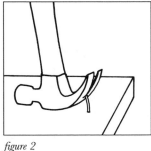

figure 1 *figure 2*

It'll probably take a few pulls to release the nail. Keep the handle upright if you need more
pulling power. (figure 2) Well done. Your first extraction.

TIP: To protect the surface of the wood, slip a piece of card under the hammer when you pull the nail.

*TIP: If your hammer keeps slipping off the nail head causing the nail to bend, it probably needs cleaning: Shine
up the striking face of the hammer with fine sandpaper.*

— SCREW IT —

There are two main types of screwdriver:

flat-head

Flat-head screwdriver for slot-head screws (they have a straight indentation in the head).

cross-head

Cross-head screwdriver (aka Phillips) for cross-shaped screws.

Screws offer a firmer fixing than nails because they have a thread that bites into whatever material is being screwed into. They're also easier to remove and reposition.

Use the right screwdriver on the right screw. Don't force the wrong screwdriver into a screw, because it won't work and you'll damage your tool.

To remove a rusty screw: Put the screwdriver into the slot and strike the top with a hammer. If this doesn't work, try heating the head of the screw with a soldering iron.

CHANT: Keep forgetting which direction to turn a screw?
Say to yourself: "Left is loose, right is tight."

— HOW TO SAW WOOD —

Place your wood on a level surface and secure it with clamps or a vise.

Grip the saw firmly, and point the first finger of the hand holding the saw down the blade to help you keep a good line.

To make a cut: Hold the saw nearly upright on the place where you are going to cut the wood. Start by drawing the saw slowly upward, using the thumb of your other hand to keep the side of the blade steady. The aim is to make a nick in the wood to guide the saw. Then push the blade forward, applying light pressure to make your cut. Continue in this way, drawing the saw back to its full extent and applying light pressure only on the forward strokes. Always make your cut on the forward stroke. Allow the weight of the saw to do most of the work. You'll need to practice—and doubtless, your saw will get stuck a few times—but persevere, and soon you'll build up a steady rhythm.

IF YOU REMEMBER JUST ONE THING: Always make your cut on the forward stroke.

DID YOU KNOW? Most lumberyards will cut wood to size for you.

TIP: Slice lengthways through some old garden hose and slip it over the cutting edge of your saw to protect it—and you.

— HOW TO USE AN ELECTRIC DRILL —

Choosing a drill

The most practical and versatile drill is one with a variable-speed facility and hammer action.
This enables you to drill into a variety of materials, including masonry, wood, and metal.
A cordless, battery-powered drill usually costs more, but there's no worries about tripping over
extension cords. It also serves as a cordless screwdriver.

Drill bits

Bits fit into the drill to make the holes. They come in various shapes and sizes, each designed to
do a specific job. It's essential to match the right bit to the material you're drilling. Start with a
basic set containing the following:

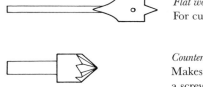

Flat wood or spade:
For cutting large holes in wood.

Countersink:
Makes a shallow round recess in wood to countersink
a screw (i.e., to ensure the head of a screw is level with
or just below the surface, so that it doesn't snag).

High-speed twist:
For making small holes in wood, metal, and plastic.

Masonry:
Toughened with a tip of tungsten carbide,
for boring holes in walls and concrete.

— DRILLING: GENERAL TIPS —

Safety first

If you want to live long enough to enjoy the fruits of your
DIY labors, always check that there are no cables or pipes where you intend to drill.
You can choose from a variety of inexpensive gadgets designed
to detect pipes and wires.

Electrics

Never drill around electric sockets or light fittings.

Hammer-drilling

Wear safety goggles, dust mask, and earplugs.

Changing drill bits

Always disconnect the drill from the power supply when you are changing drill bits.

Screws

Ensure you have the right size screw for the job.

TIP: Remove dangly jewelery, ties, and tie back long hair when drilling.

Wall plugs

A wall plug is a plug which fits into the drilled hole so that your screw
will grip firmly into the wall. Wall plugs are usually made of plastic and come in all sizes.
Select the correct size of plug and drill bit for your screw.

Adjustable depth gauge

In order to drill the hole to the required depth, you need an adjustable
depth gauge—a metal rod that fits onto the body of the drill. If you don't
have one, you can improvise: hold the wall plug up to the drill and mark
its length by winding colored tape or masking tape around the bit.

Drilling into plaster walls

This is usually quite straightforward unless the plaster is soft. Soft plaster can
turn a small hole into the Grand Canyon. If this is the case, use a wall plug with
a thread on it. When drilling masonry, the tip of the drill is liable to overheat, so
it is important to withdraw the tip every few seconds to allow it to cool,
keeping the drill running.

Drilling into a concrete wall

If you are drilling into a concrete wall you will need a drill with hammer action.

Drilling into wood

For simple DIY jobs, it's unlikely you'll need to drill a hole in wood; however a
screw will fit better into a hole if a small "starter" hole or "pilot" hole is made as a
guide for the proper hole. This can be done with a awl or a drill with a small bit.
When drilling wood, withdraw the drill bit every few seconds to clear debris from the hole.
If possible, clamp the wood to the bench so you can keep both hands on the drill and prevent
slipping and skidding.

Drilling a hole in a ceiling

Drilling into ceilings is fraught with potential danger and not recommended for beginners.

Drilling into metal

Use a metal bit when drilling into metal. Make a small dent with a awl to start you off.

Drilling into ceramic tiles

Use a masonry bit with the drill set to rotary action when drilling into ceramic tile.
Take care, as the drill could slip on the smooth surface. Mark the spot to be drilled
with a cross made of masking tape. Never use hammer action on tiles.

Drilling into plastic laminates

A hard material with a smooth surface makes drilling tricky. Put a cross made of masking tape
over the area and mark the spot you want to drill. Use a sharp wood drill bit and drill a small
starter hole first. Drill down through the top of the laminate to prevent splitting it.

*TIP: To remove a wall plug from a hole, push a screw in partway, grip both screw and wall plug with pliers,
and yank both out together.*

— How to Drill —

Drilling your first hole is a lot like your first kiss: thrilling, satisfying, and you can't wait to do it again! Let's start with something simple like fixing a chandelier to the ceiling. Not keen? All right, how does a picture hook grab you?

1. Check for hidden pipes and electrical cables using an electronic pipe and wire detector.

2. Hold the framed picture to the wall, mark the top of the frame, and measure down to the picture wire so that you know where to make your hole.

3. Mark the center point of the hole on the wall with a pencil.

4. If you don't have an adjustable depth gauge, hold the wall plug up to the drill and mark its length by winding colored tape or masking tape around the bit so you know what depth to drill the hole.

5. Set the drill to hammer setting. Position the point of the masonry drill bit on the mark at right angles to the wall.

6. Turn on the drill. Holding it steady and keeping it as straight as possible, push the drill bit carefully into the wall. No need to apply much pressure; let the drill do the work. Keep pushing the drill bit into the wall. You'll probably have to remove the drill from time to time to remove debris that builds up in the hole. Continue drilling until the hole is drilled to the correct depth as indicated by your depth gauge or colored tape.

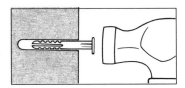

colored or masking tape

7. Press the wall plug into the drilled hole with your hand, ensuring that it is level with the wall. You might need to tap it lightly with a hammer to make it flush.

8. Place the hook against the wall so that the drilled hole and screw hole are aligned. Insert the screw, and tighten with a screwdriver. The screw should go straight into the wall plug, not at an angle. The wall plug will expand to fill the hole. Hang your picture. Sit back and admire the view.

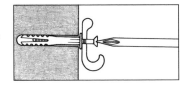

Piece of cake, wasn't it? Today, picture hooks—tomorrow, coat hooks, towel rails, toilet-paper holders, chandeliers . . . it's a hole new world.

TIP: Use a good sharp drill bit to ensure a good, clean hole. A dull drill bit forces you to exert more pressure, which can lead to slippage and scratches.

— HOW TO FILL IN CRACKS AND HOLES IN PLASTER —

1. Scrape out any loose plaster with a putty knife. Don't worry if any cracks in the plaster split open, just rake out the dust and debris. Better to happen now than after you've painted. (figure 1)

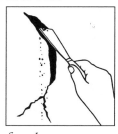

2. Press the filler into the hole, holding the knife at 90 degrees to the crack. (figure 2)

3. Remove any excess filler with a knife. Brush over the surface with a paintbrush dipped in water. This will soften the filler so you can smooth it into the crevices. When the surface is dry, sand down the wall so it is completely smooth.

figure 1

MOISTURE: Never paint over damp walls. Black or brown specks on the wall and a musty smell suggest fungal growth. (See "Dealing with moisture" on pages 141–142.)

NOTE: If the cracks in the plaster keep on reappearing even after you have filled them in, the problem might be a slight shift in the foundation of the house.

figure 2

— HOW TO UNCLOG A SINK OR BASIN —

SYMPTOM: Water is slow to drain away; in a complete blockage, water will not drain away at all.

CAUSE: Buildup of household debris such as hair, scum, or cooking grease.

CURE: The first thing to do is to check that only one sink is blocked. If all of them are affected, your problem is likely to be a blocked drain.

If it is just one sink, try pouring a good handful of washing soda followed by boiling water down the drain. Repeat if necessary. The use of cleaning chemicals like caustic soda is best avoided.

If the washing soda doesn't do the trick, you'll need a plunger. This is a bell-shaped rubber cup on a handle—cheap, cheerful, and readily available from any hardware store.

1. Fill the sink half full of water, if it is not already because of the blockage.

2. Stuff a cloth into the overflow (the little letterbox-slit in the top of the basin). This will block the airflow and prevent dirty water spurting back out at you when you put the plunger into action.

TIP: Keep a footstool beside the sinks in the house so the kids can step up to brush their teeth or help with the washing up.

3. Press the plunger down tightly to form a seal over the drain. Begin to pump the plunger energetically up and down about 10 times. The idea is to create a vacuum to dislodge the obstruction. (figure 1)

4. If this tactic fails, it means the blockage is in the U-bend and for this you'll need to remove the waste trap under the back of the sink. Don't panic, it's quite simple. The trap is a bend in the waste pipe, which "traps" water to make a seal, preventing bad smells drifting up from the sewer into the house. They come in various shapes and sizes. Modern plastic traps can be unscrewed without any need for tools; others might need the aid of a screwdriver to undo the nuts keeping it in place. Either way, make sure you put a container underneath the trap to catch the filthy water that will inevitably pour out. (figure 2)

figure 1

5. Just removing the trap may be enough to clear the obstruction. If not, poke a length of stiff wire such as a straightened wire coat hanger into the outlet pipe.

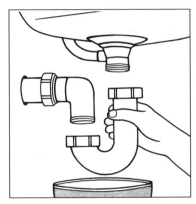

6. The trap, once removed, will be grungier than a hippie at Woodstock, so give it a thorough wash with detergent, but don't do as I once did and turn on the taps of the very sink you are trying to unblock— you'll cause a flood! Once clean, screw the trap carefully back in place. Not too slack but not so tight that you'll never be able to remove it again.

figure 2

7. Turn on the taps and flush with disinfectant. Niagara restored.

WARNING: Never pour fat, candle wax, tea leaves, coffee dregs, or vegetable peelings into the sink. Pour cooking oil into empty cans or margarine tubs and dispose of with household rubbish.

TIP: To prevent further problems, pour boiling water periodically down sinks to keep pipes clear.

— HOW TO RECOVER AN OBJECT DROPPED DOWN THE SINK —

There's an old music hall ballad ominously titled,
"My Baby has Gone Down the Plug Hole."
Hopefully, you weren't quite that clumsy, but it can still be
devastating to see your precious ring or some other item of
sentimental value tumble headlong down the drain.

1. Turn off the water as soon as possible to prevent the object
being washed away down the drain.

2. The object is likely to be in the trap so follow step 4 of
"How to unclog a sink or basin" on page 139.

3. Place a container under the trap, and, wearing gloves,
sift through the debris until, with a bit of luck, you see the object.

4. Wash object carefully and reassemble trap.

— HOW TO COMBAT CONDENSATION —

Condensation is one of the most common problems in homes. It occurs when water vapor in
the air comes into contact with a cold surface and leaves a deposit of water droplets on the
surface. You can see the effect on mirrors and windows which get steamed up when you take a
bath or shower. A certain amount of condensation is normal, but excessive condensation can
lead to mold growth that not only ruins your decor, but also eventually damages the structure of
your house.

— WHERE DOES THE WATER VAPOR COME FROM? —

1 person breathing and perspiring over one day: 3 pints
1 household plant in one day: 1 pint
Cooking one meal: 1 pint
Shower: ½ pint

Multiply these figures by the number of people, plants, meals, and showers taken
per day in the average household, and that's an awful lot of moisture hanging in the air.
I'm not recommending you stop breathing—that's a bit too drastic—
but there are some simple measures you can take to minimize the problem.

Open the windows! Let the moist air out and the dry air in.
Allow your house to breathe.

Don't block air vents in walls and windows.

When cooking, keep lids on saucepans and open a window.

If you have an extractor fan in the kitchen or bathroom, use it.

TIP: To prevent the bathroom mirror fogging up, run some cold water in the bath before you run the hot.

Close the door when you are cooking or when you are having a bath
so steam doesn't escape into other rooms.

After you have had a bath, close the door and open the window a little.

Paint steamy rooms, such as the kitchen and bathroom, with
anticondensation paint.

In the bathroom, run the cold water before the hot water to reduce steam.

Don't dry washing indoors—especially not on radiators. If you must dry clothes
indoors, use a drying rack and keep a window open so
steam can escape.

Vent your dryer to an outside wall.

Keep the whole house at an evenly warm temperature, especially
during colder weather, so no "cold spots" can occur to allow condensation
to form. Having the heat on high for just a few hours a day can
create condensation.

Install double glazing. Glass in single panes becomes very cold in winter
and it can take an entire morning to mop up those soggy windowsills.
If left damp, wooden window frames will rot.

If you have a bad condensation problem, invest in an electric dehumidifier.

— DEALING WITH MOISTURE —

SYMPTOMS: Black specks on walls; a musty smell.

CAUSE: Condensation or moisture.

How to test for moisture: Tape a piece of foil over a damp patch, ensuring it is well stuck down.
After a day or two, peel away the foil. If the surface of the foil is wet, the moisture is caused
by condensation. If the surface of the foil is dry but the underside is wet, the cause
is penetrating moisture.

CURE: If the cause is condensation, see "How to combat condensation" on page 140.
If penetrating moisture, check for defective brickwork, blocked gutters, or
faulty pointing.

To remove mold from paintwork, such as a window frame: Treat with a fungicidal wash.
Bleach will have no lasting effect.

To remove mold from a wall: See "Dealing with mold on walls" on page 89.

To remove mildew from a shower curtain: Remove from the rod, soak in a solution of bleach (one part bleach to four parts water). Rinse thoroughly, then machine-wash. If just the bottom is soiled, leave the curtain on the rod and hang it in a bucket of water with a few squirts of bleach.

To prevent mildew: After showering, pull the curtain all the way along the rod to dry so moisture doesn't hang inside it.

CLEAN GREEN: Scrub the shower curtain with a paste of lemon juice mixed with bicarbonate of soda.

— TOILET TROUBLE —

"What's with the people who put carpeting on the lid of their toilet seat? What are they thinking: 'Gosh, if we have a party, there may not be enough standing room; I'd better carpet the toilet too.'"
—Jerry Seinfeld

Toilet traumas can be some of the most traumatic domestic disasters to befall us.
The good news is that many of them can be resolved quite easily . . .

— HOW TO UNCLOG A TOILET —

SYMPTOMS: Water rises in the rim and drains slowly.

CAUSE: Main cause is flushing something unsuitable (e.g., disposable diaper).

CURE: Remove the blockage.

Do NOT keep flushing a blocked toilet. It will simply overflow.

1. Turn the water off, flush the toilet, and bail out any remaining water using a disposable cup.

2. First of all, try throwing a bucket of very warm water all at once from a great height down the toilet. If it looks like it's draining, try a couple more buckets.

3. It this doesn't work, it's plunger time again (it's not called "the plumber's friend" for nothing). The general principle for unblocking a toilet is the same as that for unblocking a sink, but, in the case of the toilet, you'll need a special long-handled plunger (rent one or improvise one out of a plastic bag tied tight round a mop head).

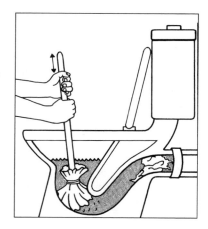

TIP: Soak a new or newly cleaned shower curtain in salted water for a few hours, then allow to dry before rehanging. This will protect against mildew.

4. Bail out some water, leaving the bowl about half full.

5. Position the plunger down inside the bend at the base of the bowl. Pump it vigorously up and down quite forcefully about a dozen times. Listen for the telltale gurgling sound that tells you your toilet trouble's cured.

6. Flush the toilet a couple of times.

If this doesn't do the trick either, you will need to buy or rent a snake—a flexible rod especially designed for the purpose. Insert the rod into the toilet trap and crank the handle.

DID YOU KNOW? If you want to find out the date your house was built, a good guide is to look at the date stamped on the inside of the toilet-cistern lid, since the toilet is likely to have been installed at the time of building.

— FLUSHING NO-NOS —
Very cheap toilet paper that doesn't dissolve well

Facial tissues

Cigarettes

Insects and bugs

Sanitary pads

— HOW TO PLAY TOILET-SEAT SEESAW —
Does the man of the house always forget to put the toilet seat down? Paint the logo of his *least* favorite sports team on the underside of the seat; paint the badge of his favorite sports team on top of the seat. Instant cure.

— HANGING TOILET PAPER ROLL —
A source of domestic strife as prickly as the toilet seat left up is the dilemma of which way to hang the roll of toilet paper on the holder. Should it hang over or under? It's a debate that's been raging since toilet paper was invented. One school of thought argues that under is best because, they say, it keeps the roll tucked away. An opposing school of thought argues that over is best because, they say, it is more hygienic: Your hands come into contact with fewer sheets and do not touch the wall. Also, if your roll is patterned, the decoration will face the right way.

HOW TO SAVE YOUR MARRIAGE: If you and your partner can't agree on the hanging dilemma, but are fortunate enough to have two bathrooms, why not compromise? Hang the toilet roll *over* in one bathroom and *under* in the other.

TIP: One of the main causes of toilet blockage is dental floss. Harmless as it may seem, it becomes entangled in other waste matter, so dispose of it with household rubbish.

— How to Synchronize the Sheets of Two-Ply Toilet Roll —

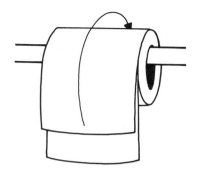

A common problem, especially with cheap toilet tissue, is that the perforations on the top sheet and bottom sheet don't match. No matter how many sheets you rip off, the two just won't get back in synch. The solution is simple when you know how: Pick up the top sheet and pass it over the roll (one revolution). Rip off the sheet and presto, the sheets will be perfectly aligned again. Now you can get on with the job in hand.

— FIXING A COLD RADIATOR: HOW TO BLEED A RADIATOR —

SYMPTOM: When the furnace is on, the radiator is noticeably cooler at the top than it is at the bottom; there might also be a rushing or gurgling sound.

CAUSE: Trapped air. Yes, even radiators suffer with it.

CURE: A couple of Tums won't do the trick here. You need to "bleed" the radiator.

1. Turn the furnace on and as soon as the water in the radiator feels warm, turn it off.

2. Locate the air valve on the radiator; it's usually on the top corner. Put a radiator bleed key (or sometimes a flat-head screwdriver will work) onto the valve. Place a cloth close to the valve to catch any water.

3. Open the valve by turning the key no more than half a turn counter-clockwise. Don't be alarmed if you hear a hissing sound—that's good; it means the trapped air is escaping.

4. As soon as water trickles out, close the valve by turning the key half a turn clockwise. Don't over-tighten.

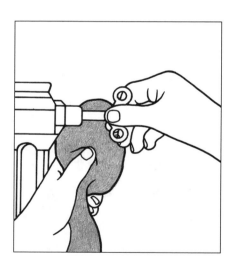

Q: How many men does it take to change a roll of toilet paper?
A: Nobody knows; it's never been done.

— HOW TO REPLACE A BROKEN PANE IN A WINDOW —

After you've reprimanded the irresponsible so-and-so who kicked the football through the window, you'll want to see about replacing the pane of glass. Unless the window is very large or a stained-glass Tiffany original (oops), it's not difficult to replace the glass yourself.

What you need: New glass, universal putty, glazing paints, protective gloves, safety goggles, chisel, pin hammer, pliers, putty knife, or old household knife.

Take a piece of the glass with you to the hardware store so they can match the thickness. Measure all four sides and the diagonals too before you buy the glass, as the window might not be dead square. Install the window from the OUTSIDE. Easier said than done if your broken window is on the second floor. It might be possible to remove the entire window from the frame. Failing that, you'll need scaffolding—and possibly, a professional.

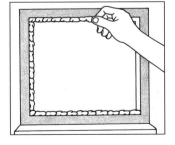

1. Wearing safety goggles and protective gloves (thick gardening gloves will do), remove the remaining glass from the window. This you can do from the inside of the window so that the glass falls outside. Crisscross the remains of the pane on both sides with strips of masking tape to make the task easier and less messy. Starting at the top, carefully tap out any remaining shards with a hammer or chisel. Wrap broken glass in newspaper before disposing of it.

2. Chip out all the old putty from around the frame. Hold a chisel at an angle to the window frame and tap it firmly with a hammer. Take care not to damage the frame itself. In a wooden window you will come across "glazing paints,", which are small, triangular-shaped nails used to hold the glass in place while the putty sets. Pull these out with pliers. (A metal window will have metal clips instead, which also need removing.)

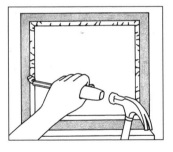

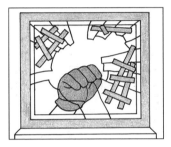

3. Knead a ball of universal putty in your hands until it is soft, then roll it into a long thin roll. Press the roll of putty into the recess all the way around the window.

TIP: Use a thick slice of bread to clear up broken glass. It picks up tiny shards better than a paper towel.

4. Wearing your gloves again, insert the new pane. Put the bottom of the pane into place first, bedding it in against the putty. Press the edges, not the middle of the glass, or it might break.

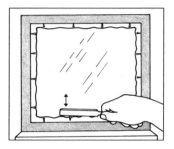

5. Use the side of the chisel to tap in glazing paints, about 6 inches apart around the window frame, to secure the glass. Slide the chisel up and down, flat against the glass. (If the window has a metal frame, replace the metal clips.)

6. Knead and roll up more putty and press it against the edge of the glass all around the window frame, covering the glazing paints. Trim any surplus with a putty knife or flat-bladed knife (wet it if the putty sticks to it), and smooth the edges to a 45-degree angle to create a neat, beveled finish.

7. Allow the putty to harden for a day, then clean the window with paint thinner. Leave for a week or two, then paint over the putty. Overlap the paint onto the glass to seal the edges. If you don't, the putty will crack.

TEMPORARY FIX: If you cannot do the repair immediately, seal the window with a sheet of plastic or, if security is a concern, use thin hardboard or plywood. Leave the broken glass in position, measure the window space, and cut a piece of wood. Fit the board into the window and tap panel pins into the wood around it.

TIP: To stop birds from eating the newly set putty around your window, sprinkle black pepper into the putty before use, or go for a synthetic putty, which doesn't contain linseed, as this is what attracts the birds.

— HOW TO CURE A DRIPPING TAP —

SYMPTOMS: Drip, drip, drip, drip—usually late at night when you're trying to sleep.

CAUSE: Worn washer (a washer is a disc usually made of rubber or metal with a hole in the middle).

CURE: Is there anything more annoying than a dripping tap—apart from Mariah Carey, of course? Fortunately, a dripping tap is easier to silence. This problem is best dealt with as soon as possible, as the continuous dribbling will stain the sink, and, if you're on a water meter, that's your hard-earned cash getting washed down the drain.

— HOW TO REPLACE THE WASHER ON A TAP —

1. Turn off the water supply at the mains (often located under the kitchen sink), then turn the tap fully on to drain the system.

2. When the water stops running, put the plug in so you don't lose parts down the drain.

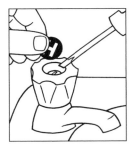

3. There are many different kinds of taps and they all dismantle slightly differently. Modern taps usually have red or blue hot indicators on the top to show hot or cold water. Use a small screwdriver to pry off the indicator to reveal a small screw. (figure 1) On a conventional tap, you unscrew the bell-shaped cover either by hand or with a screwdriver.

figure 1

4. Undo the screw and remove the head of the tap. You will see the "headgear" assembly (another name for the tap mechanism) inside.

5. Undo the headgear nut (the largest nut you see) with an adjustable wrench. (figure 2)

Keep a firm grip on the spout of the tap to prevent the fixture moving. If you have chrome or gold-plated taps, wrap PVC tape around the jaws of the wrench to prevent scratching the gilt finish.

On pillar taps, you will have to unscrew the headgear nut to reach the headgear assembly. If the nut feels stiff, don't try to force it as you might damage the sink or inlet pipe. Put a little oil around the join and let it soak in, then give it another try.

figure 2

DID YOU KNOW? "Chinese water torture" is the name given to a torture technique where water is slowly dripped onto a person's forehead, eventually driving them insane. There is no proof such torture was ever used in China.

6. Lift the whole headgear assembly out of the body of the tap.

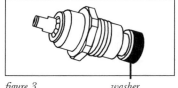

figure 3   *washer*

7. The worn washer is at the base of the headgear assembly. (figure 3) It may be joined to the "jumper" valve, pushed over a small central button, or it may be in the body of the tap. You might need to unscrew a nut to remove the old washer, or use a screwdriver to lever the old washer over the stud.

8. Fit the replacement washer of the correct size.

9. Reassemble the tap; do not over-tighten the screws. Turn the tap off, then turn the water supply back on.

TEMPORARY FIX: Wet a length of string and tie it to the spout. The drip will soundlessly flow down the string until you can solve the problem.

— HOW TO REMOVE LIME SCALE FROM A TAP —

Fill a plastic bag or yogurt container with white vinegar, citric acid, or a commercial descaling product and tie over the affected part of the tap using an elastic band or masking tape. The spout needs to be suspended in the solution. Leave for a few hours or overnight until the scale dissolves. Remove bag, turn on the tap to rinse.

Use an old toothbrush to clean the base of the tap.

Clean chrome taps by rubbing with half a lemon, then buff.

TIP: You can extend the life of your washers by not turning off your taps with too much force.

— HOW TO UNCLOG A SHOWERHEAD —

If your shower lacks power, the likeliest cause is a buildup of lime scale in the showerhead.
If it isn't too clogged up, you can use the same technique used to remove limescale
from a tap (see page 148). But if it's become very clogged, it will be better to unscrew
the showerhead from its hose, and dismantle it (keep the rubber washer safe).
Under warm running water, scrub away the lime scale with an old toothbrush.
To loosen the lime scale, soak the showerhead in a container of lemon juice, or neat
white vinegar or commercial descaler. Scrub blocked holes again using a toothbrush or
needle under warm running water. Replace the head and turn on the shower to wash away
any residue. In hard water areas, you might need to repeat this procedure every two weeks.

GIVE IT A TRY: If you live in a hard water area, it might be worthwhile fitting a
water-conditioning unit to the supply pipe of your electric shower. Two types are available:
an electromagnetic conditioner or a chemical-dosing softener. Both are easy to install.
Follow manufacturer's instructions.

— HOW TO APPLY A WATERPROOF SEAL TO A SINK OR BATH —

Over time, with wear and tear, the waterproof seal around baths and basins starts to peel off
and perish. If water seeps through the gaps, this can cause mold growth and damage to the
floor, so it's best to tackle the problem as soon as possible.

A good quality silicone sealant is what you need. It comes in clear, white, and various colors so
you can match your fixtures. Go for one with fungicide to prevent mold growth.

1. Clean the wall and surfaces thoroughly with household detergent, then denatured alcohol.
   If there is any existing silicone sealant, chip it away carefully with a knife.

2. Silicone sealant usually comes in cartridges and is
   applied with a hand-held gun. Use a piping action
   to fill the gap between the tiles/wall and sink or bath.
   Smooth it with a wet finger or a putty knife.

Use the same technique on a shower stall.

NOTE: If the gap is wider than ¼ inch the silicone
will just keep sinking into the hole so use
self-adhesive plastic sealing strips instead.

*DID YOU KNOW? Empress Poppaea, wife of Nero, took a train of 500 asses on her travels so that she would
always have a fresh supply of milk in which to bathe each day.*

— HOW TO FIX A STICKING DRAWER —

1. Remove the drawer. Look in the opening of the cupboard/cabinet where the drawer slides in. The culprit might be something as simple as a stray sock (so that's where it went!). Another possibility is that a screw has worked itself loose on the drawer runners. This is a very common problem with self-assembly furniture.

2. Easy glide: Rub the drawer and the frame with a candle. On metal drawers, apply a little lubricating oil to the runners.

NOTE: If the drawer is wooden you might find it sticks in damp or humid weather, as moisture makes it swell a little.

— HOW TO FIX A WOBBLY TABLE —

Take the cork from a bottle of wine (good excuse to buy one) and, using a sharp knife or scalpel, cut it to the same width and depth as the other table legs, then glue it to the base of the leg using a strong wood glue.

— HOW TO STOP WOODEN FLOORBOARDS FROM CREAKING —

Sometimes two wooden boards chafe together or against a nail, causing a creak. Sprinkle a liberal amount of talcum powder along the joint between the squeaking floorboards. Rub it in well with a knife until the creaking stops.

— HOW TO STOP A DOOR FROM SQUEAKING —

The likeliest cause is a rusty hinge.
Open the door and squirt a few drops of lubricating oil at the top of each hinge.
Use a rag or kitchen towel to wipe off the excess.
Swing the door back and forth a few times to work in the oil.

If the door is still not silenced, prop the door open
and pull out the pin from inside one hinge.
Clean off the rust and use a pipe cleaner to clean the hole in
the hinge where the pin goes. Apply lubricating oil and reassemble.
Repeat for all the hinges.

STICKING LOCK: Put a little oil on the key, then put the key in the lock a few times to lubricate it. Or rub the key over the point of a soft pencil, then slide it in and out of the lock.

TIP: When replacing the pins into the hinge of a door, don't knock them down so far that you can never get them out again.

— STEPLADDER SAFETY —

The most common DIY accident is falling off a ladder. Every year 12,000 people are injured, some fatally, on ladders. Most of these accidents are caused not by the ladder but human error, and many could be easily prevented by following a few simple guidelines.

Ensure that stepladder is in good condition.

Make sure the steps are clean, dry, and free of grease.

If the ladder has rubber or plastic nonslip feet, make sure none are missing.

Ensure your ladder is long enough for the job. Don't try to extend the height of the ladder by balancing it on boxes. Get a bigger ladder!

Wear flat shoes with nonslip soles and good grip. Never work in heels, slippers, or bare feet.

Check to be sure there are no hazards overhead before carrying the ladders.

Open out stepladders so they are fully extended. Check that the platform is locked into position before use. Check the manufacturer's instructions.

Never use a stepladder when it is folded and propped up against a wall.

Position the ladder on a firm, level surface.

Always face the steps of the ladder as you climb and keep a grip on the sides.

Never stand on the top platform of the ladder.

Keep both feet on the ladder at all times. Never have one foot on the ladder and one foot on something else. You could be in danger of overbalancing.

Face your work front-on as you stand on the ladder. Do not turn to the side to drill, for instance.

Don't lean or overreach. Get down and move the ladder closer to the work.

Never have more than one person on the ladder at one time.

Come down the ladder backwards, keeping a firm hold of the rail.

— Choosing a Stepladder —

A 4–7 step, folding stepladder is suitable for most needs around the house.
Look for wide steps, a platform on top, and a grab rail.
Aluminum ladders are lighter than wooden ladders.

TIP: If you have high ceilings and you need to reach the loft, go for a combination ladder, which converts to a ladder or stepladder.

— FOOD & DRINK —

"You are what you eat. Which makes me cheap, quick, and easy."

—DAVE THOMAS

— HOW TO BE A SAVVY SUPERMARKET SHOPPER —

Ever wondered why, when you run into the supermarket for a carton of milk, you leave with a cart full of goods but without the one item you went in for in the first place? Supermarkets use many scientifically calculated strategies to make us spend, some of which are so simple, so subtle, and so sneaky that you might not even notice them.

Captive audience
What we call aisles, supermarkets call "prisons," because there is only one way in and one way out of them, making the customer a virtual prisoner in a crowded aisle.

Eye level is buy level
The most expensive, most profitable items are placed at eye level and sell twice as well as other products. The only exceptions are children's snacks, which are placed at a kid's-eye level.

Anchor displays
These are the products at the top and tail of each aisle. They are given prominence either because they are high-profit products or because the supermarket wants to shift them—quickly. Profit margins on these items can often be more than 500 percent.

Eyes down
For the best bargains, look down: Food placed on the lower shelves (and least likely to catch your eye) is the least expensive, and the least profitable.

On impulse
Placing complementing products such as tomato sauces and spaghetti together may seem like a thoughtful gesture on the part of the supermarket, but their real intention is to get you to impulse-buy.

From moo to you
Milk is deliberately placed far from the entrance since it is a popular item and the supermarket wants you to pass other foods to get to it.

Sell-by date
Dairy produce with the latest sell-by date is always placed at the back of the shelf, so for the freshest possible milk, reach back through the front cartons and grab the one furthest behind.

Frozen assets
Don't buy food from a chest freezer that has been filled above the freezer line, as it's likely to have thawed and defrosted a few times. Avoid frozen food covered in ice crystals— a sign it may have defrosted and then refrozen.

Can can
Never buy dented, bulging or rusty cans as they might contain bacteria that could lead to food poisoning. Never buy jars that are sticky for the same reason.

TIP: Make a shopping list. Keep it on the fridge and keep adding to it throughout the week. Don't forget to take it with you to the supermarket. And most important of all, stick to it!

Special offers
Offers like "two for one" and "three for two" are selling techniques used by supermarkets to offload surplus stock that isn't selling. You buy more than you need and increase your purchases by up to 150 percent.

Store brands
Don't dismiss supermarket brands—the quality is often as good as some of the top brands; in fact, they're often made by the same manufacturers who make the top-selling brands. Supermarkets can charge less because they don't have to pay for advertising.

Bargain baskets
Pile 'em high and sell 'em expensive! Goods heaped all together in a large basket are designed to give the impression of being a bargain but may not always be so. Check carefully to ensure the bargain is genuine.

Habit-forming
Most of us shop on automatic pilot—buying the same products week after week. Break the habit! Don't stay loyal to one brand! Stay flexible and keep your eye out for alternatives that might be better or cheaper, or preferably both.

Pester power
"Child-friendly" supermarkets with kiddie-sized carts for the little darlings to fill with their favorite foods—it all encourages you to spend more. If possible, leave the little darlings at home while you go shopping. It will work out to be a lot cheaper and you'll get back to them a lot quicker.

Packaging
Some packaging costs more than the food inside it. Choose food that is loose; it is likely to be cheaper and fresher.

Basket case
If you've just popped in for a couple of items, pick up a basket rather than a cart.

Check your receipt
Do it after every trip, especially if you've bought a "special offer." Many millions of dollars are spent by customers every year because of scanner errors.

Next to godliness
Look for a high level of cleanliness in your supermarket—check floors, counters, carts, staff, and, always a giveaway—the restrooms.

Hunger pains
Don't shop for food when you're hungry. Not only will you buy more, but you'll also buy to eat in the car so you won't have anything left for dinner when you get home!

DID YOU KNOW? Sylvan Goldman invented the shopping cart in 1936, and put them in his Piggly Wiggly stores in Oklahoma. They were not an instant success, so Goldman hired models to push the carts around the store to demonstrate their usefulness. They caught on and Goldman made his fortune.

REMEMBER: Convenience food usually means food that is convenient for the producer and the supermarket, NOT for you, the customer.

DID YOU KNOW? Background music played in supermarkets is designed to influence the way we shop. Music played at 60 beats per minute slows us down. During busy periods when supermarkets want a faster turnover of customers, music is played at 100 beats a minute, so we pick up our pace and move through the store faster.

— HOW TO OPEN A SUPERMARKET PLASTIC BAG —
Opening flimsy supermarket plastic bags can be a nightmare, particularly if you're hassled at the checkout and there's a line forming behind you . . .

Method 1: THE LICK
Lick the tip of your finger and thumb, then tease open the bag.
Effective but not very hygienic.

Method 2: THE SNAP
Take hold of the bag between your third finger and thumb like you're going to click them together, then "snap" the bag open using friction. I think there must be a knack to this because I've seen people do it successfully but have never been able to master it myself.

Method 3: THE STRETCH
Take hold of the bag where the top joins one of the handles and pull it very slightly so that the plastic stretches just a fraction. This loosens up the two sides, allowing easy opening.

— HOW TO STORE FOOD —
If food is stored properly, it will last up to twice as long, so it's worth spending a little time when you get home from the supermarket, putting your groceries in the best place . . .

Always take fruit and vegetables out of their original wrapping so air can circulate around them.

Fruit bowls are handy when you want to reach for an apple, but they are not the best place to store fruit. If fruit is piled high, it will bruise and perish quicker.

GIVE IT A TRY: Store onions in an old pair of nylons. Place the onions in the legs of the tights and tie a knot between each one to prevent them touching. Hang in a cool, dry place and cut off an onion when needed. (Garlic and apples may also be stored this way.)

RIPENESS IS ALL: To ripen fruits like peaches, nectarines, plums, and apricots, put them in a paper bag with a ripe unpeeled banana. Fold over the top of the bag so that some air can still circulate and leave at room temperature for a day or two. Bananas release a gas called ethylene, which speeds up the ripening process in other fruits.

DID YOU KNOW? The onion is a member of the lily family.

— REFRIGERATING FOOD —

"Salome, dear, not in the fridge!"
—Marion Hill

The refrigerator temperature should be between 32° to 41°F. Use a fridge thermometer to check the setting. Leave it on the middle shelf overnight, and if the temperature is not correct, adjust the thermostat dial.

— WHAT TO STORE WHERE IN THE FRIDGE —

Bottom shelf
The coolest zone, so keep the most perishable foods here, such as uncooked meat, fish, and poultry, and milk. Cover or wrap raw food so it cannot touch or drip on other food.

The crisper
Store fruit, vegetables, and salad items in here—unwrapped. Unless they're very dirty, don't wash fresh produce before storing, as it may destroy precious nutrients.

Bottle rack in door
This zone is subject to the most fluctuations in temperature as the door is opened and closed. For this reason, avoid storing milk and eggs here. Use it for preserves, pickles, condiments, salad dressings, fruit juices, soft drinks, beer, etc.

Center and top shelves
Good place for sauces, cooked meats, ready-to-eat foods, and leftovers.

Eggs
Don't keep eggs in the egg-rack in the door of the fridge even though it seems the logical thing to do. They'll last longer if you keep them in their carton on the lowest shelf in the fridge. Store them with the pointed end downwards. Use within three weeks of purchase. Eggs absorb odors through their shells so keep them away from strongly flavored food.

What to cover
Milk, strong cheese, cream, yogurt, margarine.

A good rule of thumb: Store raw food below cooked food.

NOTES:
Frost-free fridges do not have hot and cold zones. They have an even temperature throughout.

Don't overload the fridge. The air needs to circulate freely or pockets of warm air will form.

TIP: Line the crisper drawer with bubble wrap and the increased air circulation will keep fruit and vegetables fresher for longer.

Don't put hot food straight into the fridge as it will warm up the air in the fridge. Allow it to cool down in a cool place in the kitchen, then refrigerate within an hour. The exception is rice, which should be cooled down under a running cold tap, then refrigerated immediately.

Chilled food doesn't taste as flavorful as food that is at room temperature. So, if you're planning a salad, take out lettuce, tomatoes, etc., before eating so they have time to warm up a little.

HOW TO ELIMINATE REFRIGERATOR ODORS: Clear out all food. Clean the interior with a solution of bicarbonate of soda. If the smell lingers, clean again. Keep the fridge door open until the smell has gone.

To keep the fridge smelling fresh: Smell-absorbers (often egg-shaped) are available, but these need replacing regularly, which can be expensive. An open dish of bicarbonate of soda will be just as effective and last a couple of months. *Make your own smell-absorber:* Wash out an empty film canister. Make holes in the lid with a needle. Fill the canister with activated charcoal or bicarbonate of soda. Stick a label with the date on the canister and place in the fridge. Replace every two months.

CLEANING TIP: Don't let the fridge or freezer grille at the back get clogged up with dust as they will run less efficiently. When the appliances are turned off, clean using the crevice tool or dusting brush on your vacuum.

Site your fridge away from the stove and radiators or it will have to overcompensate to maintain the correct temperature, thus using up more energy.

Don't push the fridge right up against a wall. Air must be allowed to circulate at the back.

— FREEZER —

The freezer temperature should be between 0° to 10°F.

Unlike fridges, freezers work more efficiently if kept well packed with food.

WHAT NOT TO FREEZE: Avocados, aubergines, bananas, fizzy drinks (they might explode), fish—unless straight from the net—fresh milk, garlic, hard cheese, mayonnaise, hard-boiled eggs, cooked potatoes (but not mashed), meringue, single cream, lettuce, cucumber, tomatoes, yogurt.

NOTE: Cooked potatoes turn brown in the freezer. They're still edible, but not very appetizing.

STORING FOOD IN THE FREEZER: Use airtight, moisture-tight freezer bags or heavy-duty kitchen foil. Squeeze all the air out of the plastic bags before sealing unless it contains liquids, in which case you should leave about, $\frac{1}{2}$ inch space to allow for expansion. Wrap food tightly in kitchen foil. Label packets clearly with the date and contents to prevent UFOs (Unidentifiable Frozen Objects).

DEFROSTING A FREEZER: To speed the process, place containers of hot water inside. If you're in a real hurry, blow hot air from a hair dryer over the ice.

DID YOU KNOW? The riper the banana, the more calories it contains.

— Defrosting Tips —

Allow frozen meat or poultry to thaw out slowly in the fridge, preferably overnight. Never thaw meat on the kitchen counter. Never run meat under cold water to speed up defrosting.

Cook food as soon as it has defrosted. Never refreeze uncooked food after it has been defrosted. Never refreeze cooked food that has already been thawed once.

Never freeze food that is not in perfect condition. The freezing process will not kill any bacteria already in the food; they will lie dormant and attack once the food is defrosted.

REMEMBER: Freezing cannot *improve* the quality of food; the best it can do is to retain the quality.

— FOOD SOS —

Help! How can I tell if an egg is fresh?
Immerse the egg in a bowl of salted water. If it sinks, it's fresh; if it floats, it's bad.

Help! My cereal's soggy.
To keep the snap, crackle, and pop in your cereal, transfer the contents from a new packet into an airtight container. Problem then is, what are you going to read?

Help! My bread is stale.
If it's not too stale, stick it in a steamer for a few minutes to revive it.
Alternatively, turn it into croutons for soup, use for breadcrumbs, or make bread pudding.

Help! How do I chop an onion without crying?
Try any of these: Chill the onion in the fridge for one hour before slicing; peel under running water; leave the root on; suck a marble; light a candle; chew gum; sing!

Help! How can I stop bottles rattling against each other in the truck of my car when I've been shopping?
Keep a few odd socks in your trunk and slip the bottles inside.

Help! How can I stop my cookies from going soggy?
Transfer cookies from a new packet into airtight metal box to keep them from going stale.
Place a small piece of bread in the container to preserve the crispness of the cookies.
To revitalize soggy cookies, put them on a baking tray in a hot oven for a few moments.
Or put them in the microwave for 30 seconds.

Help! The recipe calls for a clove of garlic—how much is that, exactly?
A clove of garlic is one segment of the garlic. You buy the garlic as a BULB and divide it into CLOVES. Crush it with a garlic press if you don't mind the washing up after, or simply squash the clove under the broad side of a chopping knife.

Help! How can I get rid of my garlic breath?
Chewing parsley or a coffee bean are often recommended, but neither has much lasting effect.
In France, they chew cardamom seeds—and they should know.

TIP: Fill a plant mister with cooking oil and use it to coat your frying pan when frying. You'll use far less oil.

Help! How can I prevent cheese from sticking to the grater?
Before grating, spray the grater with cooking oil. This will prevent the cheese sticking and make washing up easier.

Help! How can I get rid of kitchen odors?
Bake orange peelings at 350°F for a few minutes.

— OVEN TEMPERATURES —

TEMPERATURE	°F
	200
	225
	250
Very Low	275
Low	300
Low	325
Moderate	350
	375
Moderately hot	400
Hot	425
Very hot	450
Very hot	475

— ESSENTIAL KNIVES —

CHEF'S KNIFE
If you can have only one knife, choose this all-around utensil for chopping, mincing, dicing and slicing meat and vegetables. Use to make french fries, too.

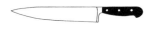

CARVING KNIFE
A long, broad blade ensures even slices from your roast, and as the farmer's wife knows, it's just the tool for cutting off the tails of blind mice.

BREAD KNIFE
The serrated edge cuts effortlessly through crusts and glides gracefully through soft fruits like tomatoes and cucumbers.

PARING KNIFE
Nifty and neat for peeling and paring fruit and vegetables, as well as fiddly jobs like making garnishes and coring. Also good for chopping herbs.

BONING KNIFE
Does what it says (i.e., bones meat), but is just as handy for cutting soft fruit like tomatoes.

TIP: Keep a dishcloth in your apron strings around your waist. Each time you use the knife, wipe it clean and dry.

KNIFE CARE

What blunts a blade is not the cutting but the continuous striking against surfaces. Your knife will stay sharper longer if your chopping board is made of something soft like wood or plastic rather than a hard surface like glass or marble.

REMEMBER: A blunt knife is likely to be more dangerous than a sharp one because you will need to apply more pressure. Keep your knife sharp.

NOTE: Knives with serrated edges are designed to never need sharpening.

WASHING KNIVES: See page 184.

— ANATOMY OF A KNIFE —

Bolster
The guard between the blade and the handle.
Can be made of stainless steel, wood, or plastic.

Tang
The unsharpened piece of the blade that extends down into the handle and is fixed by rivets.
A full tang runs the entire length of the knife for greatest strength;
a half tang runs partway through the handle;
a whittle tang is shortest.

Stamping
The most common process used for making knives,
where many knives are cut out of a piece of steel.

Forging
Knives are shaped from their own single block of steel,
making them very strong and durable.

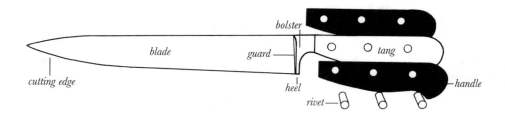

TIP: Your knife is not a can opener. Don't use it to pry open that can of beans, because you're bound to snap the tip off.

— What to Look for in a Knife —

Blade
Stainless steel is the most common.
Carbon steel is what the pros use.

Handle
Should feel secure.
A wooden handle sealed with heat-resistant plastic is best.

Balance
Place the knife on your finger under the bolster.
The weight should feel evenly balanced between handle and blade.

Weight
Choose the heaviest knife you can comfortably handle.
With a heavy blade, the knife will be doing most of the work for you.

Handle
For a chef's knife, make sure that the handle is long enough for you
to grasp it firmly with your thumb and fingers.

— OPENING JARS AND BOTTLES —

"On the one hand, we'll never experience childbirth. On the other hand, we can open all our own jars."
—Bruce Willis

Prevention is better than cure: The reason many lids stick is because they become congealed with sticky food. Before resealing a jar, always wipe off residual food with a paper towel.

Bottle lid
If the bottle has a narrow neck, use pliers or a nutcracker.

Jar lid
Is there anything more frustrating than a little bit of what you fancy so near and yet so far? The temptation is to smash the glass in sheer frustration, but stay calm. Put on rubber gloves to stop your hand slipping, or try using a towel or damp cloth. Hold the jar firmly and twist the lid. If it is a metal lid, immerse it in hot water so the metal will expand and loosen.

Decanter stopper
Pour a few drops of cooking oil around the neck of the decanter and leave in a warm place. When the oil has trickled between the stopper and the neck, use a warm cloth to gently loosen and remove the stopper.

TIP: Once opened, store jars and bottles of food in the fridge.

— NUTRITION: VITAMINS AND MINERALS —

Vitamins and minerals are vital to maintain our bodies in good working order, for growth and repair of cells.

Vitamin	Why you need it	Good sources
VITAMIN A (RETINOL)	Essential for healthy skin and maintaining mucous membranes. Also vital to good eyesight. It's true that carrots help you see in the dark!	Liver, oily fish, butter, cheese, dandelion leaves, sorrel, carrots, spinach, sweet potatoes, watercress, broccoli.
B VITAMINS (INCLUDES B1, B2, B3, B6, B12 AND FOLIC ACID)	Convert carbohydrates into energy. The more carbs you eat, the more B vitamins you need. Also important for healthy skin, hair, and red blood cells.	Meat, fish, milk, cheese, eggs, wholegrain bread and cereals, leafy green vegetables.
VITAMIN C (ASCORBIC ACID)	For healthy skin, bones, muscles; important for protecting against infection, and absorption of iron.	Red peppers, black currants, parsley, green pepper, citrus fruits, strawberries, kiwi fruit, watercress, and other green vegetables.
VITAMIN D	Nicknamed the "sunshine vitamin" because it can be produced by sunlight on oils in the skin. Needed to absorb calcium and phosphorus, and for healthy bones.	Oily fish, dairy products such as milk, cheese, eggs, butter.
VITAMIN E	Helps to maintain body cells and prevent circulatory problems.	Vegetable oils, wheat germ, nuts, seeds.
VITAMIN K	Vital for normal blood clotting.	Green leafy vegetables, especially cabbage, sprouts, broccoli, spinach, and peas; also cereal grains.

TIP: One of the greatest benefits to health is also one of the most overlooked: water. Aim to drink at least 5¼ pints a day. Plain tap water is as good as bottled water.

Mineral	Why you need it	Good sources
CALCIUM	Vital for healthy bones and teeth.	Cheese, especially Parmesan, spinach and green vegetables, milk, fish.
MAGNESIUM	Vital for healthy bones and teeth.	Present in most foods.
PHOSPHORUS	Vital for healthy bones and teeth.	Present in most foods.
SODIUM	Regulates fluids and amount of water in body cells. Deficiency is rare; excess is more common, leading to high blood pressure and risk of heart attack or stroke.	Vegetables, fruit, meat, cereal.
POTASSIUM	Works with sodium to regulate fluids in the body and maintain a normal heartbeat. Deficiency can lead to heart attacks.	Blackstrap molasses; dried fruit, such as apricots, bran, prunes; wheat germ, avocados, bananas, and oranges.
IRON	Vital for formation of red blood cells.	Liver, kidneys, blackstrap molasses, bran, sardines, egg

Other minerals, such as copper, zinc, manganese, chromium, and iodine are needed only in minute quantities and are present in most foods.

— FIBER —
See "How to keep regular" on page 196.

— HOW TO GET THE MOST GOODNESS OUT OF YOUR VEGETABLES —
Many of us are trying to eat a healthier diet. That means plenty of fresh vegetables. But did you know that the way you prepare food can destroy essential vitamins and minerals before they even make it inside your body?

Follow the guidelines on pages 164–165 and you can be sure you're getting the most out of your greens.

DID YOU KNOW? Vegetarians have 30 percent less risk of heart disease and 40 percent less risk of cancer than meat eaters. They also have lower rates of obesity, high blood pressure, and non-insulin-dependent diabetes.

— BUYING VEGETABLES —

Choose homegrown vegetables rather than less tasty and less nutritious foreign imports.
Frequent your local farmers' market or grow your own!

Buy produce in season.
The vegetables will be cheaper and taste better, too.

In supermarkets, choose the vegetables with the least packaging.

Don't pick the vegetables right on top of the display.
They're directly under the light, and light destroys nutrients.
Reach underneath for the pick of the crop.

— COOKING VEGETABLES —

Leave vegetables intact wherever possible. Tearing, shredding, and grating exposes
them to light, which destroys vitamins and minerals. Place uncut cabbage leaves flat
on top of other vegetables when steaming and they'll keep help keep in the steam.

Don't peel or scrape vegetables (except celery); simply scrub with a vegetable brush
under running water. Most of the goodness is concentrated in or just beneath the skin.
They'll taste better, too. And think of how much time you'll save in the preparation!

Keep any water left from cooking vegetables to make gravy, stocks, sauces, or soups.
The exception is spinach water; it contains oxalic acid, which prevents absorption
of calcium and iron in the body.

Steam, don't boil. Keeping vegetables out of water means valuable nutrients don't seep into
the cooking water. A steamer is a worthwhile investment. You can also use an inexpensive
stainless steel vegetable steamer, which expands to fit most saucepans, but you have to
keep an eye on it, as the water is apt to boil away quickly.

Don't automatically discard the outer leaves of green vegetables such as cabbage,
lettuce, and spinach. These are often the greenest and therefore the most nutritious.

Prepare salads and vegetables as close to the time of eating as possible.
Don't leave them soaking in water as some vitamins dissolve in water.
Use an inexpensive yet indispensable salad spinner to 'tumble dry' ingredients.

Serve vegetables as soon as possible after cooking.
Greens lose their vitamin C if kept warm after cooking.

Extracting the juice is better than nothing, but eating the whole vegetable is best.
The chewing action is good for your teeth, and you'll also get the fiber content.

DID YOU KNOW? Boiled vegetables lose up to 50 percent of minerals and 50 percent of vitamin C.

— Peeling Tips —

"Beulah, peel me a grape!"
—Mae West

Tomatoes
Place in a heatproof bowl and pour boiling water over them. Leave for a couple of minutes, then plunge into cold water. The skins will split and allow easy peeling. (Also works for peaches, cherries, and grapes.)

Oranges
To remove both peel and pith, place the orange in a heatproof bowl, pour boiling water over them, and allow to soak for about 5 minutes.

Apples
To prevent peeled apples turning brown, put them in water with a squeeze of lemon juice.

— HOW TO SLICE A PINEAPPLE —

Making pineapple rings
1. Cut off the top and begin slicing from this end. (figure 1)

2. Cut off a slice as thick as you want the ring to be.

Use a sharp knife, such as a grapefruit knife, to trim around the
pineapple between the rind and the flesh. (figure 2)

3 Discard the rind. Cut off any "eyes." Remove the hard, indigestible
central core with a knife (or a cookie cutter). (figure 3)

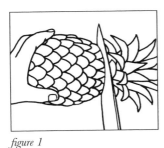

figure 1

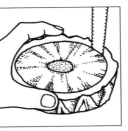

figure 2

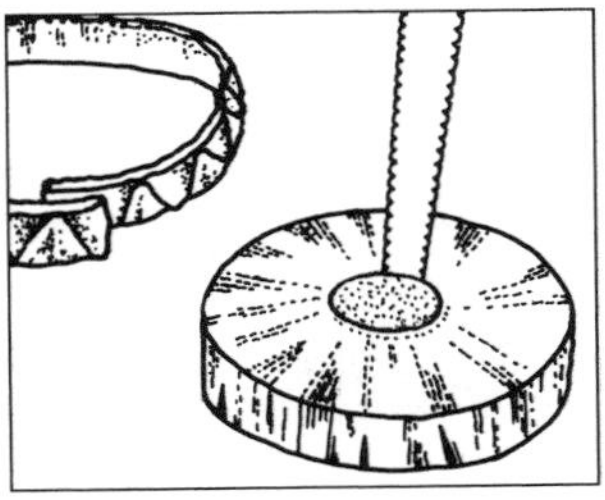

figure 3

Party time
Slice off the top of the pineapple, hollow out the flesh, and pile in fruit salad
for an exotic party dish. Keep the top to use as the "lid."

TIP: To test if a pineapple is ripe:
When you pull out a leaf from the middle of the crown, it should come out quite easily.

— CARVING —

Carving the Sunday roast has traditionally been a job for "the man of the house," and as such has acquired a certain mystique. But there's nothing difficult about carving. Follow a few simple rules and you too can become a culinary Zorro—just remember to remove your mask when wielding the blade.

— Is It Cooked? —

No matter what people say about inspecting the juices of a joint, the only really safe way to tell if meat is cooked is to use a meat thermometer.

A meat thermometer measures the internal temperature of food, and also prevents overcooking. It can also be used when cooking casseroles, egg dishes, etc., but be sure to wash it well after each use.

— General Carving Tips —

Meat is best carved after a rest. That's the meat, not you!

Take the roast out of the oven, cover it loosely with foil, and leave it be to "rest" for 10–15 minutes. This allows the succulent juices to permeate the flesh, makes carving easier, and allows you just enough time to make the gravy!

A carving fork (a long, two-pronged fork) is useful to stop the meat from skidding around the plate.

Use the knife in a gentle sawing motion. Lay slices to overlap on a warm serving plate.

All meat is best carved across the grain. It not only looks better, it tastes better.

Cut beef in very thin slices.

Cut poultry as thin as possible.

Cut pork fairly thin.

Cut lamb and veal in thick slices.

Cold meat is usually sliced more thinly than hot meat.

IF YOU REMEMBER JUST ONE THING: Use a sharp knife.

DID YOU KNOW? That fatty flap of flesh on the rump of a cooked fowl is known in Britain as the parson's nose, in America as the pope's nose, and in the Middle East as the sultan's nose.

— HOW TO CARVE A CHICKEN/TURKEY/GUINEA FOWL/PHEASANT —

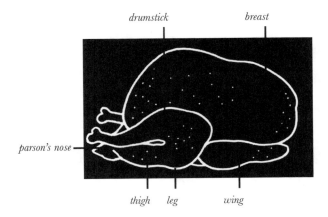

drumstick *breast*

parson's nose

thigh *leg* *wing*

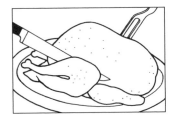

1. Remove the leg first. To do this, steady the bird with a carving fork and cut through the skin between the thigh and the body. Keep cutting until you hit the bone, then grasp the thigh and twist it outward at the joint to remove the entire leg from the body.

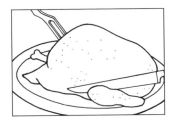

2. Next, remove the wing. To do this, waggle the wing to find the joint, then cut down through it, keeping as close to the breast as you can. Remove the wing.

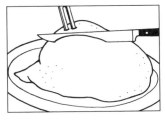

3. Now it's time to remove the breast meat. Carve downwards in long, thin slices parallel to the breastbone.

TIP: Carve all the meat off the chicken or turkey carcass and place in the fridge immediately. Consume leftovers within three days. Use the carcass for soup.

4. Turn the bird around and repeat steps 1 to 3, removing leg, wing, and breast in turn.

5. Put the legs flat on a chopping board. Divide each leg into one drumstick and one thigh by cutting down halfway between the drumstick and thigh.

6. You can either leave the drumstick whole, or, if it is big enough, carve it by holding the knuckle end of the drumstick and slicing downward.

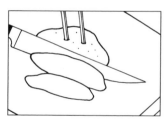

7. Place the thigh on a plate and slice thickly parallel to the bone, ensuring you avoid any gristle. Don't serve the bone.

Excellent! You didn't fowl up. Give yourself a pat on the back (but put down the knife first).

— How to Carve a Leg of Lamb —

1. Position the leg with the outer side of the leg down and the thick end away from you. Carve even slices at an angle, starting from the narrow end of the leg and working toward the top of the leg. (figure 1)

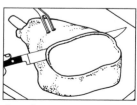

figure 1

2. When you've carved all you can from the top, turn the meat over. Start at the top and carve horizontal slices along the leg. (figure 2)

3. Finally, cut away any meat left on the bone.

Serve with mint sauce or red currant jelly.

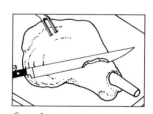

figure 2

TIP: When you buy loin of pork, ask your butcher to "chine" it for you—that is, loosen the backbone but leave it joined so that you can cut it away before you carve.

— How to Carve a Loin of Pork/Lamb/Veal —

Remove the crackling. Carve through the chine bone (backbone) and remove so that you can carve straight down through the joint.

The meat will be easier to carve if you remove part of the crackling. Slice downward.

NOTE: Pork should always be cooked right through to the center.

— How to Carve Sirloin of Beef —

Position the meat with the thick part up and the chine bone to your right. Cut off the chine bone. Loosen the meat by running the knife blade between the meat and the main rib bone. Carve down toward the bone.

— HERBS —

"Pounding fragrant things—particularly garlic, basil, parsley—is a tremendous antidote to depression."
—Patience Gray

— How to Dry Herbs —

Drying is an easy and effective method of preserving herbs such as parsley, sage, and thyme.

The best time to pick herbs for drying is in early summer when they are in bud and just about to flower. Choose a dry, warm morning after the dew but before the sun, when the oil content will be at its peak. Discard imperfect or discolored leaves and stems.

To oven-dry: Rinse herbs in cold water, shake off moisture, and pat dry on paper towels. Lay them on a baking tray. (It may be easier to pull the leaves off large-leaved herbs like mint and sage and spread them out flat on the tray.) Bake in a low oven—260°F. Turn the herbs over after about 30 minutes for even drying. When crisp (it will take about an hour), remove from the oven. Allow to cool.

To air-dry: After picking, dip the herbs in boiling water for a few seconds to clean them and help preserve their color. Shake off excess water and pat dry on paper towels. Tie in small bunches (about 5–6 stems) and hang upside down in a warm, dry place, such as an airing cupboard. They are dried when the leaves feel brittle, which is usually after about 2–4 weeks, depending on the temperature.

To dry in the microwave: A fast method if you only have small quantities to dry. Rinse herbs in cold water, shake off moisture, and pat dry on paper towels. Put 4–5 stems of the herb between paper towels in the microwave (it's not necessary to put them on a plate). Heat on high for 2–3 minutes. If not brittle after that time, continue heating in 30-second bursts, then checking, until dried.

TIP: Keep a pot of basil on your windowsill to ward off flies and mosquitoes.

After drying: Strip the leaves off the stems, and discard the stems. Herbs are best crushed just before you use them. Rub the herbs between your fingers, and crumble the leaves into a powder over a bowl. Discard stalks and any husks. Place in small airtight containers, label with contents and date, and store in a cool, dry, dark place. Whole herbs keep their flavor for about a year.

NOTE: Dried herbs are stronger than fresh. One teaspoon of dried herbs is equivalent to 2–3 teaspoons of fresh.

— WHAT GOES WITH WHAT? —
Beef and lamb
Bay, marjoram, mint, oregano, rosemary, thyme

Fish
Bay, chervil, dill, fennel, lovage, parsley

Poultry
Parsley, rosemary, tarragon, thyme

Pork and veal
Caraway, marjoram, rosemary, sage

Salads
Chives, oregano, parsley

Vegetables
Chives, fennel, lovage, parsley

— GENERAL TIPS —
To freeze herbs, wrap in aluminum foil and freeze in bunches,
or cut them up, cover them with water in an ice tray, and freeze. Defrost as required.

For a delicate flavor, chop herbs finely. For a stronger flavor, chop coarsely or tear the leaves.

Tear basil by hand. If you chop it, the leaves turn black.

Add herbs to salads to pep up the flavor.

If you wish to lower your salt intake, thyme, marjoram, or lovage make serviceable substitutes.

Herbs like lemon balm and angelica can be used to replace sugar in cooking.

Herbs can make fragrant and decorative additions to flower arrangements.

TIP: Basil loses its flavor quickly when cooked, so don't add it until the last 15 minutes or so of cooking.

TIP: Gather sweet-scented rose petals from the garden in the early morning and float them in your bath. The heat of the water will release the oils in the petals onto the surface of the water.

— THE MAGIC OF HERBS —

The magical properties of herbs and flowers have been known for centuries. Elizabethans used herbs for everything from removing warts to warding off witches. I can't vouch for how successful the recipes were, but some are definitely worth a try, like this one, which dates from 1600 and is held in the Ashmolean Museum in Oxford . . .

— To Enable One to See the Fairies —

A pint of sallet oyle and put in into a vial glasse; and first wash it with rose-water and marygolde water; the flowers to be gathered towards the east.

Wash it till the oyle becomes white, then put into the glasse, and then put thereto the budds of holly-hocke, the flowers of marygolde, the flowers or toppes of wild thyme, the budds of young hazle, and the thyme must be gathered near the side of a hill where fairies use to be; and take the grasse of a fairy throne; then all these put into the oyle in the glasse and sette it to dissolve three dayes in the sunne and then keep it for thy use.

— PASTA MASTER —

"Everything you see I owe to spaghetti."
—Sophia Loren

Pasta comes in more than 350 different shapes and sizes, but the reason for this is not purely decorative. This edible geometry is designed to complement certain sauces or fillings and so improve flavor. Match pasta shape with pasta sauce and you have a marriage made in gustatory heaven.

SHAPED PASTA: Marries well with most sauces, but has a particular affinity with chunky, textured sauces. Hunks of meat, vegetables, or beans cling to the curves and twists, and collect in the nooks and crevices. They're also suitable for baked dishes. The smaller shapes are ideal for broths.

Fusilli *(little springs)* — Campanelle *(bell flowers)* — Ruote de carre *(wheels)* — Conchiglie *(shells)* — Strozzapreti *(priest stranglers)* — Farfalle *(butterflies)*

DID YOU KNOW? Pasta has less fat and more energy than the same amount of baked potato.

TUBULAR PASTA: Suits thick and chunky sauces. Penne rigate is ideal with a rich and creamy carbonara sauce, and the bits of pancetta (bacon) cling to the ridges. Smaller tubes, like macaroni, would be better with a simple tomato sauce.

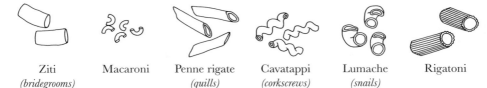

Ziti	Macaroni	Penne rigate	Cavatappi	Lumache	Rigatoni
(bridegrooms)		*(quills)*	*(corkscrews)*	*(snails)*	

LONG AND RIBBON PASTA: Are perfect with oil-based sauces, as the slippery texture coats and lubricates the long strands. Spaghetti suits pesto sauce, but also a light seafood sauce like *vongole* (clam sauce). Team thicker pasta, like tagliatelle, with tomato, meat, or creamy sauces. Cut vegetables long and thin to complement the pasta.

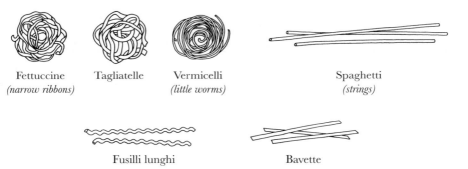

Fettuccine	Tagliatelle	Vermicelli	Spaghetti
(narrow ribbons)		*(little worms)*	*(strings)*

Fusilli lunghi	Bavette

FILLED PASTA: Are stuffed, so work best with simple sauces like melted butter and sage, or lemon and parmesan.

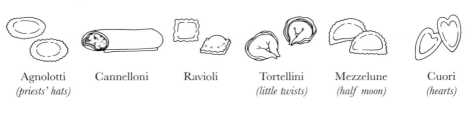

Agnolotti	Cannelloni	Ravioli	Tortellini	Mezzelune	Cuori
(priests' hats)			*(little twists)*	*(half moon)*	*(hearts)*

DID YOU KNOW? Leading Italian car designer, Giorgio Giugiaro, was asked by a pasta manufacturer to design the perfect-shaped pasta. The result was a short tube with ridges. It is known as marille.

TIP: Run out of long matches? Uncooked spaghetti will reach the parts other matches cannot reach.

— DRIED PASTA OR FRESH PASTA? —

Fresh pasta is nearly always made from eggs and is highly perishable,
which is why you find it in the refrigerator at the supermarket.

Fresh pasta cooks much quicker than dried pasta, usually in less than 3 minutes.

Dried pasta is not, as you might think, fresh pasta that's been dried.
Dried pasta rarely contains eggs. Dried pasta is a simple mix of flour, water,
and salt and has a much longer shelf life.

Neither is better than the other; it's down to personal taste.

— HOW TO COOK PERFECT PASTA —

Always cook pasta just before serving it.

Don't use second-rate pasta. If you are using dried pasta, choose a reputable brand. Some of the best are made from durum wheat semolina. Measure about 4 ounces of pasta per person.

Use a large saucepan. Pasta needs a lot of space to move around or it will be sticky.

The critical thing in cooking pasta is to use plenty of water. Allow at least 1¾ pints water per 4 ounces of pasta. It's often recommended to allow 1 teaspoon of salt per 1¾ pints water, but since pasta already contains salt, you can reduce the amount according to your taste. Bring the water to a full rolling boil before adding first the salt, then the pasta. (An Italian chef once told me the water should be "singing Aïda".) If you add the pasta too early, it will stick together.

If you're cooking long pasta like spaghetti, take a bunch in your hand, fan it out, and ease it slowly down into the pan as it gets softer.

Boil up the water again and cook uncovered. The pasta should be submerged in the water.

Don't add olive oil to pasta unless it's the flat type, like lasagne. If you do, the oil will coat the pasta and prevent the sauce from sticking to it.

Give the pasta a stir from time to time with a fork. Cooking times vary, so check the package. Dried pasta usually takes between 8–12 minutes, depending on shape and size. The only way to tell if it's cooked is by tasting it. It should be *al dente,* meaning tender but firm, with some "bite" in it. There's only a brief moment between *al dente* and soggy, so it's vital to keep your eye on the pot.

Drain the pasta in a large colander so it will drain quickly without cooling. Never rinse it under either hot or cold water, as it will wash away the starch coating.

TIP: To discover if your pasta is cooked, throw a piece against the wall. If it sticks, it's cooked.

— THE PERFECT TOMATO SAUCE —

There are endless variations on this theme.
Here's a quick, delicious, and foolproof recipe that works with most pasta dishes.

2 tablespoons olive oil
1 large onion, finely chopped
14 oz. can Italian chopped tomatoes or 1 lb. skinned, chopped fresh tomatoes
2¾ fl. oz. red wine or vegetable stock
1 teaspoon tomato purée
4–6 fresh basil leaves, chopped, or 1 teaspoon dried basil
sea salt and freshly ground black pepper
pinch of sugar

Serves 4

1. Heat the oil in a saucepan. Add the onion and fry until soft, but not brown.

2. Add the tomatoes, wine or stock, tomato purée, and basil. Cover the pan, and simmer for about 15 minutes until the sauce is thick.

3. Remove the lid and continue simmering until the sauce is the thickness you prefer. The longer you simmer, the thicker it will be. Purée the sauce in a blender if you like it smooth.

4. Season with salt and pepper and add a pinch of sugar.

5. Toss the pasta with the sauce and serve with grated Parmesan cheese and a garnish of shredded basil leaves.

NOTE: Italians would never serve pasta drowning in sauce—enough to coat the pasta, and no more. Allow any leftover sauce to cool, then refrigerate or freeze.

Buon appetito!

REMEMBER: The simplest sauces are usually the best. Don't over-complicate—use three or four of the very best ingredients.

How to eat spaghetti like an Italian: Take a small number of strands and use your fork to drag them over to the side of your plate. Hold your fork upright on the plate and twist it round and round the strands of spaghetti until you have a neat, bite-sized cluster.

TIP: If you only have canned whole tomatoes, snip them with scissors to make chopped.

— TEA: THE CUP THAT CHEERS —

Tea is the most popular beverage in the world after water.

More than two billion cups are consumed each day and, not surprisingly,
it's the British who drink the most.

Tea is that rare combination—something delicious that's healthy too.

Natural, fat-free, and calorie-free, it contains less than half the caffeine of coffee.

That quintessential British housewife, Mrs. Beeton,
summed up the appeal of the amber nectar perfectly:
"the cup that cheers but does not inebriate."

— HOW TO MAKE THE PERFECT ALL-PURPOSE CUP OF TEA —

1. Use a teapot and loose tea, if possible, which is better quality than tea bags.

2. Fill the kettle with fresh clean water and boil.

3. Warm the pot by swirling a little hot water around the inside.

4. Allow one teaspoon or one tea bag per cup, and "one for the pot".
Wake up tea leaves with a stream of boiling water.

5. Cover with a tea cozy and brew for 3–5 minutes, depending on taste.
To change the strength, alter the number of tea leaves rather than the
brewing time. Tea left longer to brew will taste bitter, not stronger.

6. Pour the tea through a strainer into individual cups.

7. Serve with milk or lemon (thinly sliced) and sugar if desired.
It makes no difference to the flavor whether you add the milk
first or last, but sticklers for etiquette dictate the milk goes in last.

ICED TEA: For small quantities, proceed as above and pour over ice.
Serve with lemon, mint leaves, or cucumber slices.

TIP: To prevent lip prints on the teacup, blot your lipstick before drinking.

DID YOU KNOW? Each year in Britain there are, on average, 37 injuries involving tea cozies.

Tea	Origin	Flavor	Recommendations
DARJEELING (Black)	Darjeeling, India	"Champagne of teas"; muscatel bouquet, piquant	Good all-purpose tea
ENGLISH BREAKFAST (Black)	Blend	Rich, smooth, malty	Nice wake-up tea; drink plain or add milk
LAPSANG SOUCHONG (Black)	Taiwan	Smoky, rich; leaves are smoked over pine embers	Traditional, smoky drawing-room tea
EARL GREY (Black)	Blend	Fragrant citrus flavor from oil of bergamot	Perfect for afternoon tea; milk may be added
MACHA (Green)	Japan	Bittersweet	Used in Japanese tea ceremony
DRAGON WELL (Green)	China	Nutty, sweet chestnut flavor; tangy	Morning or afternoon pick-me-up
FORTNUM & MASON'S	Blend	Scent of ripe peaches and muscat grapes	Served at the Queen's garden parties
TETLEY'S	British blend	Full-bodied; subtle orange flavor	Perfect late-night brew

DID YOU KNOW? All true teas are made from the same plant, camellia sinensis. *In China, monkeys were trained to pick leaves from inaccessible tea plants. Today, women do most of the harvesting.*

— HOW TO DRINK TEA LIKE PRINCE CHARLES —

Presentation

The handle of the teacup should point at an angle of 3 o'clock.
The teaspoon must be placed on the right-hand side of the saucer, facing out at 5 o'clock.
The crest on the crockery should point to 12 o'clock.

Method

Take hold of the teacup by "pinching" the handle between your first finger and thumb.
Don't curl your fingers inside the handle. And don't cock your little finger in the air.
When picking up the cup always lift the saucer with it unless you are
seated at a table, in which case the saucer may be left on the table.
Sip, don't slurp. Enjoy!

— TASSEOGRAPHY: THE ART OF READING TEA LEAVES —

When there is only about a teaspoon of tea left in the cup, turn it around three times and place it upside down on the saucer. Turn the cup upright and look deep into the grounds left inside for symbols:

Crown	. . .	success
Mouse	. . .	bad luck
Bird	. . .	good luck
Ring	. . .	marriage
Anchor	. . .	hope
Apple	. . .	long life
Dog	. . .	friendship
Flower	. . .	happiness

— VERSATILITEA —

To enhance the flavor of dried fruit, soak in tea instead of water.

To tenderize meat, add $\frac{1}{2}$ cup of tea to your stews.

To marble boiled eggs: Boil the eggs for a couple of minutes, and then remove from the pan. Tap the eggs gently with a spoon to crack the shells. Return the eggs to the pan with five tea bags and simmer for a minute. Remove the eggs and let them cool.

To add shine to brown hair, use cold black tea as an after-shampoo rinse. Cold camomile tea does the same for blonde hair.

To soothe tired eyes, place tea bags soaked in warm water over closed eyes and leave for 10–15 minutes.

To tint a print sepia: Soak 4 tea bags in 1 cup of hot water. Allow to cool. Soak the print for 10 minutes. Remove and rinse off excess liquid. Allow to dry hanging up, not flat.

TIP: Remember the teakettle—it is always up to its neck in hot water, yet it still sings!

To make mirrors sparkle and chrome gleam, use a cold infusion of tea to polish.

Save tea grounds to put around acid-loving plants (e.g., rhododendron, azalea).

— HOW TO STORE TEA —

An airtight, opaque container (not plastic) prevents tea from absorbing moisture and odors, and preserves flavor. Don't keep tea in the refrigerator—the leaves may absorb moisture from condensation. Properly stored, tea should keep for up to a year.

If you want to store a silver or stainless steel teapot and don't want it to smell, drop four or five sugar lumps in the pot.

— HOW TO BE SUSHI SAVVY —

DID YOU KNOW? Sushi means "'to vinegar" and it originated as a way of preserving fish. The fish was salted and put on a bed of vinegar rice. After a year, the rice would be discarded and only the marinated fish was eaten.

Do you feel like a fish out of water when you go to a sushi bar? Use this guide to arm yourself with everything you need to know, so next time you go, you can order like a pro.

Let's clear up one common misconception right away: Sushi is *not* raw fish. Sushi means "to vinegar," and it's about vinegared rice. The rice is combined with other ingredients, one of which might be raw fish, but is just as likely to be vegetables (I've eaten some delicious vegetarian sushi). The rice functions a bit like the bread in a sandwich, so to imagine that sushi is solely about fish would be like believing that all sandwiches are fish paste!

A sushi meal comprises many bite-sized dishes that complement each other. You can order as few as three dishes or as many as six. By the end of your meal, you will feel pleasantly satisfied without feeling stuffed.

— WHAT'S WHAT ON THE TABLE —

Soy sauce (*shoyu*) is provided as a condiment, together with a tiny ceramic dish.
Pour a tiny drop into the dish and use it as a dipping sauce.
Dip the fish side of the sushi into the sauce, not the rice side.

Oshibori is a towel resembling a tiny washcloth.
Hot or cold depending on the weather. Use it to wipe your hands.
Keep it folded or return it to the waiter.
Request a clean one whenever necessary.

What to drink: You don't want to taint the delicate flavors of the sushi,
so choose a drink that cleanses the palate—tradition dictates sake, and green tea,
but beer, wine, and water are all good.

DID YOU KNOW? Sushi is perfect if you're health-conscious, because it's generally low-fat, high-protein, and packed with vitamins and minerals.

— SUSHI BAR LINGO —

Nori
Thin sheets of dried, toasted seaweed used to wrap rolled sushi.

Sushi rice
White, short grain, sticky rice in sweetened vinegar.

Daikon
A white radish (shaped like a large white carrot), served shredded with sashimi.

Wasabi
Hot, fiery, pungent horseradish paste.
Only a tiny amount is needed to bring out the flavor of the sushi.
It's a bit of an acquired taste, so use sparingly until you get used to it.

Soy sauce (shoyu)
Fermented soy bean sauce.

Sake
Japanese rice wine, served hot or cold.

Mirin
Sweet rice wine used solely for cooking.

Rice vinegar
Adds flavor to sushi rice.

Miso
Fermented soya bean paste, used to flavor soups.

Fish
Mild flavored: *tai* (red snapper);
Stronger flavored: *hamachi* (Japanese yellowtail) or *aji* (Spanish mackerel).

EATING SUSHI: Sushi is designed as finger food, so it's fine to use your fingers, but chopsticks should be used when eating sashimi.

CHOPSTICK ETIQUETTE
Snap your disposable chopsticks open and lay them
together on the rest, uncrossed. It's impolite to rub them together as this implies the
chopsticks have splinters and are inferior. If you're not comfortable with chopsticks,
don't feel embarrassed about asking for a fork.

DID YOU KNOW? It takes 10 years' training to qualify as a sushi chef in Japan. They are highly esteemed, and sushi-making is considered an art.

ORDERING: You don't order all courses at once; each dish is ordered individually.
The traditional way to start your meal is with sashimi.
Omakase means "chef's choice"; it's the best sushi that day.

Don't order anything but sushi and sashimi from the chef. It would be like
going into a Chinese restaurant and ordering fish and chips.

— Know Your Sushi —

The names of different sushi dishes and types of sushi vary from country to country and sushi
bar to sushi bar, so things can get a bit confusing. Here are some of the main varieties you're
likely to encounter . . .

Maki-zushi (mah-kee-zoo-shee)
A general term for rolled sushi and the one most familiar to Westerners.
There are various types:
Futo-maki-zushi (foo-toh-mah-kee-zoo-shee)—thick-rolled sushi
Hoso-maki-zushi (ho-soh-mah-kee-zoo-shee)—thin-rolled sushi
The inside layer may be raw fish like salmon or yellowtail, or thin strips of crisp vegetables
like cucumber or carrot, surrounded by a layer of rice, then a thin layer of nori.
Gunkan-maki-zushi (gooh-kahn-mah-kee-zoo-shee)—battleship roll
Seafood, but particularly fish eggs, are wrapped in seaweed and moulded and
often placed on a nugget of rice. So called because the rolls resemble boats.

Nigiri-zushi (nee-gee-ree-zoo-shee)
A shaped, bite-sized block of rice topped with raw fish or seafood and bound together with a
strip of nori. It was originally sold on the streets of Toyko as a snack—eaten by men only!

Chirashi-zushi (chee-rah-shee-zoo-shee)
Scattered sushi. Rice is cooked, then placed in a bowl, and pieces of raw or cooked fish
are mixed with it. Pieces of omelet or vegetables are scattered on top.
Served with wasabi, soy, and ginger.

Inari-zushi (ee-nah-ree-zoo-shee)
Pouches of tofu (bean curd), omelet or cabbage leaves in which are wrapped rice,
fish, vegetables, or herbs.

Temaki-zushi (the-mah-kee-zoo-shee)
Roll shaped like an ice-cream cone and filled with fish such as *anago* (eel)
and/or vegetables, then wrapped in nori.

Sashimi (sah-shee-mee)
Not strictly sushi, this is slices of raw fish without rice.
It is served with soy sauce, wasabi, shredded daikon, and aromatic perilla leaves.
Fresh fish is always used, as frozen fish lacks the subtle flavors.

*TIP: Make you own sushi! The only specialized equipment you need is a bamboo rolling mat to roll out the
sushi. Sushi rice is now available in supermarkets.*

Oshi-zushi (oh-shee-zoo-shee)—pressed sushi
The rice is pressed into a sushi mold, commonly with marinated fish
such as smoked salmon or haddock. Once it is compressed, the sushi is
removed from the mold, unwrapped, and sliced into bite-sized pieces.

California rolls
An "inside-out roll," basically; a type of *maki-zushi* invented in Los Angeles
for Americans who felt a bit squeamish about eating raw fish.
They consist of cooked fish rolled in rice and wrapped in nori.
The original combination is crabmeat, avocado, and cucumber, but
numerous variations occur, none of which are popular in Japan.

— COFFEE SHOP LINGO —
If you've ventured into a coffee shop lately, you'll know that the choice of coffees is
overwhelming, and it's easy to become confused, befuddled, if not intimidated.
Use this crib sheet and you'll soon be speaking coffeehouse lingo like a barista
(no, they don't wear wigs).

Americano: Espresso diluted with hot water

Americano misto: Americano with steamed milk

Barista: Trained espresso maker

Brevé: Espresso with semi-skimmed milk

Café au lait: Equal quantities of dark-roasted coffee and hot milk

Cappuccino: Espresso mixed with steamed milk, topped off with the foam from
the steamed milk and dusted with cinnamon or cocoa powder

Con panna: Espresso with whipped cream

Corretto: Espresso with a liqueur added

Crème: Espresso with thick cream

Decaf: Decaffeinated coffee

Demitasse: Small espresso cup

Doppio: Double espresso

Double: another name for Doppio

*DID YOU KNOW? There's still an awful lot of coffee in Brazil. They produce 30 percent of the
coffee in the world.*

Espresso: Small shot of rich, full-bodied coffee, always served black

Frappuccino: Iced cappuccino

Freddo: Chilled espresso in a glass, ice optional

Granita: Latte with frozen milk

Harmless: Decaf espresso

Latte: Half espresso and half hot milk

Lungo: Espresso using a long pull to extract the most flavor from the bean

Macchiato: Espresso topped with a dash of steamed milk

Medici: Doppio poured over chocolate syrup and orange peel, topped with whipped cream

Mocha: Latte with chocolate and whipped cream

Mochaccino: Cappuccino with steamed chocolate milk,
topped with foam from the steamed chocolate milk

No Fun: Decaf latte

On a leash: To go

Shot in the dark: Regular coffee with a shot of espresso

Skinny: Nonfat or skimmed milk latte

Skinny harmless: Decaf, nonfat or skimmed milk latte

Speed ball: Another name for "Shot in the dark"

Thunder thighs: Double, tall mocha made with whole milk,
topped with whipped cream

Unleaded: Decaf

Viennese: Strong coffee and melted chocolate whisked until
frothy and served with whipped cream

Why bother: Another name for "Skinny harmless"

With wings: To go, in a cup with handles

*TIP: Store coffee in an airtight container, in a cool, dark place. Coffee absorbs flavors, so don't keep it near
strong-smelling food like cheese or onions.*

— WASHING UP —

"Three roommates, and still nobody washes a dish in my apartment.
Last week I was thirsty and I had to get out my Yahtzee game for a clean cup."
—Dobie Maxwell

— HOW TO WASH DISHES BY HAND —

1. Scrape all residual food off plates and dishes into the wastebasket.

2. Rinse all items under a tap of hot, running water.

3. Put heavily stained pans and dishes aside to soak
(i.e., add a squirt of dishwashing liquid and fill with hot water).
The exceptions are pans with starchy food residue like
mashed potato, milk, or egg, which should be soaked in cold water.
Put these to one side and tackle them last.
If a pan is badly soiled, let it soak overnight.

4. Put on rubber gloves.

5. Fill a dishpan with the hottest water your hands can
stand and mix in just a squirt of dishwashing liquid.
Don't use too much, as it will leave a film on the dishes.

6. Start washing up. The idea is to start with the least dirty and work up to the
dirtiest, which is logical, but use your common sense. This is the recommended order:

Glasses

Lightly soiled dishes

Cups and mugs

Soiled dishes

Cutlery

Cooking pots, pans, and dishes

7. Use a scrubbing pad or brush for ground-in stains.

8. Change the water as soon as it loses its clarity.

9. Don't pile glasses all together into the dishpan.
Wash individually. See page 184.

TIP: Too much dishwashing liquid is worse than too little. Be frugal!

10. Rinse each item after you wash it under hot, running water.

11. Don't lay plates horizontally on the draining board.
Get yourself a proper drainer for cutlery and a rack for plates so you can stack vertically.
That way they will drip-dry and there's no need for drying
(though you can polish glasses with a soft cloth if you want them sparkling).
It's much more hygienic.

12. When you're done, empty and clean the dishpan,
retrieve the stray teaspoon, which will inevitably be lurking at the bottom,
and clean the surrounding work surfaces.

SINK STINKS: Pour down a solution of boiling water and a cup of bicarbonate
of soda every few weeks to keep your sink smelling fresh and drains
running smoothly.

— WASHING SPECIFIC ITEMS —

Glasses
Need to be spotlessly clean, and free from any dishwashing liquid or odor. This is particularly important with champagne glasses, where detergent will destroy the bubbles, just like soap in your bubble bath.

The best way to wash glasses is to place them sideways into the water and wash each glass separately, using a brush. Rinse thoroughly in clean, warm water. Allow to drip-dry. If you must use a towel, ensure it is clean and lint-free.

Knives
Wash knives with wooden handles by hand in hot, soapy water even if they are dishwasher-safe. Wash and dry carbon steel blade knives immediately or they will rust. Don't leave knives soaking at the bottom of the dishpan. They'll go rusty, and you might just forget they're there and slice off a finger. That will really cloud your water.

Saucepans
To remove burnt-on stains without the need for soaking, put a squirt of dishwashing liquid in the pan, fill with water, and simmer on a low heat for about 10 minutes. This will loosen the burnt deposit for easy removal. Rinse and dry.

CLEAN GREEN: Cover a burnt pan with lots of salt and some water, leave overnight, then wash.

Milk pan
Leave to soak in cold water.

TIP: Rinse the pan in cold water BEFORE you heat the milk, and it will be easier to clean.

TIP: The method for cleaning saucepans also works for roasting pans.

Chopping board
Plastic—Can be washed in the dishwasher. Wooden—Scrub under running hot water with a brush. Don't leave to soak or it could warp. To remove the onion or garlic taste from a board, rub it with cut lemon.

Teacups and mugs
To remove brown tannin stains from inside cups and mugs, rub with salt.

Blender
Add hot water and a tiny squirt of dishwashing liquid and give it a whizz. Empty, refill with water to rinse.

Thermos
Use a tablet of denture cleaner.

— WASHING DISHES IN THE DISHWASHER —

Use only the detergent recommended for your machine and check the manual for the correct amount to use.

Scrape off food residue and rinse all dishes and cutlery under the hot tap before putting them in the dishwasher.

Stack according to your dishwasher instructions.

Stack knives with their blades pointing downward.

Don't put plastic items near the heating element as they will melt.

Don't overload the washer. Space is needed so the water can circulate.

Check your manual but, as a rule, avoid washing: fragile china, ceramic dishes, hand-painted ware, kitchen knives, silverware, cutlery with ivory or wooden handles.

Never wash silver and stainless steel cutlery together, as the steel may stain the silver.

Also avoid washing crystal glasses as the strong detergent will result eventually in "etching"—white marks that won't come off.

Place half a lemon among the dirty dishes and they'll emerge zinging with freshness. It also helps control lime scale.

DID YOU KNOW? A national survey found that, given the choice, women would rather see a man washing dishes than dancing nude.

— STYLE & GROOMING —

"My grandmother took a bath every year, whether she needed it or not."

—BRENDAN BEHAN

— HOW TO TAKE BODY MEASUREMENTS FOR CLOTHES —

— MEN'S MEASURMENTS —

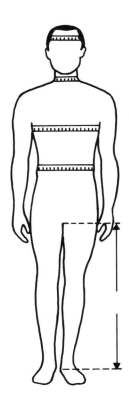

Hat
Wrap a tape measure around your head, level with the middle of your forehead. For a more precise measurement, get a friend to do it.

Collar
Wrap a tape measure around your neck, where the center of the collar would be if you were wearing a shirt. Allow some slack for comfort and personal preference.

Chest
Measure around the fullest part of your chest, keeping the tape taut across your back and close up under your arms.

Waist
To find your true waistline, tie some string loosely around your middle, then measure around where it comes to rest with a tape measure. For belts, add 2 inches to your waist size.

Inside leg
Measure down the inner side of the leg from the crotch to the anklebone.

Sleeve length
Unless you're a contortionist, you'll need a helping hand for this one. Bend your elbow and measure from point A, just below the center of the neck, along the elbow, and down the arm to the wrist, point B.

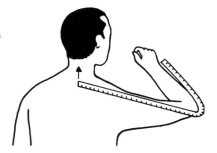

DID YOU KNOW? More than 100 measurements are taken when fitting an astronaut for their space suit—including knees and knuckles.

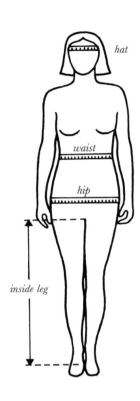

hat

waist

hip

inside leg

— WOMEN'S MEASUREMENTS —

Hat
As for men (see page 187).

Bust
See "How to buy the perfect bra" on pages 189–190.

Waist
To find your true waistline, tie some string loosely around your middle, then measure around where it comes to rest with a tape measure. For belts, add 2 inches to your waist size.

Hip measurement
Stand with your feet together and measure around the fullest part of your hips, which is about 8 inches below your natural waistline.

Inside leg
Measure down the inner side of the leg from the crotch to the anklebone.

— CLOTHES SIZES —

American	British	Continental
6	8	38
8	10	40
10	12	42
12	14	44
14	16	46
16	18	48
18	20	50

— SHOE MEASUREMENTS —
Measure the sole of your foot from the tip of your big toe to your heel.

TIP: Stand up straight when taking all measurements.

— SHOE SIZES —

Men

British	6½	7	7½	8	8½	9	9½	10	10½	11	11½	12
American	7	7½	8	8½	9	9½	10	11	11½	12	12½	13
Continental	40	41	41	42	42	43	44	44	45	46	46	47

Women

British	3½	4	4½	5	5½	6	6½	7	8	9
American	5	5½	6	6½	7	7½	8	8½	9½	10½
Continental	36	37	37	38	39	39	40	41	42	43

NOTE: Shoe sizes are approximate, as continental sizes vary between countries.

— HOW TO BUY THE PERFECT BRA —

Nine out of ten women do not wear the correct bra size, and frankly, I'm not in the least surprised. Have you ever tried working out your bra size? You need to be Gisele Bundchen crossed with Einstein to make any sense of all the different size charts and puzzling mathematical formulas.

The truth is, measuring for a bra is not an exact science. The size of bra you need varies according to the brand, style, and fabric.

The best way to measure your bra size is to forget all the charts and scientific calculations, chuck out the tape measure, grab yourself a big bundle of bras in various sizes, and keep trying them on until you hit on the right one. Here are a few guidelines to help . . .

When you do up the bra at the back, put it on the first set of hooks. As the bra becomes looser with wear, move down to the second or third hooks. If the bra you try on feels more comfortable in the third hook, try on a smaller bra.

Make sure the cups encompass your breasts. If the fabric is saggy, the cup is too big. If your breast bulges over at the front or sides (the so-called "double-bubble" effect), it's too small.

Make sure the center seam of the bra lies flat against your breastbone.

Check the tension of the underband. If the back of the band rides up, it's too loose; the shoulder straps will have to bear more weight and will dig in. The back of the underband should be equal with the front. Remember, it's the underband, *not* the straps, that gives a bra most of the support.

DID YOU KNOW? Most women wear bras out of habit or because they believe they are necessary for support. In fact, medical research has shown that bras do not stop breasts from sagging.

Adjust the straps for comfort. Straps should not be so tight that they cut into your shoulders nor so loose that you lose support.

Jump up and down to test the support. Don't be shy. No one has to see you in the fitting room!

Never buy an underwired bra if the wires rest on the soft tissue of the breast. Not only is this uncomfortable, but it could also damage your breast tissue. The wires should lie flat on your rib cage; that is, on hard bone only. They should also stretch around your breast, not cut into it.

Try a top on over the bra to see that it flatters your shape. If you wear tight-fitting tops, avoid bras with frills and bows which will show through. Go for a seamless bra instead.

Your bust size fluctuates during the month, so choose a stretch fabric with some give in it.

WARNING: Many stores offer a free "professional" bra-fitting service, but they are not always reliable.

TIP: You know you have the right bra if you're not aware you're wearing it.

— MEASURING YOUR POOCH —

Since you're looking so dapper, we can't have your pooch letting the sartorial side down, can we? Here's how to measure your faithful friend for their coat and collar.

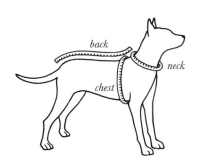

NOTE: Fido should be standing up when measurements are taken.

Neck: Measure loosely all the way around the lowest part of the neck at the top of the shoulders.

Chest: Measure loosely around the broadest part of the chest behind the front legs.

Back: Measure from the base of the neck, where the collar would fit, to the base of the tail (not the tip).

TIP: If you want to dress your faithful friend in designer collars and leads, T-shirts, tank tops, and hair bows, try the Internet. There's a whole host of sites selling dog togs.

— GERM WARFARE —

"Keep yourself clean and bright; you are the window through which you must see the world."
—*George Bernard Shaw*

Bacteria and viruses lurk everywhere, and some can live on surfaces like bedsheets, elevator buttons, and stair rails for days if conditions are favorable. You come along, touch the bedsheet, elevator button or stair rail, and pick up the bacteria on your hands. All you have to do next is rub your eye, or touch yoour nose or mouth with the infected finger, and it's atishoo, atishoo, atishoo for the next week or, maybe something even worse—flu, a tummy bug, Hepatitis A, or, if you're in the hospital, MRSA (Methicillin-Resistant Staphylococcus Aureus).

So, what can you do in the war against germs? Health professionals are unanimously agreed: The single most effective thing you can do is also one of the simplest—wash your hands. Or to be more specific, wash your hands properly. If you do, your chances of catching a virus are slashed by 40 percent.

DID YOU KNOW? In Victorian times, it was not uncommon to sew children into their underwear at the onset of winter and not to let them out again until spring. It was believed that colds and chills could be kept at bay if the body was not exposed to the air or washed. Come to think of it, I know a few guys who are keeping this tradition alive.

— COMMON BREEDING GROUNDS FOR GERMS —
Shared computer keyboard and mouse
Restaurant menus
Parking meters
ATM buttons
Elevator buttons
Light switches
Stair and escalator railings
Peanuts on counters of bars
Shopping cart handles
Telephones
Money
Hands of supermarket checkout operators
Doorknobs (especially in public restrooms)
Taps and soap dispensers in public restrooms
Hospital beds

DID YOU KNOW? The average sneeze travels at 90 mph spreads over a distance of 30 feet, and projects 100,000 flu germs into the air.

— HOW TO WASH YOUR HANDS —

No need for fancy wipes and scrubs when you frolic with the carbolic: nothing works better than good old-fashioned soap and water. Avoid antibacterial soaps as they can also destroy friendly bacteria.

1. Remove any rings. Keep a "ring bowl" by the sink at home for when you need to wash your hands.

2. Wet your hands and wrists under HOT running water.

3. Apply plenty of soap and work up a good lather, rubbing palm against palm.

4. Rub your right hand over the back of your left hand. Swap hands and repeat.

5. Interlace your fingers so soap reaches between them.

6. Rub your right fingertips into the palm of your left hand. Swap hands and repeat.

7. Rub your right thumb in a rotary motion with your left hand. Swap hands and repeat.

8. Rub your left wrist in a rotary motion with your right hand. Swap hands and repeat.

DID YOU KNOW? Billionaire business tycoon, Donald Trump, does not shake anyone by the hand for fear of catching their germs.

9. Rinse your hands thoroughly under running WARM water. Make sure you rinse off every last bit of soap as soap does not kill germs; all it does is trap them.

10. Dry your hands on a clean towel. In a public restrooms, disposable paper towels are preferable to electric hand dryers, which can blow microbes onto your hands. Dry your hands thoroughly because bacteria thrive in damp conditions. Pat your hands rather than rub them to avoid chapping.

11. Turn off the tap with the towel or your elbow to prevent possible recontamination.

12. Use the towel to open the door if you're in a public toilet. Avoid touching the door handle.

NOTE: From steps 4 to 8, repeat the number of strokes at least 5 times.

You need to spend at least 20 seconds washing your hands for it be effective.

NOTE: When you are washing your hands at home, use a nailbrush to scrub beneath your fingernails.

— WHEN TO WASH YOUR HANDS —

Before . . .
handling food
eating
putting in or taking out a contact lens
tending someone who is sick

After . . .
using the toilet
handling uncooked foods, especially raw meats
touching pets
sneezing or coughing
changing a diaper
handling money
petting an animal
being outside

DON'T PANIC: A little bit of dirt won't hurt you—in fact, there are scientists who claim it actually does you good! They argue that without exposure to bugs in infancy, the immune system is never "trained" to combat foreign invaders, leaving it weak and vulnerable to allergic disorders such as asthma. The watchword is common sense. Don't live your life in a bubble of ultracleanliness. Practice good basic hygiene and instill the rules into your kids from an early age.

DID YOU KNOW? A survey revealed that 1 in 5 adults don't wash their hands after using a public restroom. Men are worse than women and, oh dear, students are worst of all.

— PERSONAL HYGIENE —

DID YOU KNOW? There are more than 3 million sweat glands around the human body.

The sweat glands are situated mainly in the armpits and between the legs. They kick into action at puberty and gradually slow as we get older. That's why the very young and the elderly rarely suffer from B.O.

Washing daily with soap and water goes a long way to controlling B.O. So too does wearing clean clothes. But is there a need for deodorants and antiperspirants?

Deodorant works by taking away the smell, and when it is perfumed, that disguises body odor.

Antiperspirant contains chemicals to inhibit odor-causing bacteria.

Commercial products are often a combination of the two.

HEALTH CHECK: There have been reports pointing to a possible link between certain antiperspirants that use an aluminum base and breast cancer. If you are concerned, steer clear of antiperspirants containing chemicals such as aluminum and zirconium.

Try an all-natural, cheap, and safe deodorant made out of bicarbonate of soda, also known as baking soda. (Don't confuse it with baking powder—they're two different things.)

To make the deodorant: Sprinkle a tiny amount of baking soda into the palm of your hand. Add a tiny amount of water—just enough to dissolve the baking soda entirely—and create a smooth paste. Apply to your underarms.

— KEEPING CLEAN AND FRESH —
Bathe or shower at least once a day.

Freshen up in the bathroom as many times as you need to during the day.

Don't eat garlic or spicy food. The odor is emitted through the pores.

Wash clothes regularly.

TIP: Wear loose-fitting clothes, in natural fibers such as cotton and linen, so air can circulate freely around your body.

— BASIC FUNCTIONS —

Who needs instruction on what is a natural function? Surely, it's common sense? Well, if that is so, why did an online survey of "bottom-wiping techniques" find that 56 percent of people polled were doing it incorrectly? And why are urinary tract infections (UTIs), such as cystitis, among the most common infections in women? Considering that one of the main causes of UTIs is incorrect bottom-wiping, this strongly suggests that many women *do* need instruction. So, ladies—and gentlemen,—are you sitting comfortably?

— How to Go to the Toilet —

"How long a minute is depends on which side of the bathroom door you're on."
—*Zall's Second Law*

1. Sharing a toilet seat is like sharing your toothbrush with strangers, so if you are in a public restrooms, don't sit directly on the seat. Some public facilities provide paper liners to cover the seat; if not, line the seat with toilet tissue. Don't be tempted to squat over the seat because you won't empty your bladder properly

2. Pull your underwear right down around your ankles. Half-mast is not good enough.

3. Sit down on the toilet. Keep your legs slightly apart and place your feet flat on the floor.

4. Bend forward slightly.

5. Do what comes naturally.

6. Now it's time to wipe your bottom. Stay sitting while you do this. Take a wad of toilet paper, scrunch it up, and begin wiping. There is a common misconception that it doesn't matter *how* you wipe your bottom, but there IS a right way and a wrong way. Choose the wrong way and you'll be endangering your health.

RIGHT WAY: Wipe from front to back. This keeps bacteria away from the urinary tract where infection can occur.

WRONG WAY: *Never* wipe from back to front. This spreads bacteria from the back passage and can lead to infection. That goes for women *and* men, although women are more susceptible to infection.

IDEAL WAY: Wipe back *then* front, using fresh toilet tissue for each. Keep wiping until the paper is totally clean.

7. Flush the toilet.

8. Now wash your hands—see "How to wash your hands" on pages 192–193.

TIP: Dentists recommend you keep your toothbrushes at least 6 feet away from the toilet to avoid contamination from airborne bacteria during flushing.

— HOW TO GET RID OF BATHROOM SMELLS —

Strike a match or light a candle and the flame will burn away the unpleasant gases. Put out the match or candle and leave it in the room in a dish for 10 minutes.

— HOW TO KEEP REGULAR —

Fiber has very little nutritional value, but it plays a vital part in the digestive process. A daily ration of fiber prevents constipation and reduces the risk of bowel problems.

TOP SOURCES OF FIBER	g per 100g
Bran	44.0
Dried apricots	19–24.0
Dried figs	19–24.0
Prunes	16.0
Shredded Wheat	12.0
Frozen peas	12.0
Oatmeal	7.0
Wholemeal bread	6.0
Muesli	6.0

— HOW TO CLEAN THE TOILET —

If the bowl is badly stained, you first need to remove the water from the bowl. Use a plastic disposable cup to bale it out. Then pour thick, neat bleach directly on the stain and rinse off immediately, as it could discolor the glaze. Continue until the stain is gone. Never mix different brands of toilet cleaner in the bowl together.

CLEAN GREEN: Flush the toilet, then sprinkle bicarbonate of soda around the bowl, add white vinegar (it will start fizzing), and clean with paper towels and plenty of elbow grease.

DID YOU KNOW? In Japanese homes the toilet is always separate from the bathroom. They also change into special slippers to visit the toilet.

— HOW TO BREATHE —

We breathe, on average, 18 times a minute, 1,018 times an hour, 25,920 times a day. With all that practice, you'd think we'd all be experts, wouldn't you?

Are you breathing properly?
Try this simple test: Place one hand on your chest and the other on your stomach. Take a normal breath. Notice which hand rises more. Probably neither hand moved much, but if anything, the one on your chest rose a little more. If that's so, you are not breathing correctly. You are what is known as a "chest breather".

You're not alone: A doctor in the U.S. who is an expert on respiratory matters, estimates that up to 80 percent of Americans are chest breathers. That figure can probably be extended to include most Westerners, since we all follow a similar lifestyle.

What is a chest breather?
Chest breathers take shallow breaths. They use less than 20 percent of their lungs' capacity. Less oxygen enters the lungs, so the body is deprived of energy and bodily funtions are comprised. Chest breathing is stressed breathing, and this in turn leads to more stress because you need to take more breaths, and so it becomes a vicious circle.

How breathing works
Put very simply, you breathe in air to give the cells of your body the oxygen they need, and you breathe out the unwanted carbon dioxide.

So, what is good beathing practice?
For an object lesson in good breathing, watch a baby or an animal sleeping. See how their whole body is used in the process. Their tummy slowly rises and falls with each breath in and out. This is because a muscle called the diaphragm is used. The diaphragm is a strong sheet of muscle between the chest cavity and the stomach.

Why do we lose our instinctive good breathing practices?
As we grow up, we're always being told to hold our stomach in and puff out our chest. A flat stomach with tight, inflexible abdominal muscles inhibits the action of the diaphragm.

Is it worth learning to breathe better?
You bet. Even more than diet or exercise, better breathing has extraordinary health benefits, both physical and mental: lower blood pressure, increased blood circulation, reduced stress, increased concentration, more efficient digestive system, boosted metabolism, weight loss, reduction in back and neck pain, improved sleep—how long do you have?

If better breathing is such a miracle worker, why haven't I heard more about it?
While the healing power of breathing has been known for centuries in Eastern medicine, it is still new in Western medicine, so not many scientific studies have been done. Another reason is that, unlike a new diet, say, breathing is not a marketable commodity. A pair of lungs cannot be patented, which means there is no potential to make money. So, until they can find a way of charging us to breathe, there won't be much funding for research projects.

DID YOU KNOW? Seventy percent of the body's waste is eliminated through breathing. A clinical study showed that the single most important factor in living a healthier and longer life was how well you breathe.

— HOW TO IMPROVE YOUR BREATHING —

The aim: To make your stomach rise more than your chest as your diaphragm expands, so you are using your full lung capacity.

The technique
Good breathing starts with good posture. You cannot breathe efficiently if you are slumped, slouched, or stooped. Keep your spine straight and the crown of your head up. Focus on lifting your rib cage up off your hips. Draw your shoulder blades on your back close together to open up your chest cavity, ready to take in the oxygen.

Breathe in slowly through your nose. Focus on drawing air down into the base of your tummy first, then your middle chest, and lastly, your upper chest. That way you will use all your lung capacity. Imagine you're pouring a glass of water—the water goes down to the bottom of the glass first, then the middle, and finally the top. To feel this happening, put your hands on your ribs with your thumbs at the front and your fingers twisted round to the back. As air fills your body, you should also feel your tummy being pushed down and out.

When you feel as if your lungs are full, hold it for a second, then slowly breathe out through your nose. Imagine you're emptying the glass of water. You empty the top first, then the middle, and finally, the bottom. You should feel your stomach deflate as air is pushed out.

REMEMBER: Your stomach should expand as you inhale, and contract as you exhale.

When you first try this it will probably feel very strange—and very difficult! But, with practice, you can make good breathing as automatic as bad breathing.

Should you breathe through your nose or your mouth?
Generally speaking, you should breathe in and out through your nose. Your nose warms up and humidifies the incoming air, and is equipped with little hairs that filter out dust particles and other bacteria in the air. Breathing through the mouth is usually just a bad habit.

GIVE IT A TRY: Next time you have to climb a flight of stairs, instead of huffing and puffing, try to control the tempo of your breathing: As you go up the first two stairs, breathe in; as you go up the next two stairs, breathe out. Keep this rhythm going—two in, two out, two in, two out—and when you reach the top, you won't be breathless.

A WORD OF CAUTION: Deep and full breathing is a powerful technique. If you have any history of respiratory problems or a known medical condition, check with your doctor before attempting.

FIND OUT MORE: Go to www.breathing.com and you can try synchronizing your own breathing with a moving model of a diaphragm. Enroll in a yoga or Pilates class, where you will learn conscious and controlled breathing techniques.

DID YOU KNOW? Hollywood celebrities are now hiring "breath-control coaches" to help them improve their breathing technique.

— HOW TO GET THE PERFECT SMILE —

"Love conquers all things—except poverty and toothache."
—Mae West

An attractive smile is one of the best assets you can have.
To ensure you keep yours dazzling, get your teeth into these top tips.

— HOW TO USE DENTAL FLOSS —

Flossing is an essential part of a proper teeth-cleaning routine. It is not an optional extra.
Flossing reaches the bacteria between teeth that brushing cannot reach.

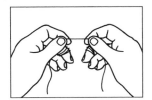

1. Break off about 20 inches of floss and wind most of it around the middle finger of one hand. Wind the rest around the middle finger of your other hand. Leave a gap of about 2 inches between.

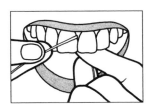

2. Keeping the floss taut between your thumb and first finger, slide the floss between your teeth using a gentle zigzag motion. Never snap it between your teeth. Don't use the floss like a cheese grater, or you could damage your gums and cause cavities.

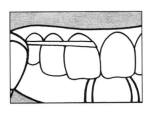

3. Curve the floss into a "C" shape around the base of the tooth and carefully under the gum line. Hold the floss tight against the tooth and slide the floss up and down the side of the tooth several times, gently wiping the plaque from the tooth and gums.

4. Carefully remove the floss from between your tooth.

5. Wind a little more floss from one middle finger to the other so you have a fresh piece of floss.

6. Repeat the flossing process between each of your teeth, using a new section of floss each time.

7. Finally, rinse your mouth to remove any leftover plaque.

Which teeth should you floss? Just those you want to keep.
When to floss? At least once a day, **BEFORE** brushing.

DID YOU KNOW? The electric chair was invented by a dentist named Albert Southwick.

— WHICH TOOTHBRUSH? —

Brushing gets rid of the bacteria that lead to tooth decay and the plaque
that can cause cavities and gum disease.

Choose a brush with soft or medium bristles. A small head is best as it will
reach into all corners of your mouth more easily.

An electric toothbrush is the dental equivalent of an electric floor-polisher,
and will therefore do a more efficient job than a regular toothbrush.

Change your toothbrush every 3 months but don't throw out your old one.
Use it for household chores.

— TOOTHSOME TIPS —

Don't smoke. Smoking not only makes your breath smell like an ashtray,
but it also promotes serious problems such as gum disease and oral cancer.

Eat crunchy, raw foods such as apples or carrots, which cleanse and refresh your mouth.
Pineapple is also a good choice as it contains an enzyme which helps to clean your mouth.

Rub your gums and teeth with a sage leaf for a natural clean and polish.

If you have a toothache, a drop of clove oil applied to the tooth may offer
some relief until you can see a dentist.

— BRUSHING —

Vary your brushing pattern occasionally, otherwise you'll miss the same bits.
If you're right-handed, try brushing your teeth with your left hand from time to time,
and vice versa.

When to brush
Ideally, you should brush your teeth after every meal,
because bacteria start attacking your teeth moments after you eat.
Of course, this isn't always practical, so aim for at least twice a day,
before breakfast and before bed.

How long to brush for
To do a thorough job you need to clean your teeth for 2–3 minutes.
Many electric toothbrushes are equipped with timers which
let you know when your time is up—and it's a lot longer than you might think.

*TIP: When you think you're out of toothpaste, snip the tube in half and you'll find enough for a few more
brushes. (This applies to any creams packaged in tubes.)*

— HOW TO BRUSH YOUR TEETH —

A pea-sized amount of toothpaste is quite enough to get your teeth clean.

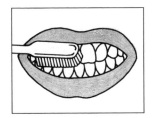

1. Place the brush at a 45 degree angle to your teeth.
   Direct the bristles to where your gums and teeth meet.

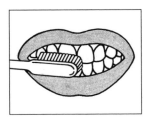

2. Move the brush in a gentle, circular motion.
   Dentists recommend what they call a "gentle scrub."

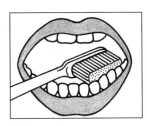

3. Clean your teeth tooth by tooth.
   Brush every surface of each tooth, front and back.

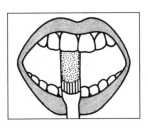

4. Clean the inside surface of your front teeth using the top of
   the brush, moving it gently up and down the teeth.

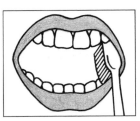

5. Back teeth need cleaning just as thoroughly as front teeth.

TIP: As a temporary measure, in an emergency, stick your broken crown back in place using denture fixative.

— FOOT NOTES —

"My husband refuses to try anything on. Even shoes.
He just holds the box up to the light and says, 'Yeah, these fit fine.' "
—Rita Rudner

— How to Choose the Perfect Pair of Shoes —

DID YOU KNOW? A study in America found that 90 percent of women wear shoes that are too small for them.

Check your shoe size. Your feet don't stop growing as you grow older. If you haven't checked your size for 10 years or more, you might be in for a surprise.

Check the weight of the shoes. This might sound silly, but heavy shoes are harder to walk in, put strain on your muscles, and make walking feel like you're wearing leaded boots.

Your foot size varies during the day. The best time to shop for shoes is late in the afternoon when feet are at their largest.

Try shoes on both feet. Most of us have one foot bigger than the other.

Everyday shoes? Go for rubber soles—they act as shock absorbers and take the strain off your knees.

Find a pair of shoes you like? Buy two pairs.

Find a pair of shoes you like and are comfortable too? Buy every pair!

GIVE IT A TRY: The Egyptians carved the names of their enemies on the soles of their sandals so they could literally walk all over them. The perfect revenge.

When going out to buy shoes, put on a pair of socks or tights similar to those you intend to wear with your new shoes. Never try shoes on bare feet.

Don't wear the same shoes day in and day out—particularly if they're high heels. Alternate shoes of different heel-heights so your feet are not always stressed in the same place.

Flat shoes are not necessarily better for your feet. Chiropodists recommend a heel between $\frac{1}{2}$ to $\frac{3}{4}$ of an inch.

Don't wear sneakers constantly. Continuous wearing encourages toes to spread and feet to widen.

Wear socks with at least 70 percent cotton content rather than all-nylon or acrylic, to allow your feet to breathe.

TIP: Ladies! If you've ever attended a garden party or an outdoor wedding, you'll know that damp grass can wreak havoc on your heels and spoil an expensive pair of shoes. Try wrapping clear sticky tape round the heels before you set foot on the lawn. Afterward, simply peel off the tape. Or paint the heels with clear nail polish.

— How to Polish Leather Shoes —

"Unshined shoes are the end of civilization."
—Diana Vreeland

1. Lay down lots of newspaper in a ventilated room.

2. Wipe off any dirt with a soft cloth before you start to polish. Stubborn stains can be removed with a little dab of vinegar on a damp cloth.

3. Put shoe-trees in the shoes or stuff them with newspaper so they'll keep their shape.

4. Use a good-quality shoe polish. Choose one that most closely matches the color of your shoes.

5. Put a smidgen of shoe polish on the tip of a round shoe-polish brush (or a soft toothbrush if you must) and spread evenly all over the shoe.

6. Give the polish time to sink into the shoe and "feed" the leather.

7. Use the same brush to brush off the polish.

8. With a lint-free cloth, buff up the shoes to a high shine, top, back, and sides. Give it some elbow grease.

9. Step out into the world with your head held high but not so high that you can't see what you're treading in—oops! Too late. Where's that polish?

SUEDE SHOES: Use a suede-brush to remove dirt. Brush the suede lightly in one direction, not to and fro. Allow wet suede shoes to dry naturally.

PATENT LEATHER: Spray with a thin coat of furniture polish, wipe dry, and buff to a shine.

DRYING WET SHOES: Stuff with newspaper and allow them to dry out naturally. Don't put them by a warm radiator.

— How to Refresh Smelly Sneakers —

Method 1
Sprinkle a teaspoon or two of bicarbonate of soda into each shoe right down to the toe.
Seal in a plastic bag in the freezer overnight.

Method 2
Fill with cat litter and leave overnight.

Method 3
Wash in the washing machine on a gentle wash cycle with plenty of fluffy towels or a duvet.

TIP: To prevent your shoelaces coming undone, dampen them with water before tying or rub with wax polish.

— HOW TO CUT YOUR TOENAILS —

An ingrown toenail is a common, painful condition where the nail grows into the skin. One of the main causes is trimming toenails incorrectly.

Here's how to do it correctly:

Use a pair of good-quality nail clippers.

Cut your toenail straight across.
Don't make one long cut as this could split the nail.
It's better to make a few little cuts along the nail.

Don't cut toenails too short.

Don't cut the edges or sides so short that they dig into your skin.

After trimming, file the nail to a square shape so the edges
won't snag on your socks or tights.

Use an emery board rather than a metal file.

HOW TO USE AN EMERY BOARD: Use the coarse-grade surface for shortening and shaping your nails. Use the finer-grade surface for smoothing the edge of the nail. Hold the emery board at a slight angle to the nail and file from side to center on both sides of the nail. Never scrape the main nail surface.

Trim your toenails at least once a month.
After bathing is a good time, as your nails will be softer and easier to cut.

— JEWELRY —

DID YOU KNOW? The more you wear pearls, the more they will shine, as the oils in your skin improve their sheen.

Apply makeup, perfume, and hair spray before putting on jewelry as the chemicals in the cosmetics could damage it.

Keep a file of receipts and insurance information and photographs of precious pieces.

— HOW TO CLEAN JEWELRY —

There are many commercial jewelry cleaners on the market, but this method is simple, effective, nontoxic, and safe for most stones, including jet, amethyst, diamond, rubies, and sapphires. Exceptions are pearls, coral, cameos, emeralds, ivory, mother of pearl, simulated pearls, marcasite, opals, and turquoise. It goes without saying, but I'll say it anyway: If you treasure a piece, don't take any risks with it.

DID YOU KNOW? A Victorian lady would instruct her maid to wear her pearls for a few hours so they would "warm up" and not feel cold against her own skin when she put them on.

1. Fill a plastic bowl with a solution of warm water and dishwashing liquid. Don't use hot water because when the metal expands, the stones may fall out.

2. Immerse your jewelry in the solution, ensuring they are not touching each other.

3. Allow the jewelry to soak for a few minutes.

4. Remove the jewelry and brush gently with an old toothbrush.

5. Rinse the jewelry thoroughly and lay it on a clean towel. Allow to dry or blow with a hair dryer on a low setting.

6. Check the washing solution for any stray stone or earring before pouring it away.

> *TIP: Never wash jewelry under a running tap or in the sink for obvious reasons.*
> *If you do happen to drop your wedding ring down the drain*
> *see "How to recover an object dropped down the sink" on page 140.*

> *TIP: Always rinse silver stud earrings with water after cleaning with silver polish.*
> *Paint the posts of silver earrings with clear nail polish to prevent tarnishing*
> *from causing an allergic reaction and possible ear infection.*

To clean pearls and coral: Rub carefully with a chamois leather. Handle with care as they scratch easily.

> *GIVE IT A TRY: To clean shell jewelry, give it a quick swoosh in the sea.*

— JEWELRY TIPS —

To untangle a knotted chain
Lay the chain on a piece of paper on a flat surface. Dust the chain with a little talcum powder (or add a drop of baby oil), then use a couple of sewing needles to ease the knots apart.

To remove a ring that's stuck on your finger
Wet your hand and rub soap-lather around the ring. Slide the ring carefully over the knuckle, turning it as you do so.

To keep your jewels safe from burglars while you're away on vacation
Place items in the ice cube tray, fill with water, and freeze. Don't forget to unfreeze them on your return.

> *TIP: When cleaning jewelry make sure you do it in an area where you can easily recover any piece*
> *that becomes detached.*

— SCENTS AND SENSIBILITY —

"What's left when you turn out the light? A woman's femininity and her perfume."
—*Jean-Paul Guerlain*

The scent you choose is as much an expression of your personality as the clothes you choose. We talk about "wearing a scent" just as we talk about "wearing a dress." It's worth putting a little effort into choosing the right one for you.

— HOW TO CHOOSE THE PERFECT PERFUME: DOS AND DON'TS —

Don't eat garlic or spicy food 24 hours before you go shopping for a new scent because your pores will still bear traces of the strong flavors, and this will affect the smell of the perfume on your skin.

Don't try any more than three scents in one shopping trip or you will overwhelm your sense of smell. The alcohol in the perfume anesthetizes your nose.

Do smell the perfume properly. It's not enough to just sniff the top of the tester (which is probably stale) or spray some in the air and smell that. The best way is to lightly mist the perfume over a paper card, give it a few seconds, then sniff the card.

Don't buy the perfume immediately even if you love the smell. Allow the scent to develop for at least an hour. Sniff the card again once the scent has settled. If you still like it, go back and test the perfume on your skin. Don't blast the vapor so it puddles the skin: lightly mist the inside of your wrist. Don't rub it in as this will "flatten" the scent. Live with it for a day to see how it feels at different times of the day.

Don't buy a perfume because you like the smell of it on your friend. Perfume smells different on different people.

Don't be seduced by fancy packaging and celebrity endorsements: The best reason to buy a perfume is because you like the smell of it.

"Where should one apply perfume? Wherever one wants to be kissed."
—*Coco Chanel*

APPLYING PERFUME: Spray about three short puffs of perfume directly onto your skin.

WHERE TO APPLY PERFUME: Wrists, the crevice in your collarbone, and the inside of your elbows are the best places. Behind the ears is the worst place, as many sweat glands are located there and they kill the effect.

Perfume lasts longer if sprayed onto damp skin, so spritz after bathing.

TIP: If you're going out to dinner on a romantic date, spray a little scent behind your knees. The heat will make the scent—and his temperature—rise.

STORING PERFUME

A French perfumier or "nose" once told me that a good perfume, like wine, will mature and even improve with age. But that applies only if you look after it. Perfumes don't like extreme hot or cold, but most damaging of all is light. Keep your perfume with its lid tight on, in its box, out of direct sunlight. If you don't it could "turn" in a matter of weeks. By the way, keeping your perfume in the fridge won't make it last any longer.

ARE YOU GETTING UP SOMEONE'S NOSE?

In America, there is a growing campaign for "aroma-free zones" similar to smoke-free zones. Restaurants will seat you by the door or the extractor fan if you're reeking of scent. Overwhelming scents can trigger an asthma attack, and in extreme cases, prove fatal. So, if you're planning a trip to a public space, like a restaurant, theater, or church service, be considerate and don't drown everyone in your pungent perfume. Go for a more subtle scent; after all, a little mystery is always more alluring.

TIP: Don't throw out your empty perfume bottles.
Place them, lids off, in your linen cupboard or drawers to fragrance your linen.

— HAIR FLAIR —

The first thing people notice about your appearance is your hair. If your hairstyle is sending out the wrong signals about who you are, you need to change it. But where do you start? Tailor your haircut to suit the shape of your face.

— HOW TO DETERMINE YOUR FACE SHAPE —

1. Tape a piece of tracing paper to a mirror.

2. Sit or stand facing the mirror.

3. Pull all your hair away from your face and clip or tie it back.

4. Use a thick pen at arm's length to draw around the outline of your face as reflected on the tracing paper on the mirror.

Check the diagrams below to find out which face shape matches your outline.

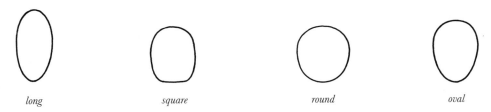

| long | square | round | oval |

DID YOU KNOW? Hair grows faster in summer than winter, and faster during the day than night.

— FINDING THE HAIRSTYLE TO SUIT YOUR FACE SHAPE —

LONG
AVOID: Volume on top; long, straight bobs all one length; any style cut level to above chin-level.

CHOOSE: A shoulder-length style to widen your face; wispy bangs to shorten the length of the forehead.

CELEBS: Sarah Jessica Parker, Gwyneth Paltrow

ROUND
AVOID: Sleek or curly styles that widen your face; severe styles.

CHOOSE: A soft cut with feathery layers brushing your cheeks will make your face look slimmer; volume on top and short bangs will add length to your face.

CELEBS: Kate Winslet, Drew Barrymore

SQUARE
AVOID: Geometric or symmetrical cuts, close crops, severe styles, full bangs, and styles with a center part.

CHOOSE: An asymmetrical cut to soften the angles; an off-center part to draw attention away from your jawline; a bob with long layers or soft curls will soften hard lines.

CELEBS: Sandra Bullock, Demi Moore

OVAL
CHOOSE: Long or short, straight or curly; any hairstyle will suit your classic face shape.

AVOID: Bragging too much about having the perfect face shape!

CELEBS: Catherine Zeta Jones, Kate Moss, Julia Roberts

TIP: Gather all your hair tightly at the back of your head and place in a ponytail or bun. Stretching your face and forehead gives you an instant facelift!

— HAIRBRUSHES AND COMBS —

Once you have the perfect hairstyle, you'll want to maintain it in tiptop shape.
As with any job, choose the right tools and you're nearly there.

*DID YOU KNOW? Brushing is good for your hair: it sloughs off dead skin
from your scalp and increases blood flow. The rhythm of brushing can also help to relieve stress.*

Brushes and combs come in all shapes and sizes.
There's one to suit every hair type and style.
As a general rule of thumb, the longer your hair, the bigger your brush should be.
If you have hair of different lengths, it's a good idea to have several brushes.

Vent brush
Good for blow-drying as it lets air circulate around the
brush to add volume and lift the hair.

Paddle brush
Good for detangling and creating smooth, straight hair.

Radial / round / curling brush
Adds curl, wave, and volume when blow-drying.
The smaller the brush, the tighter the curl.

Bristle / nylon brush
Use on curly or coarse hair to ease through tangles.

Classic styling brush
Adds lift without tangling when blow-drying.

Large-toothed comb
Use on curly or wet hair or for combing conditioner through.

Tail comb
Ideal for creating your part, and for dressing hair.

TIPS
Bewildered by the choices out there?
Choose the same brand your hairdresser uses and you'll be sure it has the professional seal of approval.

Use a comb to detangle wet hair. Never use a brush, as it will damage wet hair.

*TIP: When you tie your hair in a ponytail, tilt your head backward and you'll catch all your hair at once
in a neat bunch.*

— HOW TO SHAMPOO YOUR HAIR —

Choosing a shampoo

A moisturizing shampoo suits dry, colored or permed hair. Greasy hair formula will control the buildup of sebum in oily hair. Combination formula is ideal if your scalp is greasy and the ends are dry. A gentle shampoo is kind to hair that is washed frequently or if you have a sensitive scalp.

METHOD

1. Brush your hair so it is free of tangles.

2. Wash your hair under running water, such as a shower, or by kneeling down with your head hanging over the edge of a bath using a showerhead connected to the taps. Never wash your hair in the bath—dirty water won't give you clean hair. The water should be *warm*, not hot.

3. Squeeze a little shampoo into one palm, rub your palms together, and apply to your hair. Don't squeeze it directly onto your hair. Use the pads of your fingers to massage the shampoo gently into your scalp and through to the ends of the hair. Work it up into a lather to loosen the dirt, but don't rub; hair is at its most vulnerable when wet.

4. Rinse hair thoroughly under the flow of *warm* water.

TIPS

The main cause of dull and lank hair is too much shampoo and not enough rinsing.

Over-washing hair strips it of its natural oils.
There's no need to shampoo your hair twice every time you wash it—unless it is particularly dirty.

HAIR CONDITIONER: Apply to the ends of the hair and rub in well. Avoid the scalp area as it will clog the roots.

"To maintain the golden sheen, rinse your blonde hair in flat champagne."
—Diana Vreeland

Wash your brushes and combs in a little shampoo and warm water as often as you wash your hair.

HOW TO USE HAIR SPRAY: Don't spray it straight onto your hair. You'll achieve a more natural look if you spray it on your brush and comb it through.

TIP: In an emergency, if you have dark hair and need to cover a little amount
of gray hair but don't have time to dye it, use mascara.

REMEMBER: The products you use on your hair also affect your body. Hair may be dead but your scalp is alive and, like a sponge, soaks up any product you put on your hair. Read the labels on products carefully.

TIP: Hair adapts to the oils in a shampoo after a while, so vary your brand of shampoo to keep it refreshed,
or keep a few different bottles and alternate them.

— How to Dry Your Hair —
— Towel-drying —

Take small sections of hair and squeeze the towel around
them to soak up the water. Don't rub hair or it will be dull.

— Blow-drying —

Towel-dry your hair first, until it's about 80 percent dry.
If you style wet hair, any shape you give it will drop out very quickly.
Use a nozzle on the hair dryer. Keep the hair taut with the brush, and dry.
For a fuller effect, use your fingers like a comb.
If you have longer hair, bend your head down toward your knees to dry the roots.

— Scrunch-drying —

When your hair is almost dry, apply a pea-sized amount of mousse or gel into your hair.
Scrunch handfuls of hair, a section at a time.
When nearly dry, apply mousse or wax and work through the hair.

— Electrical Hair-Drying Equipment —

Hair dryer: If you're having a bad hair day, it might be because of your hair dryer; if you're
having a good hair day, it might be because of your hair dryer. That's how much difference it
can make. Invest in the best you can afford. Choose one with a long cylinder and long cord
so you can reach a mirror. It should feel comfortable to hold and not too heavy. Power
varies—the average is 1600 watts—more wattage will dry your hair faster but not necessarily
better. Look for a dryer with a nozzle and diffuser attachments to give you more choice in
styling.

Nozzle: An attachment that slots on to the end of your hair dryer and concentrates the airflow
on a small section of your hair, giving a smooth and shiny effect.

Diffuser: A large, dish-shaped attachment that slots onto the end of your hair dryer. Whereas the
nozzle concentrates airflow, the diffuser disperses air over a wider area. Use it on naturally
curly hair to minimize frizz. Place handfuls of hair inside the diffuser to dry it gently and give
more lift and body. Hair takes longer to dry because of the slower airflow.

Curling iron: Creates waves and curls.

Using a hair dryer: Heat can damage your hair. Use your fingers to gauge the correct temperature
to dry your hair: If it's too hot for your fingers, it's too hot for your hair.

Use a mousse or conditioner to protect your hair from the heat. If you have greasy hair, use the
hair dryer on a cooler setting, as the heat stimulates the sebum-producing glands.

TIP: If you get hair dye on your skin, put a little milk on a tissue or some cotton wool and gently rub off.

— HOW TO MAKE A THREE-STRAND BRAID —

If the word *braid* makes you think of Heidi or giggly schoolgirls, think again. Braiding is cool. It can be a beautiful and elegant way to dress long hair, and even better, it's easy.

Start with clean, dry, tangle-free hair. If your hair is flyaway, smooth in some styling gel to keep it under control.

1. Divide your hair into three neat and equal strands. (figure 1)

2. Cross strand A to the right, over strand B. Push strand B to the left, out of the way. (figure 2)

3. Cross strand C to the left, over strand A. Push strand A to the right, out of the way. (figure 3)

4. Cross strand B to the right, over strand C toward strand A. (figure 4)

5. Cross strand A back to the left and over strand B. (figure 5)

6. Continue braiding in this way until you reach the end of your hair. (figure 6)

7. The finished three-strand braid. Secure with a hair scrunchie. (figure 7)

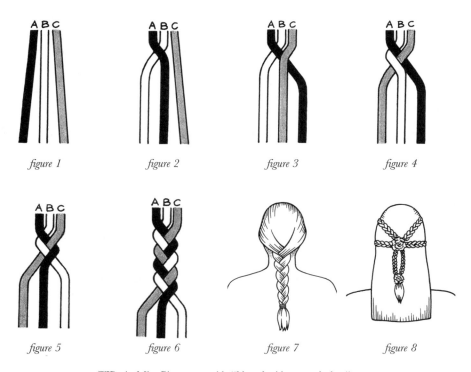

figure 1

figure 2

figure 3

figure 4

figure 5

figure 6

figure 7

figure 8

TIP: As Miss Piggy once said, "Never braid your eyelashes."

CHANT: To remember the sequence, just say to yourself: left strand over center strand, right strand over center strand, left strand over center strand, right strand over center strand, and so on . . .

Once you've mastered the basic technique, get creative! Try a four-strand braid, or five or six or more. You'll need an extra pair of hands for the more complex braids. You can also change the look by varying the thickness of the braid and where you make the part on your head. (figure 8)

— UNDERBRAIDING —

Use the same method as braiding, but instead of crossing the hair *over*, cross it *under*.

The finished braid lies on top of the hair instead of being a part of the hair.

— CORNROWS —

These braids are made using lots of parallel parts, with fine, three-stemmed braids.

It's a good idea to sleep with a satin scarf on your head to protect the braids.

They should last for up to a fortnight.

GIVE IT A TRY:
Add pizzazz to braids by weaving in colored ribbons: Instead of separating your hair into three sections, divide it into two sections and the ribbon becomes the third section.

TOP TIP: The secret to a good braid is pulling the hair evenly so the tension remains the same. If you don't, the braid will be lopsided.

TIP: Use "hair scrunchies" in your hair. Plain rubber bands are the quickest way to split ends ever invented.

— *General Braiding Tips* —

If you are a complete beginner, before braiding your own hair, practice on three pieces of different colored ribbon.

It's best not to use a mirror because the reversed image can confuse you. Better to rely on your sense of touch.

— CRIMPING —

To give your hair a rippled, "corrugated" effect without using crimping irons: Separate your hair into sections. The smaller the sections, the finer the crimp will look. Braid three-strand braids from root to tip, evenly around your head, and secure each with covered elastic bands. Leave in overnight, then unravel.

— STAR HAIR STENCIL —

What you need: Stencil, paintbrush, washable body paint or spray-on hair color, narrow paintbrush, glitter powder, hair spray

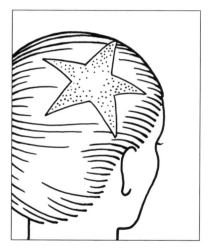

1. Choose a stencil design to coordinate with your look. You can either buy a ready-made stencil or make your own by tracing a design onto stiff card and cutting it out.

2. Hold the stencil on your hair and dab on the paint with the brush or use a spray-on hair paint. Choose a color that will show up on your hair. Shield your face if you use the spray.

3. When the stencil is filled in, sprinkle on the glitter powder.

TIP: Enlist a friend to help, as it's vital to keep the stencil steady so the design is not smudged.

DID YOU KNOW? Rhino horn is made of compacted hair and keratin.

— HAIRDRESSING SOS —

Help! My hair is full of split ends; how can I repair them?
Unlike skin, hair is not living, so it cannot repair itself when it is damaged.
The only way to get rid of the split ends is to cut them off.

Help! I've recently moved and I've noticed that although I use the same shampoo,
it doesn't lather well, and my hair feels dry and rough.
Sounds like you've moved from a soft water area into a hard water area. Soft water gives you
soft, silky hair and good lather. Hard water won't damage your hair but it might be a good idea
to use a conditioner after you shampoo.

Help! My bobby pins are always slipping out of my hair.
Apply a light covering of hair spray to the bobby pin before use.

Help! My hair is dull and lifeless.
Add shine by rubbing a silk scarf gently back and forth over your hair The molecular structure
of silk flattens and smoothes the hair cuticles. Or, give your scalp a good rub with the tips of
your fingers from front to back. It will release the sebum and restore shine.

Help! How can I control my flyaway hair?
Spray hair spray on your comb and run it through your hair.

Help! How can I avoid "bed-head" hair?
Switch from a cotton pillowcase to a satin pillowcase. Your hair will glide slinkily over satin;
cotton creates friction, which disturbs the hair follicles. If you're already using a satin pillowcase
and still have "bed-head" hair there must be some other explanation . . .

Help! How can I achieve the "bed-head" hair?
Yes, some people do find it attractive. Sleep on a cotton pillowcase and
just before going to bed, damp your hair a little and apply mousse.
Of course, there might be other ways of achieving it also . . .

GIVE IT A TRY:
We tend to be squeamish about human hair clippings, but not so the practical
Victorians. They recycled clippings to make "hair art." Hair artists created intricate pictures
of scenes such as mountain landscapes and portraits using different-colored hair. So, when
you next get a haircut, why not ask your hairdresser for a doggie bag of clippings and turn
them into a family heirloom.

TIP: Styling curly hair can be bothersome. Curly hair needs to be well hydrated and is better if left to air-dry.

— HOW TO GET THE PERFECT SHAVE —

Men usually learn to shave by watching a member of their family (rarely the mother).
This means that they also pick up all the bad habits of their teacher.
So, what's the best way to achieve that perfect, precision shave?

What to use

A manual razor will give you a closer shave than an electric razor. Use a clean, sharp blade so
you won't have to apply much pressure, minimizing the risk of nicks and cuts.

Shaving technique

Use short, gentle, quick strokes. Never scrape the razor over your skin. Always shave in
the same direction as the hair growth to ensure fewer ingrown hairs and a closer shave.
Never shave against the grain of the hair growth, or you risk causing razor burn (taking
too much skin off).

If you do happen to nick your skin, don't stick bits of tissue or toilet paper over the cuts
because the bleeding will only start up again when you remove them. Clean off the blood, then
apply a styptic pencil, which contains alum and will stem the bleeding. Alternatively, put a dab
of shaving cream or foam on the cut.

The best time to shave is right after a shower or bath when
your skin is soft and your pores are open.

Always look in a mirror to shave. A steam-free magnifying mirror is a useful asset.

1. Wash your face with soap and hot water to clean the skin and remove excess oil.

2. Wet your beard with **HOT** water to soften the hair and make it easier to cut.

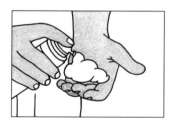

3. Apply shaving cream, foam, oil, or gel to lubricate your
skin. Put it on with your fingers or, better still, a shaving
brush. Use a brisk circular motion as this will raise the
hairs and prepare them for cutting.

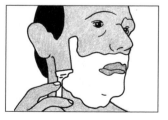

4. Rinse your manual blade in hot water, then start to shave.
Start with the areas around the cheeks first. This allows
time for the more resistant hairs to soften up. Growth is
densest on the upper lip, so leave this till last.

TIP: Change your blade as soon as it starts to dull. This could be after only a couple of shaves.

5. Rinse the blade in warm water after every couple of strokes to remove debris from the razor so it doesn't clog up.

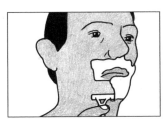

6. Shave around the neck and chin areas next.

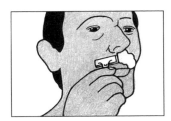

7. Lastly, shave your upper lip.

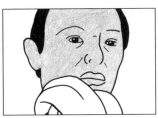

8. When you're done, rinse your face thoroughly in *cold* water to close the pores, then pat dry with a towel. Don't forget to rinse the blade, too, in cold water. Don't wipe it on a towel—a sure way to dull the blade. Finish up with an after-shaving moisturizer or balm.

TOP TIP: For the perfect shave, use a sharp, clean blade.

— HOW TO USE AN ELECTRIC SHAVER —

An electric shaver won't give you the close shave of a wet shave, but it's convenient and handy if you're pushed for time . . .
Use on dry skin only.
Shave in the same direction as the hair growth.
Don't press the shaver against your skin. Let it do the work for you.
Rinse your face in cold water afterward.

TIP: Use a shaving oil instead of foam for more lubrication and a clearer view of where you're shaving.

– Scarves & Ties –

"With an evening coat and a white tie, anybody, even a stockbroker, can gain a reputation for being civilized."

—Oscar Wilde

— HOW TO WEAR IT WITH STYLE —

What separates us from the animals? Our ability to accessorize, of course. Here are some ideas to inspire you to dress up and look divine.

— HOW TO TIE SILK SCARVES —

A silk scarf has to be the most versatile fashion accessory a woman could ever own. It can be an accent on an outfit or the main focus, it can pull an outfit together, add glamour to evening wear, and even cover up a bad hair day. I own 365 of them.

— *Classic Chic* —

A simple and stylish way to fill in the neckline of a jacket, suit, or coat, or wear it over a sweater to flatter the shape of your face.

1. Take a long scarf or fold a square scarf on the bias (see "How to fold a square scarf on the bias" on page 220). Hang the center of the scarf around your neck and cross end B over end A.

2. Twist end B once around end A, leaving it quite loose.

3. Pass the two ends around to the back of your neck and tie in a reef knot at the back (see page 247 for "How to tie a square knot").

4. Shape the front so that it sits nicely on the neck.

GIVE IT A TRY: For a touch of extra glamour, twist a long pearl necklace into a long scarf.

— How to Fold a Square Scarf on the Bias —

If you want to try one of the folding techniques that requires a long scarf
but you only have a square scarf, worry not: This is how to transform your
square scarf into a long scarf.

Method 1:
Lay a square scarf facedown in a diamond shape on a flat surface.

Fold the top and bottom corners inward to meet and overlap a little in the center.

Continue folding of the same corners into the center until
the scarf is the thickness you want.

Method 2:
Fold the square scarf into a triangle.

Starting from the point of the triangle, simply roll the scarf into a slim, long scarf.

— Grace Kelly Head Scarf —

A sporty and sophisticated style, perfect for keeping the wind out of your hair as you're
motoring around the Côte d'Azur in your open-top car with a Cary Grant lookalike.
Also good for a bad hair day in Florida.

1. Fold a square scarf into a triangle and lay it over your head. Cross the two ends of the scarf
   underneath your chin. (figure 1)

2. Pass the two ends around to the back of your neck. (figure 2)

3. Tie a square knot at the back (see page 247, "How to tie a square knot"). (figure 3)

4. Shape the scarf at your neck and forehead. (figure 4)

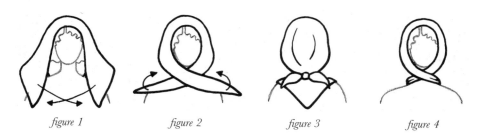

| figure 1 | figure 2 | figure 3 | figure 4 |

DID YOU KNOW? Grace Kelly was the first actress ever to appear on a postage stamp.

Versatility: When you stop off at a chic roadside bistro, create a nice effect by pushing the hood back off your head and shaping the scarf at your neck. It also looks good if you turn the scarf around. When you hit the road again, simply pull the hood back up again.

TIP: The knot also looks good tied at the side.

— Loop the Loop —

A stylish look over a sweater or blouse:

1. Drape the center of a long scarf across the front of your neck and around to the back. Cross the two ends over at the back and pass them back around to the front.

2. Let the scarf hang loosely scooped at the neck.

3. Take hold of one end and weave it slackly over and under the loop. You might need to do it three or four times depending on how long your scarf is. Leave a little bit loose at the end.

4. Repeat step 3 with the other end until both ends hang evenly.

STORING SCARVES: To prevent creases, roll your scarf around an empty tube before storing. Roll on a flat surface and ensure the tube is long enough to support the scarf. Store flat.

TIP: Before buying, feel the weight of the scarf: the heavier the silk, the better quality.

— PASHMINAS OR SHAWLS —

Whether it's a ball or a barbecue, when the evening turns chilly,
here's a way to prevent the cold shoulder.

— Bolero —

Perfect for a sleeveless dress or to show off a colorful scarf.

1. Fold a large square pashmina in half with the wrong side facing outward. Tie both ends with the smallest square knots you can (see page 247). (figure 1)

2. Turn the pashmina inside out so that the right side is now facing outward and the knots are hidden inside. (figure 2)

3. Drape the scarf over your shoulders and put your arms through the two openings. The knots should be under your arms. (figure 3)

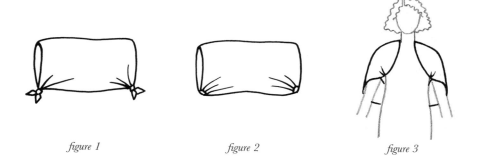

figure 1   *figure 2*   *figure 3*

— More Ideas for Tying Your Pashmina —

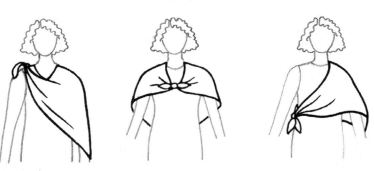

DID YOU KNOW? Pashminas were first made in India in the 15th century for the Mogul emperors.

— SUMMER DRESSING —
When the going gets hot, try these cool cover-ups.

— Halter-Neck Top —

1. Fold a large square scarf diagonally to form a triangle shape and tie a square knot at the tip of the triangle (see page 247).

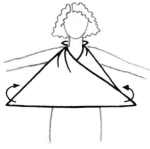

2. Slip your head between the triangle so the knot is behind your neck. Bring the other two ends of the triangle around your middle and tie at the back.

3. Neaten the halter neck at the front.

— How to Tie a Sarong/Pareo/Kanga —

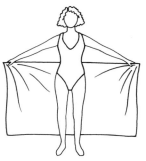

There are many variations on tying a sarong, but this is the classic . . .

1. Take a sarong and hold it horizontally behind you at the waist. (figure 1)

2. Bring the ends to the front and knot securely below the waist. (figure 2)

figure 1   figure 2

TIP: A sarong is so versatile: it can be a skirt, throw, sheet, towel, shawl, picnic blanket, beach blanket, tablecloth, curtain, or birdcage cover!

— Real Men Do Wear Sarongs —

Despite soccer star David Beckham's best efforts, the sarong for men has yet to catch on as urban wear, but it's still perfect for the beach, where it certainly makes a more modish cover-up than a damp towel around the waist.

1. Fold the sarong in half lengthways and wrap it around your waist. (figure 1)

2. Fold the outer edges into the side of your body. (figure 2)

3. Fold the outer edges again, into your waist, and tuck well in.
Secure discreetly with a pin if necessary. (figure 3)

NOTE: Sarongs demonstrated are unisex.

figure 1   figure 2   figure 3

— How to Tie Your Winter Scarf —
Cold weather is *brrr*illiant—
so long as you're wrapped up snug and warm
against those wintry winds.

That's not to say you have to look like the
Abominable Snowman when you venture out.

Check out these simple but stylish ways to wear
everyone's favorite winter fashion accessory:
the woolly scarf.

DID YOU KNOW? The Abominable Snowman, also known as the Yeti, is a legendary "bear-man" believed to roam the snowy peaks of the Himalayas.

— Country-Style —

1. Fold the scarf in half lengthways and place it around your neck so both ends hang down equally at the front. (figure 1)

2. Bring the "open" end (on the left) through the loop of the "closed" end (right). (figure 2)

3. Tighten the loop until the scarf feels comfortable and drapes nicely. (figure 3)

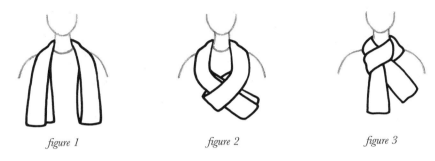

figure 1　　　　　　*figure 2*　　　　　　*figure 3*

— Snuggler —

1. Hang the scarf around your neck with one end hanging about 12 inches below the other end. (figure 1)

2. Take the longer end and wrap it once around your neck, passing it back around to the front so it is now equal in length with the other end. (figure 2)

3. Tie the two ends together in a knot and . . . bring on the snowballs! (figure 3)

VARIATION: Tie the scarves at the side of your neck to vary the styles.
NOTE: Both scarves are unisex.

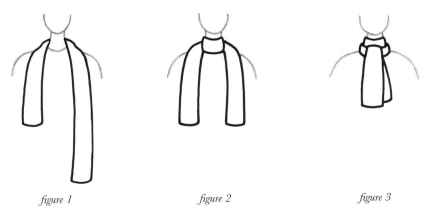

figure 1　　　　　　*figure 2*　　　　　　*figure 3*

TIP: Choose a scarf in a color to contrast with your winter coat. For extra warmth, choose a fleece scarf or, if your budget can stretch to it, cashmere.

— Ties —

"A well-tied tie is the first serious step in life."
—Oscar Wilde

Casual Friday may be spreading to other days of the week, but there is still only one article of clothing that cuts the sartorial mustard for business and formal social occasions: the tie. It needn't be a fashion noose. A tie can express your individuality in color, pattern, fabric, and design.

— How to Choose a Tie —

The best ties are made of silk. Top-quality silk will feel smooth to the touch.

On the back of a good-quality tie you will always find a "bar tack"—
a set of stitches sewn across the top of the diamond shape on the wide end.
This helps keep the shape of the tie.

As a general rule . . .

The color of the tie should be darker than the shirt.
The color of the shirt should be lighter than the jacket.
The width of the tie should be about the same as the width of your jacket lapels.

REMEMBER: A tie will make you look taller and slimmer because it
puts the accent on the vertical.

— General Tie Tips—

The top button of your shirt should always be done up when wearing a tie.

The knot of the tie should be pulled tight to lie precisely in the center of
the triangle formed by the collar.

The tip of the knotted tie should just reach to the top of the belt of your trousers.
There should be no gap between tie and trousers.

The narrow end of the knotted tie may be the same length or shorter
than the wide end, but it should never be longer.

If the narrow end hangs lower than the wide end on the finished tie, undo the knot and tie it
again, with the wide end hanging lower than you had it the first time.

For each knot demonstrated on pages 227–231, start with your shirt buttoned up to the top
(including the collar) and your collar up.

TIP: A tiepin not only finishes off the look, but also keeps your tie from dangling in your minestrone.

— The Four-In-Hand —

SHAPE: This is the classic knot we learn as children. The long and narrow knot gives the illusion of a long neck. It gives good results with both thin and thick ties, and suits any shape of collar. Looks best with button-down shirts.

1. Place the tie around your neck with the wide end on your right, hanging below the narrow end.

2. Pass the wide end around the narrow end, and bring it back to the right-hand side.

3. Pass the wide end around the narrow end for a second time, but this time leave it on the left-hand side.

4. Pull the wide end up through the loop at your neck.

5. Put the first finger of your left hand into the knot at the front to loosen it a little so that you can then slip the wide end down through the knot. Pull the wide end right down through the knot and tighten it by pulling on the wide end.

6. Straighten the tie by pulling on the narrow end with your right hand and drawing the knot up toward your collar with your left hand until it looks neat and centered.

DID YOU KNOW? The four-in-hand is so called because it was the tie worn by patrons of a 19th-century English gentleman's club of the same name.

— The Windsor Knot —

SHAPE: The wide, triangular shape exudes confidence, making it perfect for a job interview or presentation. It is best tied with a thin tie, and worn with a cutaway or "spread" collar—that is, where the tips of the collar are spread wide, leaving a large gap in which to show off the knot of the tie.

1. Place the tie around your neck with the wide end on your right, hanging below the narrow end. (figure 1)

2. Cross the wide end over the narrow end and pass it up through the loop at your neck. Then bring the wide end down on the left-hand side, and pass it around behind the narrow end as indicated by the arrow. (figure 2)

3. The wide end will now be on the right. Bring the wide end down through the loop at your neck as indicated by the arrow. (figure 3)

4. The wide end should finish up on the left. (figure 4)

5. Cross the wide end over the front of the narrow end, finishing up on the right. (figure 5)

6. Bring the wide end up through the loop at your neck again. (figure 6)

7. Slip the wide end right down through the knot at the front and tighten. (figure 7)

8. Straighten the tie by pulling on the narrow end with your right hand and drawing the knot up toward your collar with your left hand until it looks neat and centered. (figure 8)

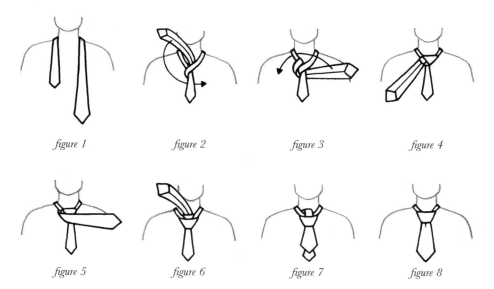

| *figure 1* | *figure 2* | *figure 3* | *figure 4* |
| *figure 5* | *figure 6* | *figure 7* | *figure 8* |

DID YOU KNOW? The Windsor knot is named after the Duke of Windsor, later the Prince of Wales, who favored a larger knot in his tie.

— The Half-Windsor —

SHAPE: A more discreet version of the Windsor knot, suitable for standard shirt collars and perfect on any occasion.

1. Place the tie around your neck with the wide end on your right, hanging below the narrow end. (figure 1)

2. Cross the wide end over the narrow end and bring it around behind the narrow end, so it finishes up on the right. (figure 2)

3. Pass the wide end down through the loop at your neck so it finishes up on the left. (figure 3)

4. Cross the wide end over the front of the narrow end to finish on the right. This will form the front of the knot. (figure 4)

5. Pull the wide end up through the loop at your neck. (figure 5)

6. Thread the wide end right down through the knot at the front and tighten. (figure 6)

7. Straighten the tie by pulling on the narrow end with your right hand and drawing the knot up toward your collar with your left hand until it looks neat and centered. (figure 7)

REMEMBER: If at first you don't succeed, tie, tie again!

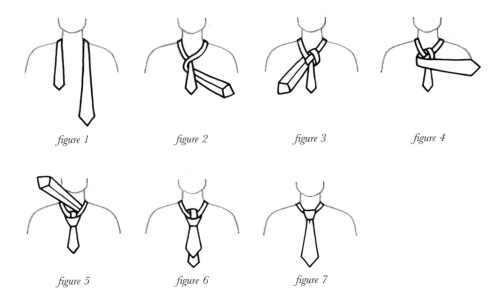

figure 1   figure 2   figure 3   figure 4

figure 5   figure 6   figure 7

TIP: When taking off your tie, always unknot it first or you could damage the fabric and alter the shape of the tie. Never slip it over your head.

230

— How to Tie the Perfect Bow Tie —

Ready-made bow ties serve the purpose, but there's something deathless about them. They're *too* perfect. Once you've learned to tie a bow tie, you'll *never* wear anything but the real thing with your tux. And you may even become a convert, dump your ties, and wear only bow ties.

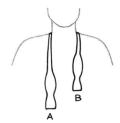

1. Place the bow tie around your neck with the left end A hanging between 1–2 inches longer than the right end B.

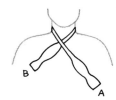

2. Cross the longer left end A over the shorter right end B.

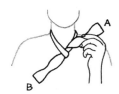

3. Pass end A up and through the loop at your neck.

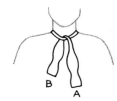

4. Tighten the knot at your neck.

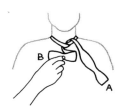

5. Now it's time to form what will become the front of your bow tie. Take end B and double it up to make the shape of a bow.

DID YOU KNOW? Some doctors wear bow ties for reasons of hygiene. A tie dangling into a full bedpan is not a good look.

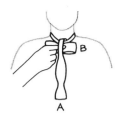

6. Place your bow shape up at your neck across the points of your collar and hold it there between the thumb and first finger of your left hand. Let end A hang down in front of it. The part of A that touches the first finger of your left hand will form the center bit of your bow tie.

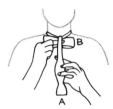

7. Now it's time to start forming the bow shape that will become the back of your bow tie. Grasp end A between the thumb and first finger of your right hand at the point where the bow flares in. Hold them in place and tuck your third finger behind end A. Now twist your wrist sharply to the right.

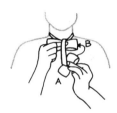

8. What you will get is a new bow shape. Still holding bow-shaped end B firmly at your neck, pass the new bow shape up behind bow-shaped end B in the direction of the arrow in the illustration.

9. Push the new bow shape right through behind bow-shaped end B. You'll need to release the thumb of your left hand just for a split second, so you can poke the new bow shape through the resulting little opening to make a knot and come directly behind bow-shaped end B.

10. Your bow tie will be uneven at this stage. Pull on the double ends to tighten the bow, and shape up the single ends too. The final bow tie will have one double end and one single end on either side. The single end will be on top on the left-hand side and underneath on the right-hand side (vice versa for the double ends).

There are no hard-and-fast rules as to how a finished bow tie should look, just so long as it has character. The knot can be large or small, the bows can be smooth or dimpled,—it's up to you. Let your individuality shine through.

To undo the bow: Pull on the single ends.

TIP: There's no sexier look than a bow tie, untied, and dangling loosely around the collar of a man's tuxedo shirt at the end of a romantic evening . . .

– HOME OFFICE –

*"If a cluttered desk is the sign of a cluttered mind,
of what, then, is an empty desk a sign of?"*

—LAURENCE J. PETER

Whether you're running a business or just keeping up with bills, a dedicated workspace is now considered as essential as a kitchen or bathroom. The biggest mistake people make when styling their work area is to model it on a corporate office with banks of filing cabinets, desks—everything, in fact, but a watercooler. Is it any wonder they don't want to spend time there?

The challenge is to make it feel homey and welcoming without losing the practicality and efficiency. When you're relaxed, you think better. Create a space you'll enjoy spending time in; after all, in this office, *you're* the boss.

— PLANNING THE PERFECT WORKSPACE —

Sort out coffee-making facilities—well, you gotta get your priorities straight.

Decide where to position your office in the house. It can go almost anywhere—in an attic, a spare room, landing, hallway, or under the stairs. One of the most successful I've seen was actually in a closet in a bedroom—it opened out into a desk and shelves, and even had space for a coffeemaker!

Plan the layout of your office. If it's in a cupboard, it won't take long. If you're lucky enough to have an entire room, go for an L-shape set up with the computer against the wall, so you can turn to face the window when writing or answering the phone. Filter the sunlight from windows with a slatted blind. If you can't eliminate glare from the computer screen, you can buy an antiglare screen that clips onto your computer screen and filters out glare.

Avoid positioning your computer in front of a window. Yes, I know it's nice to gaze at the view, but your eyes will constantly be adjusting between the bright light of the window and the darker screen of the computer.

Think vertically. A monitor, keyboard, desktop computer and printer can be stacked to economize on space. Or get yourself a laptop.

Consider the lighting. Clip-on spotlights are better than an overhead light because they can be moved around the room to illuminate different areas. If your office is a sewing room or artist's studio, use "daylight bulbs" to minimize eye strain.

Task lighting is crucial. If you are doing close work like reading, invest in an adjustable lamp that directs the beam exactly where you want it. Place the lamp on the left if you're right-handed (vice versa if you're left-handed) to reduce glare and prevent shadows falling across the paper.

Ensure there is adequate ventilation in the room. Electrical equipment can cause a buildup of heat. Some computers don't like being pushed right up against a wall. Leave a gap of at least 2 inches to avoid overheating.

Make sure there is space for hardware, telephones, and plenty of electric sockets and telephone jacks—you don't want wires and cords trailing across the floor.

TIP: Fine-tune the brightness and contrast of your computer screen by adjusting the controls on the monitor.

Fix a bulletin board on the wall to keep notes, invitations, and important telephone numbers like the local takeout place.

MOTTO: You can never have too many shelves. If you can stretch to custom-made shelves, you'll pack a lot more in.

— MAKING YOURSELF AT HOME —

What usually happens with the home office is that you blow most of your budget on the computer and office equipment, leaving precious little left to spend on design. Looks like we'll have to rely on flair and imitation.

It won't cost much for a can of a paint, but it will make a big difference. Choose soothing colors for the walls. If it's mostly evenings you'll spend in your workplace, go for a color that looks warm under artificial light, such as maroon.

Avoid large or busy patterns on furnishing fabrics, and swags and frills on curtains. A simple blind would be a better choice so you can control the flow of light.

Adorn the walls with favorite paintings and photographs. Place personal treasures on the shelves so you have something to gaze at when you need inspiration.

A desk is not compulsory. A work surface is. Revamp an old wooden desk. Use an old kitchen table. Anything will do so long as it's robust and the right height.

A desk may not be compulsory but a good chair is. If you do a lot of work at your computer, that dining chair won't do. A good office chair, height-adjustable, swivel, and on castors. If space allows, a sofa or even a chaise longue is useful when you want to snooze, I mean, think.

Make room for a few plants. Plants release oxygen, which improves air quality. The officey potted palm is not obligatory. A vase of fresh flowers will soften the edges and fill your office with fragrance.

REMEMBER: If you're on a budget, office equipment can often be found going for a song at auctions of bankrupt companies' stock. Spray those gray filing cabinets a funky color using textured metal paint and no one will ever know.

GIVE IT A TRY: Put a beveled glass-top on top of two sets of filing cabinets (one at either end) and you've got your desk and storage.

TIP: Use an old pair of tights as a cover for your computer keyboard.

— STORAGE SOLUTIONS —

Don't build a paper mountain. Store as many files as you can on computer—
but be sure you also save them on a CD as backup.

Stash papers in decorative boxes or baskets. Picnic baskets or vintage suitcases
are stylish and quirky.

Put plastic divider trays or cutlery dividers in desk drawers so pens,
paper clips, stamps, etc., are easy to lay your hands on.

Hang pocket files and racks on the back of doors to hold magazines and brochures.

A tool organizer makes a great place to store small items. Spray it to coordinate with
your color scheme.

You'll always find a use for a big wastebasket.

— SHREDDING —

What are you to do with that blizzard of old bills, bank statements, receipts, letters, and other
personal documents that inevitably accumulate even in a small home office? If you simply
crumple them up and throw them in the bin, you could become a victim of the fastest-growing
crime in the U.S.: identity theft. This is where thieves steal your name and credit details to
apply for credit or buy goods online and elsewhere. Even if the banks and credit card
companies cover you for the cost of the fraud, it can literally take years to get your finances
straightened out.

So, what can you do to protect yourself? Destroy all confidential and sensitive documents before
disposing of them. You could painstakingly tear them into little pieces and disperse them in
different bins around the house. You could burn, barbecue, or bury them. But the best solution
is to get a personal shredder. A sign of the times, the personal shredder is fast becoming as
essential as a fridge or a washing machine.

— CHOOSING A SHREDDER —

A basic shredder will set you back only 20 dollars. For this you'll get a hand-cranked model that
takes only one sheet of paper at a time. A top of the range model, costing hundreds of dollars,
will have a larger bin capacity, take 8 sheets at a time, and also shred credit cards.

TIP: Choose a shredder that crosscuts the paper for extra security.

TIP: If you have children, look for shredder with a childproof safety-lock.

*DID YOU KNOW? It takes, on average, 18 months before people they realize they have been a victim of identity
theft. Keep a close eye on your credit and bank accounts so you can spot any discrepancy and sort it fast.*

— COMPUTER CARE —

Always turn off your computer to clean it.

Use only recommended cleaning products.

Never spray any cleaning fluid directly on the monitor.
Spray the liquid onto a lint-free cloth,
then use the cloth to clean the screen.

Use an antistatic cloth to wipe the screen every day.

Use a cotton swab or soft brush (a cosmetic brush is ideal) to remove
dust and crumbs from the crevices in between the keys on the keyboard.
Rub the bristles in your hand to create static electricity, which will attract the dust.
Or blow dust off the keyboard using an aerosol of compressed air
(available at computer stores).

To keep your keyboard and monitor dust-free, cover them
with a cloth or plastic dust cover when not in use.

Keep the mouse pad clean—avoid putting any drinks on your mouse pad. Minor deposits on
the mouse pad will be transferred via the mouse-ball onto the rollers inside the mouse.

Do not use the mouse with wet or grimy hands. Both will accelerate the buildup of debris
inside the mouse.

Avoid using hand cream just before using the mouse.

*TIP: Buy a mouse with optical technology. They are not as vulnerable to the buildup of debris which
reduces the effectiveness of the mouse.*

TIP: Even if you buy a top-of-the-range computer, chances are it will come with a cheap 'n'
nasty keyboard. Manufacturers know that we spend all our time looking at the monitor and
specs of the computer, so we'll more than likely overlook the keyboard. Hence the crappy
quality. Yet, the keyboard is just as vital as the monitor. It's well worth investing in a new, good-
quality keyboard. They vary enormously in "feel," so test them out at your local computer store
and find the one that feels right for you. Keep your cheap one for emergencies.

— UNRAVELING SPAGHETTI JUNCTION —

Endless cables and wires are a health risk (you could trip over them) and they also look messy
and unsightly. Use cord control tubes to conceal your wires. Or make your own with a length
of plastic drainpipe.

DID YOU KNOW? The average computer workstation harbors more germs than the average toilet seat.

— HOW TO SIT AT YOUR COMPUTER —

Many health problems, such as back pain and carpal tunnel syndrome, can be avoided with a few simple precautions.

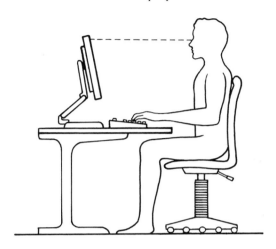

Position your chair directly in front of the keyboard.

The front of the computer screen should be about 20 inches from your eyes.
Your eyes should be just level with the top of the screen display.

The keyboard should be low enough to let your elbows make a right angle when you rest your fingertips on the keyboard. If you do a lot of typing, a wrist rest—a pad that sits in front of the keyboard—will take the strain off your wrists while you type.

Your back should be well supported by the back of the chair. Your thighs should be horizontal and your knees should be at right angles while you work. The backs of your knees should not quite touch the chair. Your feet should be flat on the floor or you can use a footrest.

Rest your eyes by looking away from the screen every 10 minutes and focusing on a distant object.

Take a break—take a walk! People who sit immobile for long periods in front of their computer can develop a DVT (deep vein thrombosis).

DID YOU KNOW? Try this when you're sitting idly at your computer: With your right foot make clockwise circles. At the same time, draw the number 6 in the air using your right hand. Your foot will change direction.

TIP: Your screen should be as glare-free as possible. Experiment with your monitor until you find the best position. You could also try using an antiglare screen.

— Leisure Time —

"Games are the last resort of those who do not know how to idle."

—Robert Lynd

— LISTENING TO MUSIC —

Forget fancy amplifiers and subwoofers—the most important consideration when it comes to listening to music is your listening environment. Yet which of us gives it a second thought? Most of us buy the equipment, plug it in, and stick the speakers any place the cat isn't sitting. But there's no point spending your hard-earned cash on a state-of-the-art sound system if you don't get the basics right.

To optimize sound quality, avoid the minimalist look. Sound is greatly affected by the objects in a room; even the position of a plant can make a difference. In an empty room, sound bounces off the bare walls, creating a brash sound. Try clapping your hand in the middle of an empty room and you'll get the idea.

To help muffle sound distortion, use heavy curtains, carpets or rugs, bookcases full of books, wall hangings, etc. These all act as sound absorbers. For maximum effect, place these behind your speakers.

The ideal listening position is triangular: a speaker at each corner and the listener at the tip. All sides of the triangle should be of equal length—about 7 feet—and the speakers should be angled toward you. Position your favorite chair at the apex of the triangle.

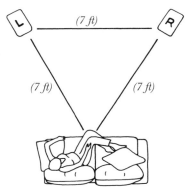

Don't put speakers directly up against a wall, as sound will bounce back into the room. For average-sized speakers, leave a gap of about 8 inches; more, if the speakers are larger.

Don't put speakers directly on the floor. Even if the floor is carpeted, there is likely to be vibration. Put speakers on stands. If they are very large, they can be fitted with "spikes," which keep them above ground level. The speakers should be at the same level as your head when you are in your usual listening position.

Don't put speakers next to the television unless they are magnetically shielded, as they could distort the color on the TV. Keep them at least 12 inches away from the set.

Settle back and enjoy the music.

TIP: If you have neighbors close by, be considerate,—put on headphones to listen to loud music.

— GAMES —

The inexorable rise of the computer game has led to a sharp decline in traditional games. Many kids today have no idea how to play Hangman or Consequences. Even Tic-Tac-Toe is a mystery to them. Rediscover the fun for yourself, then pass it on to the deprived youth of today.

— CAT'S CRADLE —

Cat's cradle is the ancient art of making figures out of a single loop of string. It is enjoyed by cultures the world over, from Aborigines to Inuits. Native peoples with strong oral traditions made the string "pictures" to illustrate their stories and legends, and also to use in their magic charms. The Navajo of America wove figures of storm clouds and coyotes; the Papuans of New Guinea made figures of sea snakes and headhunters. Various materials have been used for tying, from coconut fiber to finely braided human hair.

What you need: a piece of string or cord about 5 feet long, knotted to make a loop about 2½ feet long.

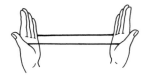

1. Place the string over your hand, keeping your thumbs free.

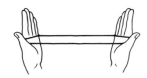

2. Loop the string around each hand. Leave your thumbs out of the loop.

3. Reach over with the middle finger of your right hand and hook it under the string on your left palm.

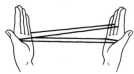

4. Pull your hands apart so the string is taut.

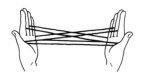

5. Repeat steps 3 and 4, using the middle finger of your left hand.

Well done! You just made the cat's cradle.

DID YOU KNOW? The name "cat's cradle" is a corruption of "cratch cradle." Cratch is an old word for a cattle trough or manger, which is a similar shape to the figure made by the strings.

— THE GARDEN GATE, AKA DIAMONDS, SOLDIER'S BED —

Follow steps 1–5 of the Cat's Cradle (see page 240).

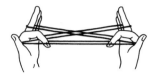

1. Put your first fingers under the X shape at the front and catch the bottom piece of string.

2. Bring the string up over your first fingers. Pull tight.

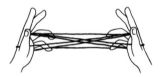

3. Put your little fingers under the X shape at the back and catch the bottom piece of string.

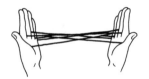

4. Bring the string up over your little fingers. Pull tight.

5. Straighten all your fingers, and keeping them held tight together, put them all through the middle of the loop so that all the tips of your fingers are touching your palms. Pull tight.

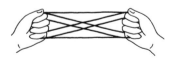

Voilà! A garden gate.

Now that you have the basic moves, the variations are endless. Try inventing your own.

TIP: Carry a piece of string with you, and you'll never be bored.

— HANGMAN —

Number of players: Two or more

What you need: Paper and pencil

How to play: One player is designated the "hangman." He thinks of the title of a film/book/song/whatever and writes down the letters as dashes. Spaces are left if there is more than one word. So, for example, *Snow White and the Seven Dwarfs* would be represented as follows:

_ _ _ _   _ _ _ _ _   _ _ _   _ _ _   _ _ _ _ _   _ _ _ _ _ _

The aim of the game is for the other player(s) to guess the name before they are "hung." A player names different letters she thinks might appear in the words. If she guesses a letter correctly, the hangman must fill in each dash where the letter appears. For example, if she says "E," the hangman fills in the dashes as follows:

_ _ _ _   _ _ _ _ E   _ _ _   _ _ E   _ E _ E _   _ _ _ _ _ _

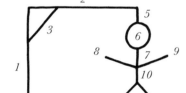

If the player names a letter that does not appear in the words, the hangman jots down the letter as a reminder and starts to construct the gallows on which to hang the player. The numbers on the illustration show the sequence in which the gallows is constructed from 1 to 11. Each number represents a wrong letter guessed. If the player is hanged before the title is guessed, the hangman wins.

— ROCK, PAPER, SCISSORS —
Number of players: Two

What you need: Nothing

How to play: Both players start by putting one hand behind their back. On the count of three, they bring their hand back around to the front as scissors (first finger and middle finger extended in a V shape), paper (hand held flat), or a rock (a closed fist). Each element beats or is beaten by another: scissors cut paper; paper covers rock; rock crushes scissors. If players use the same element, the round is a draw. Rounds can go on as long as agreed.

DID YOU KNOW? With practice, you might qualify for the Rock, Paper, Scissors World Championships. Check it out at www.rpschamps.com.

— CONSEQUENCES —

Number of players: Two or more

What you need: Pencil and paper

How to play: The aim of the game is to make up a story together without knowing what the other people have written. Each person is given a piece of paper and writes down one line of the story, the sillier and more outrageous the better. They then fold the paper over to hide the line, and pass it to the next person. They continue in this way until all lines of the story are complete. In order to give some structure to the story, it needs to follow an outline.

The following is just a suggestion—you can devise your own variations.

The _____ (insert adjective)

_____ (insert boy's name) *met the*

_____ (insert adjective)

_____ (insert girl's name) *at*

_____ (insert name of place)

He said _____

She said _____

He did _____ (insert description of something he did)

She did _____ (insert description of something she did)

The consequence was _____

And the world said _____

The fun comes at the end when each person unfolds the paper they are holding and reads it aloud to the group.

TIP: Play Picture Consequences by following the method described above, but substituting pictures for the words: head / body / arms / legs / shoes.

— Tic-Tac-Toe —

Number of players: Two

What you need: Paper and pencils

How to play: Draw a nine-square grid. Decide who wants to be "O" and who wants to be "X." Toss a coin to decide who goes first. If "X" wins, they make an X in one of the nine boxes; "O" then makes an O in another box. The object of the game is to make three Xs or three Os, either horizontally, vertically, or diagonally. Each player takes their turn trying to make their line of three while preventing their opponent from making their line of three. The person who goes first has a slight advantage. After the first game, players take it in turns to go first.

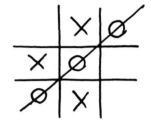

— Boxes —

Number of players: Two

What you need: Pencil and unlined paper

How to play: Draw a 10 x 10 grid of dots (100 dots in total) on a sheet of unlined paper. Each player takes it in turns to connect two dots to form a line, either horizontally or vertically. Diagonal lines are not allowed. Each time a player draws the fourth line to complete a box, they put their initial inside and have an extra turn. The game continues until no more lines can be drawn. The person with the most initials in the boxes is the winner.

— Hopscotch —

Number of players: Two or more

What you need: Flat stone, chalk, a paved, level area

How to play: On a paved, level area, one person chalks the hopscotch course. Single areas are hopped on one foot, "double" areas (3 and 4, and 6 and 7) must be straddled, left foot on the left square, right foot on the right.

Player One throws her stone or marker into area 1. If the stone lands entirely within that area without touching a line, she then hops over that area, into area 2; then, because areas 3 and 4 are double she has to straddle them with her left foot in area 3 and her right foot in area 4. She then hops into area 5, straddles double areas 6 and 7, hops into area 8, then turns around and repeats the entire sequence; that is, until she hops into area 2. When she reaches area 2, she stoops down, remaining on one leg, and picks up her marker, then hops back over area 1 without touching a line.

DID YOU KNOW? During the Roman occupation of Britain, soldiers in full armor played a form of hopscotch on a court 100 feet long as a military training exercise.

If Player One completes the course successfully, she throws her stone into area 2. If the stone lands in the area without touching a line, she hops into area 1, avoids area 2 because her marker is there, straddles areas 3 and 4, hops into 5, straddles 6 and 7, hops into 8, turns around, and repeats the entire sequence in reverse order until she reaches area 3. Here, she bends down and picks up her marker from area 2, hops back over areas 2 and 1 to the starting line.

Player One then throws her marker into area 3 and follows the same procedure of hopping and straddling. Play continues in this way until Player One makes a mistake. This could be for various reasons: if her marker fails to land in the correct area without touching a line, or if she steps on a line, misses an area, or loses her balance and puts down an extra foot when she shouldn't. When she makes a mistake, she leaves her marker in the area where the mistake was made and Player Two takes their turn.

Player Two follows exactly the same procedure as Player One, but because players must always hop over a square where a marker has been placed, Player Two must hop over Player One's marker.

When play returns to Player One, they resume where they left off. The first player to complete the course for every area wins.

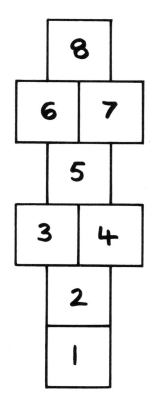

REMEMBER: Players must always hop over an area where a marker has been placed.

— ANIMAL, VEGETABLE, MINERAL, AKA TWENTY QUESTIONS —

Number of players: Two; can also be played in teams

What you need: Nothing

How to play: One person thinks of an object, person, place, or thing and tells the others whether it is animal, vegetable, mineral, or abstract. The other players then ask 20 questions to find out what the word is. The person who thought of the word can only answer yes or no to the questions. If someone makes an incorrect guess at the word, that counts as one question. If the word is guessed before the 20 questions have been asked, that player wins and chooses the next word.

TIP: If the players use up their 20 questions without guessing the object, the player with the object in mind reveals it and thinks of a new one.

— CATEGORIES —

Number of players: Two or more

What you need: Pencil and paper

How to play: Decide on about eight categories of different subjects—anything from names of countries to names of pop bands. Make a list of the categories and put a series of columns beside it:

CATEGORY	A		S
Girl's Name	Annabelle	5	Sarah
City	Amsterdam	5	Stockholm
Flower	Anemone	10	Snowdrop
Pop Song	All My Lovin'	5	Suspicious Minds
Part of the Body	Arm	5	Sternum
Animal	Antelope	5	Sloth
Film Title	Aladdin	5	Star Wars
Sport	Athletics	10	Snowboarding
Score	45		

One person picks a letter at random from a book. All players then have to fill in each category with a word starting with that letter. As soon as a player has finished, they shout "Stop" and everyone else must lay down their pencils, regardless of whether they have finished or not. If no one shouts "Stop," the round is ended after 5 minutes. Points are then awarded: 5 points if another player also has your word, 10 points if you were the only player to get that word. (There is therefore an incentive to think of an original word if you can.) If it turns out the person who stopped the game had an inadmissible answer (e.g., put the name of a country instead of a city), 20 points are deducted from their score for that particular round. The winner is the player who scores the most points.

— WHY KNOT? —

"Trust in God but tie up your camel."
—Arab saying

There are over 4,000 knots in existence. How many can you tie? Unless you were a Scout, the answer probably is, just one: the so-called "granny knot." That's the one we're all taught as kids to tie our shoelaces. Velcro fastenings on shoes mean that many children today are growing up clueless as to how to tie any knots at all. High time, then, we were reminded how really, really useful knots can be. A well-tied knot can usually do a job quicker, stronger, and cheaper than tape and glue. And knot tying is much more fun!

DID YOU KNOW? The expression tying the knot *dates back to Roman times when the bride wore a girdle secured by a knot. On the wedding night, the groom had the honor of "untying the knot."*

— HOW TO TIE A SQUARE KNOT —

Ease of tying and untying make this classic binding knot a favorite general-purpose knot. Use it for tying the perfect parcel, fastening a shoelace, securing a bandage or sling, or tying a hair ribbon around a braid.

1. Cross two ends of the same rope, left over right. (figure 1)

2. Place the left end under the right end, and bring it back over.
   Make sure you leave enough rope for the next part of the knot. (figure 2)

3. Cross the two remaining ends, right over left. (figure 3)

4. Place the right end under the left end, and bring it back over. (figure 4)

5. Tighten the knot by pulling on the two ends of the rope. (figure 5)

6. The finished knot. (figure 6)

CAUTION: Take care you don't tie the same half-knot twice or you'll end up with the unreliable granny knot.

CHANT: To remember the correct sequence, say:
   "Left over right and under; right over left and under."

TO UNDO THE KNOT: Just pull one of the free ends toward the other.
   This will turn it into a sliding knot.

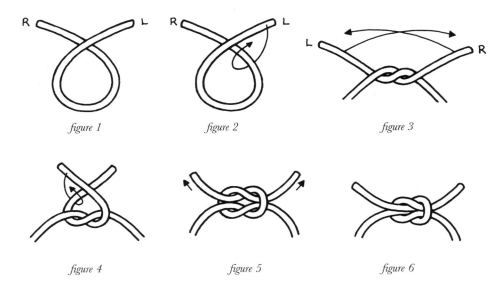

figure 1   figure 2   figure 3

figure 4   figure 5   figure 6

DID YOU KNOW? The square knot is also known as the "reef knot," named after the reefing sail on old sailboats. The ancient Romans knew it as the Hercules knot.

— BOWLINE —

Pronounced *boh-linn*, this fixed loop is strong and does not jam or slip. Place it over or around an object for hoisting or dragging; place it in your hand to hold or pull an object; join two ropes together using two bowlines.

1. Make an overhand loop in the rope by taking it between the fingers and thumb of your right hand and making a clockwise twist with your wrist near where you want the knot to be. (figure 1)

2. Bring line A up and through the loop from behind. (figure 2)

3. Take line A around the back of line B. (figure 3)

4. Tuck line A back down into the small loop, this time from front to back. (figure 4)

5. Tighten the knot by pulling on lines A and B while keeping the big loop. (figure 5)

6. The finished knot. (figure 6)

CHANT: To remember the sequence, say: "The rabbit comes out of the hole, around the tree, and back down the hole again." The hole is the small loop, and the rabbit is line A.

TO UNDO THE KNOT: Push line B forward in the direction of the knot.

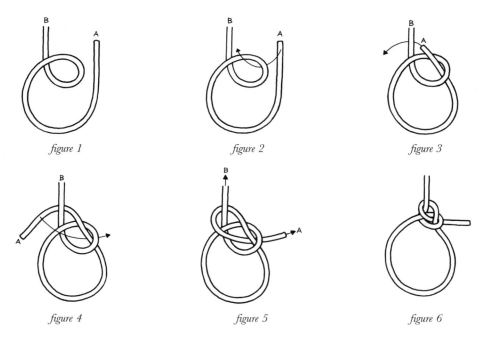

figure 1   *figure 2*   *figure 3*

figure 4   *figure 5*   *figure 6*

DID YOU KNOW? This knot was originally used to attach a rope from the bow of a ship to a sail.

— ROUND TURN AND TWO HALF-HITCHES —

Indispensable when you want to moor your yacht to a dock post. What, no yacht?
Horse? Dog? Clothesline, surely? Practically any object that needs securing to a post, pole,
stake, or handle will find a use for this knot. It can also be used to tie down or secure loads
to a car roof rack or trailer.

1. Pass the end of the rope (end A) twice around the post, pole, rail, or whatever is to be the anchorage, from front to back. (figure 1)

2. Holding end B tight, pass end A over, under, and back up through end B. (figure 2)

3. Pull end A and end B tight. This forms what is known as a "half-hitch." (figure 3)

4. Repeat step 2. (figure 4)

5. Repeat step 3 to form another "half-hitch." (figure 5)

6. The finished knot. (figure 6)

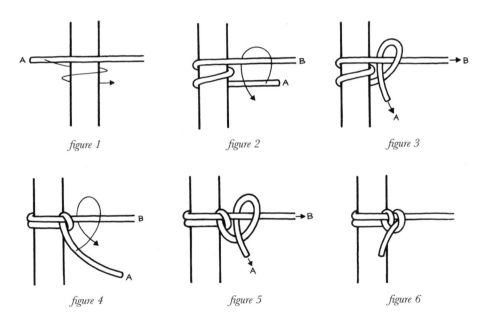

figure 1   figure 2   figure 3

figure 4   figure 5   figure 6

DID YOU KNOW? This knot was first recorded in a seamanship textbook of 1794 but likely dates back to ancient times.

— Houseplants
& Flowers —

*"One sure way to lose another woman's friendship is to try to
improve her flower arrangements."*

—MARCELENE COX

— FLOWER POWER —

*"When you have only two pennies left in the world,
buy a loaf of bread with one, and a lily with the other."*
—*Chinese proverb*

The color, form, and fragrance of plants literally breathe life into a home:
they improve the air quality by producing oxygen and absorbing carbon dioxide.
They also rid the air of toxins like ammonia, benzene, and formaldehyde,
given out by electrical appliances and man-made carpets.

— HOW TO CHOOSE THE PERFECT HOUSEPLANT —

Pick a plant to suit your home and your lifestyle. If you spend a lot of time away from home,
buy a plant that needs little watering.

Don't fit the plant to the spot, fit the spot to the plant. Decide where you want to site a plant,
take the dimensions of the spot, consider the amount of light, the temperature and humidity,
then go out and choose a plant that suits those conditions and will do well there.

Plants for sunny spots: Aloe, Bougainvillea, Cacti, Campanula, Citrus,
Kalanchoe, Pelargonium, Sedum

Plants for shady spots: Asparagus, Calathea, Ficus pumila, Maranta,
Philodendron, Sellaginella

Choose a good specimen. The plant should look sturdy with no signs of damage or
discoloration to the leaves. Steer clear of plants if the leaves look as if they have been
gnawed, or if the plant is sticky—sure signs of pests and disease.

Check the roots of the plant by giving the pot a tap and carefully tugging on the stem base.
The plant should lift out without any difficulty. Avoid roots that look dried or overcrowded.

Don't buy a plant where the soil has shrunk away from the sides of the pot, as this suggests that
the plant has dried out at some point.

Don't be tempted by the plant with the most flowers. Go for one with a few flowers open but
also some still in bud so you can enjoy an ongoing display.

Once you get your plant home, allow it to acclimatize to its new environment. Don't put a plant
from outside straight into a centrally heated room.

Group plants together. They look better and grow better too.

*TIP: Buy houseplants in spring and summer if possible, as growth is fastest and they will cope better with the
new environment. If you buy a plant in winter, wrap it well, and don't leave it in the car or it will catch a chill.*

Never use ordinary soil from your garden to pot up houseplants. Proper potting soil has a different composition to garden soil, with nutrients to encourage root development. You also risk bringing in diseases and bugs.

GIVE IT A TRY: Orchids may look exotic, but they make great houseplants. Pot-grown orchids add style and sophistication to any room.

— HOUSEPLANT CARE —
TEMPERATURE
The closer you can simulate the natural habitat of a plant, the more it will thrive. In a steamy bathroom, create a lush tropical rainforest paradise with humidity-loving ferns and bromelaids. In a sunny conservatory, terracotta pots brimming with geraniums and bougainvillea create a Mediterranean feel.

Sudden changes in temperature will seriously affect your plant. Don't place any plant in a draft or beside a fire or radiator. In winter, if you have a plant on a windowsill during the day, move it out in the evening when you draw the curtains.

WATERING
Water your plant only when it needs it. Stick your finger about a ½ inch into the soil at the side of the pot, and if it feels dry, the plant needs a drink.

THE GOLDEN RULE: Don't over-water your plant. More plants die through over-watering than neglect.

MISTING
Central heating makes many rooms too dry for plants. Every day, spray plants (except hairy-leaved varieties) with a mister filled with rainwater or tepid tap water.

FEEDING
Feed plants from spring to late summer with liquid fertilizer. Do not overfeed.

LEAF CLEANING
Dust soon builds up on houseplants. Clean shiny-leaved plants with cotton wool soaked in rainwater, but don't wet hairy-leaved plants—dust them with a paintbrush. Avoid commercial leaf-cleaning products.

VACATIONS
You may be lucky enough to have a kind neighbor who will come in and water your plants regularly. If not, fill plastic trays with moist peat and place the plants inside them. In a shady position, and given a good watering before you leave, they should last up to two weeks without adverse effects.

GIVE IT A TRY: To give a terracotta pot a weathered look, brush the surface with plain yogurt, leave in a shady spot for a few weeks, and it will soon be overgrown with beautiful mosses and lichen. An instant antique!

TIP: Talking to your plants is perfectly normal. The only time to worry is when they start talking back.

— HOW TO ARRANGE FLOWERS —

Thank goodness, modern flower arranging is no longer about contorting blooms into abnormal positions; rather, it's about working sympathetically with your flowers to create a more natural, unaffected look.

— *How to Choose the Perfect Vase* —

Often overlooked, the greatest influence on your flower arrangement is the vase. The neck and diameter are crucial to how the flowers will look. The wider the neck, the more flowers you'll need and the trickier the arranging will be. Rectangular or square-shaped vases with wide necks are least forgiving as the flowers have no support. Novices are recommended to choose a vase with a narrow neck as the flowers will fall naturally into place and need very little arranging.

It's a good idea to have at least three different-shaped vases at home so you can use a variety of flowers.

Goldfish bowl: Don't try to fill it with flowers because you'll need a gardenful! Float just a few specimen flower heads on top of the water: Cut the stems to about 1 inch so the flowers can still draw up water. If a flower has trouble floating, cut a piece of bubble wrap and stick the stem through the middle, taking care the bubble wrap doesn't show through. Or, for a clean, modern look, fill the bowl a third full and coil calla lilies around inside so that their stems are submerged but their heads are out.

Tazza (pronounced *tat-ser*): A shallow vessel originally for holding wine. Like the goldfish bowl, you would need many flowers to fill this wide neck. Better to float three specimen flower heads such as camellias and add the same number of floating candles.

Urn: This classic shape suits lilies, roses, gerberas, and snapdragons.

Small round bowl: Perfect for a dome of garden roses, anemones, ranunculus, cosmos daisies, and hellebores (Christmas roses).

TIP: If the vase/container is not watertight, hide a jam jar inside or line with plastic and use florist's foam.

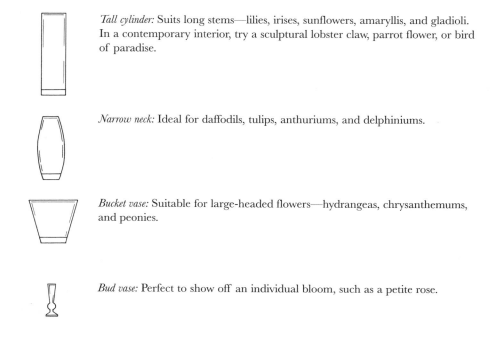

Tall cylinder: Suits long stems—lilies, irises, sunflowers, amaryllis, and gladioli. In a contemporary interior, try a sculptural lobster claw, parrot flower, or bird of paradise.

Narrow neck: Ideal for daffodils, tulips, anthuriums, and delphiniums.

Bucket vase: Suitable for large-headed flowers—hydrangeas, chrysanthemums, and peonies.

Bud vase: Perfect to show off an individual bloom, such as a petite rose.

THINKING BEYOND THE VASE: An old jewelry box, perfume bottle, teacups, teapots, cocktail glasses, shells, an old umbrella stand, antique medicine bottles, drink cans . . . can all be used to display flowers. Match the container with the flowers.

— How to Clean a Glass Vase —

Outside: Clean with warm, soapy water and dry with a soft cloth.
Inside: Method 1: fill the vase with a warm solution of detergent and leave to soak for a few hours or overnight. Rinse out thoroughly. Method 2: Soak the vase in a solution of water and bleach for about half an hour. Rinse out thoroughly.
If the vase is cloudy (this is caused by lime-scale buildup):
Method 1: Sprinkle a little automatic dishwasher liquid in the vase and fill with water.
Method 2: Swill 3 teaspoons of ammonia gently around the vase, then rinse thoroughly.
If all else fails, a commercial lime-scale remover should do the trick.

— How to Care for Cut Flowers —

As soon as you get home, plunge the flowers into a sink or bucket of warm water.
While they are underwater, use a sharp knife or scissors to cut the bottom of each stem at an angle of 45 degrees. Take off at least ⅜ inch so the flowers can take up fresh water.
Strip away all flowers, leaves, and thorns below the water level of the vase.
If left in the water, they will rot. Stems only should be submerged.

TIP: Change the water in your vase regularly to prevent it becoming encrusted with flower residue.

— How to Arrange Your Flowers —

Fill a clean vase with fresh, lukewarm water. If you have plant food, add it now.

A good rule of thumb is to keep the flowers no more than twice the height of the container. For smaller vases, keep the flowers no more than twice the height plus the width.

Aim for something well balanced but not too top-heavy. Think about color, but also texture and fragrance.

Either use lots of flowers or just a few choice blooms. An odd number of flowers will create a more pleasing visual statement than an even number.

Don't mix too many different types of flowers in a single arrangement.

Choose flowers according to the seasons—daffodils as harbingers of spring, poinsettias to brighten dark, winter days, etc. You will get better value for your money and feel more in touch with the seasons.

Harmonize shapes and textures. Sometimes, simplicity is the most stylish. Go for a single variety, such as all tulips, all roses, or all sweet peas.

Keep your color palette simple. Choose a theme, such as pastel colors or berry colors, or stick to all one color.

If your flowers are not cooperating, try crisscrossing clear sticky tape over the top of the vase and sticking the stems through the gaps.

Large freestanding vases with tall flowers look good on the floor in a corner.

In a minimalist interior, a simple vase of sculptural grasses or skeletal twigs adds a touch of drama.

GIVE IT A TRY: Scrunch up a large sheet of clear cellophane and stuff it willy-nilly into a large vase. Add a few specimen, showy flower heads, then fill the vase with water. The effect is like crackled ice on a frozen lake. It won't last long, but while it does, it will look stunning.

— Pollen Count —

The pollen stain is a notoriously difficult mark to remove. Lilies are especially hazardous, so before arranging, it's a good precaution to remove the pollen sac at the top of each stamen (that's the little stalk growing up out of the middle of the flower head). Take the stamen firmly between your finger and thumb, and pull off the pollen sac in one go. If pollen does get on your clothes, don't rub it. Put a piece of sticky tape carefully over the pollen and dab it up.
See page 23 for more hints on pollen removal.

TIP: Add a few drops of food coloring to dye the water to match the flowers.

— ENTERTAINING —

"I do wish we could chat longer, but I'm having an old friend for dinner."

—HANNIBAL LECTER

— HOW TO THROW THE PERFECT DINNER PARTY —

The secret of successful entertaining is to create a warm and affable atmosphere where guests can relax and sparkle, old friendships can flourish, and new ones be forged.

— HOW TO SATISFY GUESTS WITH SPECIAL DIETARY NEEDS —

Planning a dinner party menu can be tricky at the best of times, but how do you cater for people whose food choices are limited for ethical, medical, or religious reasons?

Diet	Won't Eat	Will Eat
VEGETARIAN	Officially, a "veggie" will not eat meat, fish, or poultry; unofficially, some veggies eat fish—I've even known ones who eat bacon sandwiches (in secret).	Eggs and milk products; however, beware "hidden" meat products in some foods; e.g., cheese may contain animal rennet (the lining of a calf's stomach), gelatine (boiled-up animal bones and skins), lard, animal fat, stocks in soup.
VEGAN	Meat, fish, poultry, also dairy products such as milk and eggs.	Vegetables, bread, cereals, fruit, tofu.
WHEAT ALLERGY	Bread, pasta, cakes made with ordinary flour.	Pastry is okay so long as it's made with rye flour not ordinary flour; wheat-free bread and wheat-free pasta are available from health food stores.
KOSHER (Devout Jews)	Pork, rabbit, and products thereof; shellfish, crustaceans, octopus, squid. Meat and dairy must not be mixed at a single meal.	Animals that chew the cud or have cloven hooves—so lamb, beef, poultry, and goat are all fine. However, the meat must have been slaughtered by a practicing Jewish butcher. Fish with scales or fins are also acceptable.
HALAL (Devout Muslims)	Pigs and products thereof, lard, food containing gelatine. Most do not touch alcohol, so beware alcohol-based sauces.	Meat slaughtered in accordance with Muslim religious practices. Buy lamb or beef from a Halal butcher.
LACTOSE INTOLERANT (lactose is a sugar found in milk)	Dairy products, such as cream, yogurt, butter and margarine.	Soya milk is a good substitute.
GLUTEN INTOLERANT (Coeliac disease, a disorder of the intestine, can make people sensitive to the protein, gluten)	Cereals, bread, pasta, cakes, biscuits; sausages and processed meat; canned food which uses wheat flour as a thickening agent; barley-based drinks including beer and malted milk drinks.	Soya-based products and products labeled "gluten-free." Thicken sauces with gluten-free flour, soya flour, or corn flour. Cheese, milk, eggs, meat, poultry, fish are all fine.

DID YOU KNOW? Socrates, Pythagoras, Leonardo da Vinci, Isaac Newton, Charles Darwin, Leo Tolstoy, Albert Einstein, and Mahatma Gandhi were all vegetarians.

— General Tips for Guests with Special Dietary Needs —

No, an omelet or an extra helping of potatoes is not acceptable.
Put a little effort into the food.

If you're short of ideas, get hold of a specialty cookbook.
If you don't want to buy a new one you might not use again,
rummage in a secondhand bookshop.
You can often pick up cookbooks at bargain prices.
Alternatively, search the Internet. Many of the TV chefs have their own
websites containing recipes and tips.

Many of your favorite recipes can be adapted for people with sensitivies/allergies by
using different types of flour and dairy product substitutes.

Ask about possible food sensitivities and restrictions in advance,
so you have time to plan your menu. People would much rather that
you asked, rather than having to tell you on the night that they don't like
or can't eat something that you've prepared.

An allergy to nuts, is very common. If you know that one of your guests is
allergic to nuts you must think carefully about your recipes, and remember
that as well as not using nuts, you must avoid using nut oils. etc.

Don't make your "special dietary needs" guest feel that they're putting you to any
trouble, even if they are. You're the host. Be gracious.
And take their needs seriously.

Shop at a health food store or a specialty butcher shop and ask their advice.

Accommodate, don't isolate. Dining is a shared social experience, and part of the
pleasure of eating is enjoying the same food together as far as possible.
Be creative: e.g., many soups work equally well with a vegetarian stock.
Whip up a veggie stir-fry for everyone and put the meat on a separate dish.

Don't be too ambitious and try new recipes for every course. It's best
to stick to a couple of recipes that you know and are tried and tested,
and just try something new for one course. Alternatively, have a trial run
before the dinner party.

The simplest way to ensure your guest will be happy?
Ask them for their favorite recipe.

TIP: When planning a menu, the golden rule is: Keep it simple.

— How to Dress the Table —

Put as much thought into dressing the table as you do yourself.

Dining table: A polished wood table looks elegant but it will need coasters and placemats. Placemats are catching up with designer trends so there's no need for the "hunting scenes" look.

GIVE IT A TRY: If you're throwing a party for close pals, get a photograph of each friend enlarged to the size of a placemat, laminate, and use as their individual placemat.

Tablecloth: If want to cover the table, a plain white linen cloth is traditional. It should be large enough to overhang all sides of the table by at least 9 inches. Ensure it is well pressed.

GIVE IT A TRY: To change the look of a white tablecloth, drape a large piece of sheer colored fabric diagonally across it.

DID YOU KNOW? To polish the wood on the great banqueting table at Windsor Castle, a "reviver" of vinegar and water is used.

— Putting People in Their Place —

Arrange the chairs around the table *before* setting it. Position the chair so that guests are seated directly opposite each other. Sit on a chair to check you've allowed enough elbow room. As the host, position your seat where you can easily get up.

If you want to follow formal etiquette, the host and hostess sit facing one another; the most important guest sits on the right of the host, and their partner sits on the right of the hostess.

If you have more than six guests, use place cards to avoid confusion.

— How to Decorate the Table —

Choose a color scheme and decorations to complement the decor of the table, the style of the room, and the type of occasion. Be imaginative, but don't clutter the table with too many decorations. Remember that people need room to eat.

Place your centerpiece on the table first. This can be flowers, fruit, a combination of both, or even an *objet d'art*. Whatever you choose, keep it low enough not to impede cross-table chat. Steer clear of heavily scented flowers and candles that will detract from the delicious aromas of your home cooking.

TIP: Seat a portly person at the end or head of a table where they can spread out without cramping anyone's style.

— How to Make a Crystal Ice Bowl —

An ice bowl is a striking way to serve ice cream, fruit salads, sorbets, iced soups, and seafood—anything that needs to stay cool. As a centerpiece for a dinner party or buffet, it will elicit gasps of amazement from your guests. Under flickering candlelight, it looks enchanting, like something from the palace of the Ice Queen in the fairy tale.

What you need: 2 freezer-proof glass bowls—one needs to be slightly smaller in order to fit inside the other, leaving a gap of at least 2 inches all around, sticky tape, water, ice cubes

Decorations: For savory version: lemon or lime slices, fresh herbs like rosemary, shells such as mussels; for dessert version: small flowers, petals, berries, leaves such as ivy, herbs, fruit slices such as star anise.

1. Fill the larger bowl with cold water to a depth of about 1 inches. NOTE: For clearer ice, boil the water first, then allow to cool before use.

2. Sprinkle a few decorations in the water.

3. Center the smaller bowl inside the larger bowl. The rims of the two bowls should be level and there should be an equal amount of space—at least a gap of 2 inches—between the two bowls all around, including the base.

4. Stick a couple of pieces of adhesive tape to crisscross over the top of the bowls at right angles, to hold them in position.

5. Tuck more decorations into the space between the bowls in a random pattern. Don't overdo the decorations. Less is more; besides, if you add too many decorations, the ice won't show through.

6. Carefully fill up the space between the two bowls with water right to the top. While you pour the water, lay something flat, like a chopping board, on top of the bowls so that they don't separate. Don't put water into the smaller bowl.

7. Place on a level surface in the freezer for 24 hours until the ice is solid.

8. Unmold your ice bowl: if you have time, let it sit at room temperature and thaw naturally to the point where you can remove the bowls. If not, carefully fill the small bowl with lukewarm water from the tap so the ice softens just enough for you to lift it out of the bigger bowl. Dip the outer bowl in warm water to soften the ice and remove the crystal ice bowl. Don't use hot water, as it might crack the ice bowl.

9. Store the ice bowl in the freezer until required.

10. Place the ice bowl on a tray or plate with a few paper towels tucked discreetly underneath, out of sight, to catch the water as it melts. Decorate around the bowl with a few flowers.

TIP: Substitute bucket-shaped containers for bowls and you have the perfect cooler for a bottle of champagne.

— How to Set the Table —

The best way to set a table is to suit the mood of the party and the food you are serving. For an informal gathering, you'll probably be happy with minimum cutlery, but for a formal dinner party, you might want to follow more formal guidelines. Don't feel you have to follow these "rules" to the letter. Even the etiquette guides can't agree on what goes where; in fact, they often contradict each other! The table in the illustration is set for:

First course: Soup
Second course: Fish
Third course: Meat
Fourth course: Dessert

Key
1. Napkin
2. Fish fork
3. Dinner fork
4. Dinner plate
5. Dinner knife
6. Fish knife
7. Soup spoon
8. Red wine glass
9. Water glass
10. White wine glass
11. Dessert fork
12. Dessert spoon
13. Bread plate

— Usual Order of Courses —

First: Soup, pâté, or starter

Second (optional): Fish

Main: Meat, or fish with vegetables

Fourth (optional): Green salad

Fifth: Dessert

Sixth: Cheese

Seventh: Fresh fruit

Eighth: Coffee, chocolates and/or liqueurs

Ninth: Indigestion tablet

TIP: To create a romantic vibe for a Valentine's supper or an intimate dinner for two, put on a bright shade of lipstick and plant a kiss on the rim of the dessert plates. Mwah!

THE GOLDEN RULE: Cutlery is always arranged in the order in which it will be used, starting from the outside. So, cutlery for the first course goes furthest away from the plate, cutlery for the second course goes next nearest, and so on.

Forks go to the left of the plate.

Knives go to the right of the plate with the blades pointing inward toward the plate.

The soup spoon goes to the right of the knives.

The dessert spoon and fork may be laid in sequence with the other cutlery (i.e., either side of the dinner plate), or they can go above. If placed above, the fork points right and the spoon points left. The fork should be nearest the plate.

The bread plate goes at 10 o'clock on the table-setting clock or it can also go to the left of your dinner plate. If there is a butter knife each, lay it across the bread plate.

REMEMBER: Work from the outside in.

Place the trio of water glass, red-wine glass, and white-wine glass in a triangular formation at 2 o'clock on the table-setting clock. If there's only a water glass and a wineglass, place the water glass above the tip of the blade of your dinner knife, with the wineglass to the right of it.

Place the napkin to the left of the plate and cutlery or, if you are using a charger plate, you can place it on that. It has become fashionable to use a charger plate. This is a larger plate placed under your dinner plate. The charger is removed at the same time as the dinner plate.

Place salt, pepper, mustard, and sauces on the table and remove them after the main course.

GIVE IT A TRY: Create a "harlequin dinner service"—one where every plate is different. It's a great excuse to buy odd plates from flea markets and yard sales, which you wouldn't otherwise know what to do with. A harlequin service looks particularly striking if the collection is coordinated using a harmonious color, pattern, or theme (e.g., all florals, all geometrics). You can do the same with glasses. And, of course, the brilliant thing about a harlequin set is that if a plate or glass gets broken, there's no problem replacing it!

When you've gone to so much effort to make the table look attractive, you wouldn't then plonk ketchup bottles, supermarket cartons, and margarine tubs directly onto the table—would you? Of course not! You'll make them look as appetizing as possible by transferring them into elegant serving dishes and pretty containers.

Soft drinks, too, taste better served from a crystal decanter or a jug with plenty of ice and perhaps a few sprigs of mint or lemon slices. And while you're on a decorating roll, why not embellish the water glasses? Tie a ribbon around the stem to match your color theme. Dip the rims in water, then into colored sugar crystals. Ginger ale never tasted so good!

TIP: Place the glasses on the table last so there's less chance of them getting knocked over.

— HOW TO CHOOSE THE PERFECT GLASS —

RED WINE: The inward curve of the rim allows the wine to be swirled in the glass without splashing and so release the aromatic bouquet. Serve half full so that the full aroma can be appreciated.

WHITE WINE: Slightly smaller and narrower than a red-wine glass, as white wine doesn't need to breathe.

SHERRY COPITA: The traditional Spanish sherry glass conserves the evocative bouquet. Fill it half full.

CHAMPAGNE FLUTE: The tall, slim shape means less wine is exposed to the air so the wine holds its fizz longer.

LIQUEUR: Spirit-based liqueurs have a high alcohol content, hence the tiny glass. Also used for schnapps and vodka (but not at the same time!). Don't stint; fill almost to the brim.

COCKTAIL: Long stem, classic "V" shape; what 007 sips his martinis out of.

BRANDY: The balloon shape means that if the glass is knocked over, the contents won't spill out. Also, the glass can be easily warmed in the hands.

WHISKEY: Flat-based tumbler shape is traditional, large enough to accommodate ice, water, or your choice of mixers.

HIGHBALL/WATER GLASS: Tall, straight-sided tumbler used for highballs, meaning drinks made with mixers; also suitable for water and nonalcoholic drinks.

PILSNER: Tall and slender, the traditional choice for beer, ale, stout, and similar drinks.

If you can't stretch to the full set, start with three basic shapes: the sherry, which is also suitable for port and liqueurs, the wineglass and a whiskey tumbler, which can improvise for beer and long drinks.

TIP: Don't serve champagne in a liqueur glass. That would be just plain mean.

— How to Hold a Wineglass —

There's a reason why the stems are tall: to keep the wine from being warmed in the hand.
Hold all wineglasses by the stem.

— Glass Know-How —

The most important indicators of quality are weight and smoothness.

Top-quality glass is made of lead crystal and will feel heavy.

To tell if a glass is made of quality lead crystal, tap the rim lightly with your fingernail.
A ringing tone proves it's the real deal.

Very cheap glass feels thick and gritty when you drink from it.

The thinner the glass and the finer the rim, the more pleasant the drinking experience.

Choose clear glasses for wines and spirits so that the color and clarity of the drink
may be seen and savored. Any drink out of a blue glass is unappetizing.
That said, colored goblets in rich jewel hues do look bedazzling on a Christmas table.

— How to Wash Glasses —

See page 184.

— Glass Storage —

Store glasses upright as the rim is the most fragile part of a glass. If stored upside down, the
glass may also pick up bacteria in the cupboard. Also, the air trapped in the bowl of the glass
releases an odor, which can affect the taste of drinks.

TIPS

Remove fine scratches on glasses by rubbing with non-gel toothpaste and wiping with a dry cloth.

Repair a chip on the rim of a glass by rubbing with extra-fine sandpaper until smooth.

— How to Choose Wine —

Q: What's the best wine to go with your meal?
A: The one you enjoy most.

Don't dismiss as inferior a supermarket brand of wine or champagne. The supermarket wine
buyer will visit wine-growing regions and put in a huge order from the wine house.
It's often exactly the same blend as the wine house's label but at a fraction of the price.

TIP: To reduce the risk of chipping your best glasses, put a rubber splash guard on your tap.

— How to Match Food and Wine —

The general rule of thumb:
Red wine with red meat, white wine with white meat or fish, sweet wine with desserts.

Match the heaviness of the wine to the heaviness of the food:
a light wine for lighter flavors, a stronger wine for richer.

TIPS

If you're having trouble getting a cork back into an open bottle of wine,
pour boiling water over the cork to soften it and press it back on the bottle.

Freeze leftover wine into ice cubes and use it in sauces and casseroles.

FESTIVE TIP: If there is snow outside, use it to fill the ice bucket.

GIVE IT A TRY: You've heard of a ship in a bottle, but how about a pear in a bottle? *Eau de Vie de Poire* is a narrow-necked bottle of French liqueur with a whole pear floating inside. The trick is to find a pear tree in summer, and place a young budding fruit, still on the tree, inside the bottle. Tie the bottle to a branch and wait for the fruit to mature. When ripe, remove the bottle and fill it with your favorite spirit. Your friends will be amazed.

— How to Serve Food and Wine —

Serve wine and water from the guest's right.

Put plates down in front of guests from the right.

Remove empty plates from the left.

Offer dishes of food from the right and allow guests to help themselves.

Sparkling wines and white wines are best served chilled. An hour in the fridge is fine.
If you forget, don't put the bottle in the freezer. It will chill faster if placed in a bucket
of cold water or a basin full of ice cubes for about 15 minutes.

Red wines are best served at room temperature.

How to open a bottle of wine without a corkscrew:
Method 1: Screw an ordinary screw into the cork.
Using a pair of pliers, pull the head of the screw.

Method 2: Hold the neck of the wine bottle until the
hot tap and carefully coax out the cork with a knife.

Method 3: Push the cork gently into the bottle with the end of a wooden spoon.

TIP: Serve your best wine first. As the evening wears on, guests will be less likely to notice any decline in quality. Hic.

— CHAMPAGNE —

"Champagne! I love it. It tastes like your foot's asleep."
—Joan Davis

— *Glossary* —

Extra-brut—driest

Brut—dry

Sec—medium dry to medium sweet

Extra sec—dry to medium dry

Demi sec—semisweet to sweet

Doux—very sweet

Cava—the generic description for *méthode champenoise* wines produced in Spain.

— *Bottle Sizes* —

Type	Capacity	Number of Bottles
Quarter	18.75 cl	$^1/_4$
Half-bottle	37.5 cl	$^1/_2$
Bottle	75 cl	1
Magnum	1.5 liter	2
Jeroboam	3 liter	4
Rehoboam	4.5 liter	6
Methuselah	6 liter	8
Salmanazar	9 liter	12
Balthazar	12 liter	16
Nebuchadnezzar	15 liter	20

A mnemonic to help you remember the bottle sizes is:
*M*y *J*udy *R*eally *M*akes *S*plendid *B*elching *N*oises

TIP: Cooking wine: If it isn't good enough for the chef to drink, don't use it to cook with.

— How to Open a Bottle Of Champagne —

Unless you're christening a ship or celebrating a Grand Prix victory, there should be no loud bang or explosion of foam. The idea is that the cork should slide slowly out from the bottleneck.

1. Chill the bottle in the refrigerator for a couple of hours.

2. Peel off the foil from the cork.

3. Keeping one hand over the cork in case it pops off prematurely, untwist the wire and remove the wire muzzle.

4. With one hand, hold the base of the bottle at a 45-degree angle, facing away from you. With the other hand, hold the cork in a towel. Twist cork and bottle in opposite directions.

DID YOU KNOW? "Sabrage" is a swashbuckling method of opening a bottle of bubbly. The blade of a saber is used to lop off the entire top of the bottle, cork and all, using a single stroke of the blade. Major James Hewitt, former beau of Diana, Princess of Wales, is reputed to be a master of the art. Could this be how he wooed the Princess?

— How to Pour Champagne —

DON'T: Tilt the glass and pour down the inside of the glass.

DO: Pour a small amount into each glass first to allow for the foam. Then top up each glass to about ¾ full.

STORING: An open bottle of bubbly will keep in the fridge overnight. No need for silver spoons in the neck and all that malarkey.

— HOW TO FOLD A NAPKIN —

An artfully folded napkin takes minutes to make but transforms an ordinary meal into a festive celebration. On pages 268–269 are two examples of napkin folds that you might like to try.

What you need: A clean napkin. Choose a heavy linen or well-starched cotton, which hold their shape well. It should be about 20 inches square. Choose a color to coordinate with your table setting. If in doubt, you can't go wrong with white.

TIP: If the bubbles do overflow when opening a bottle of champagne, simply dip your finger in the top of the bottle until the foaming settles.

— Le Chic —

1. Fold the napkin into quarters to make a square. Roll the top layer from the open corner down toward the bottom left-hand "closed" corner as far as you can.

2. Press the roll flat to make a band. Fold (don't roll) the second layer back toward the bottom left-hand corner and tuck under the roll. Leave a band the same width as the first.

3. Repeat step 3 with the third layer, folding (not rolling) the layer back and turning it under the fold, leaving a band the same width.

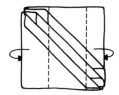

4. Fold the right and left sides to the underside of the napkin to form a rectangular "pouch."

5. The finished napkin.

TIP: As a special touch, slip a small party favor, a simple flower, or sprig of herbs into the pocket. For buffet parties, tuck the knife, fork, and spoon into each fold, side by side.

TIP: Practice your folding technique on a napkin you aren't going to use or it will look grubby by the time you put it on the table.

— Napkin Placement —

For formal dinners, place the napkin in the center of the place setting or to the left of the forks. Don't put napkins in glasses as they might be knocked over when the napkin is removed.

— Water Lily —

1. Fold all four corners of the napkin into the center and press flat. (figure 1)

2. Repeat step 1, to make a smaller square. (figure 2)

3. Taking care not to lose the folds you've made, carefully turn the napkin over. (figure 3)

4. Fold all four corners into the center for a third time. (figure 4)

5. Place a small dish or plate in the center of the napkin to prevent it unfolding. Reach behind one corner of the napkin and carefully pull out one of the folds underneath. (figure 5)

6. Pull the fold gently up and outward toward you to form a petal shape. (figure 6)

7. Repeat steps 5 and 6 for the other three corners.

8. Remove the dish. Reach under the napkin again, and pull out the four flaps between each "petal" to form the leaves of the water lily. (figure 7)

9. The finished napkin. (figure 8)

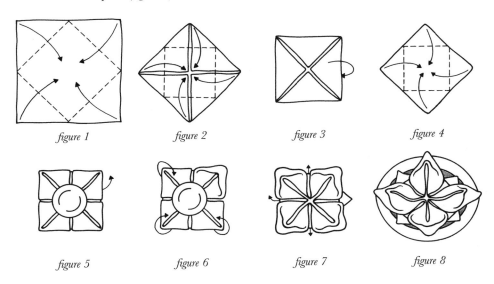

figure 1   figure 2   figure 3   figure 4

figure 5   figure 6   figure 7   figure 8

TIP: Use a colored napkin to make the water lily and coordinate with a centerpiece of floating candles and fresh flowers the same color.

— Lighting —

Keep lighting soft and subdued, but not so low that your guests can't find the bones in their fish.

Nothing beats the magical glow of candlelight—so warm, so cozy, and so kind to unlifted, unbotoxed faces. Keep candle flames below eye level so people talking across the table aren't dazzled.

GIVE IT A TRY: If the Liberace gilt candelabra look isn't you, try a mirror laid flat on the table crowded with as many tea lights as you can squeeze on. Stunning in its simplicity, it also doubles as a centerpiece. For more tips on candles, turn to page 113.

— Background Music —

Often overlooked, music can make or break the mood. Resist the temptation to play all your personal favorites; consider your guests' musical tastes too. That bad, eh? Then compromise: If there's time, make a compilation CD with a mix of mutual faves.

Music should not be so loud it drowns out the witty conversation.

It goes without saying, but I'll say it anyway: Turn off the television.

— Temperature Control —

Set a comfortable temperature in the room before your guests arrive. Check the thermostat again once the party is under way, as a large gathering of people can generate a lot of warmth. Open windows if it becomes stuffy.

— How to Prepare the Guest Bathroom —

You look fab, your dining table looks fab, even your napkins look fab, but your best efforts can all be ruined in a flush, I mean, a flash, if your powder room is not up to scratch. As well as a toilet so spotlessly clean that you could eat your dinner off it (not a serving suggestion), provide fluffy towels, soap, and a potted plant or small flower arrangement. Ensure an adequate supply of toilet paper. (No, I'm not trying to imply anything about your cooking.)

— Games —

Not everyone's idea of a good time—especially if it's strip poker and you haven't been to the gym lately. Never bully people into joining in if they don't want to. Keep it relaxed and informal. This is no time to get competitive.

REMEMBER: Relax and enjoy yourself! Your guests will take their cue from you, and if you're stressed out, they are unlikely to have a good time either.

TIP: If your dining room overlooks the garden, lace fairy lights through the branches of the trees and leave the curtains open.

— DINNER PARTY MANNERS DOS AND DON'TS —

Lay the napkin on your lap as you eat. Use it to dab the corners of your mouth.
Don't use it to wipe your mouth or spit food into. It goes without saying but I'll say
it anyway: Don't blow your nose on your napkin.

Don't smoke during a meal. If no ashtrays are provided, that means no smoking.

When drinking, look down into the glass, not out over it.

Don't blow on food that is too hot. Wait until it cools down.

Don't make noises as you chew or slurping sounds as you eat soup.

Ask your neighbor if you need the salt or some other item. Don't reach across.

If the serving spoon falls into the stew, don't roll up your sleeves and fish it out.
Leave it in and use a clean spoon.

Mothers of young children: Don't automatically turn to the person
beside you and cut up their meat for them.

Don't cut meat like you're sawing timber. Pull the knife gently toward you as you cut.

If you want to remove a bone from your mouth, discreetly take it
out with your fingers and slip it onto the edge of your plate.

Do place the napkin neatly on the table, to the right side of the plate when you have finished
eating. Don't refold the napkin, but don't leave it in a crumpled heap either.

Eating bread and rolls: Break off a bite-sized piece over your bread plate,
then use the bread knife to butter it.

Eating asparagus: Pick up a spear with your fingers, dip it in the sauce, and take a bite.
Leave tough parts on the edge of your plate. If the asparagus is very limp or already covered
in sauce, use a knife and fork.

Finger bowls may be provided at formal dinners where a hands-on course such as lobster
or fruit is served. The idea is that you dip the tips of your fingers in the bowl and then
dry them on your napkin.

AND FINALLY . . . Many of these tips don't just apply when you have guests.
Even if it's just you and Fluffy the goldfish, light a candle, fold a napkin,
and eat your beans on toast off your finest china. No, it's not sad; it's civilized.
It's only sad if you fold a napkin for Fluffy too.

TIP: If anyone breaches etiquette at your dinner party, e.g., drinking from the finger bowl, the polite reaction is to smile and act as if it is perfectly normal. Never draw attention to a faux pas as you will embarrass your guest.

GIFTS & WRAPPING

"The perfect gift for the person who has everything? A burglar alarm."

—MILTON BERLE

— PERFECT PRESENTS —

If your calendar is a mass of circled dates for this birthday and that anniversary, you'll be glad of some inspiring ideas for choosing and wrapping gifts, as well as simple techniques for tying beautiful bows and ravishing rosettes. Dahling, you shouldn't have!

— CHOOSING A GIFT —

Don't buy a gift just because *you* like it. You may think that piece of abstract art would look fantastic above your fireplace, but ask yourself, will *they* want it above theirs?

Do consider the recipient's available space at home. That life-size cuddly gorilla may be cute, but they really shouldn't have to move to a new house to accommodate it.

Don't buy noisy toys, especially for Christmas. The peace of many a happy family gathering has been shattered by a little drummer boy. Parumpapumpum.

Don't leave your purchase till the last minute. When you're desperate, stressed, and under pressure, you're more likely to spend a lot more than you intended on something that might not be wanted.

Don't buy pets. Full stop.

Do hit the ATM if all inspiration fails. Ready cash rarely disappoints.

Don't just hand out cash straight from your wallet. Slip it discreetly inside an appropriate greeting card, or better still, a bouquet of their favorite flowers.

Do give an "ethical gift" to support a charity. Oxfam/America will make a donation on your behalf to buy a gift for someone in need. They range from goats to camels, beehives to shares in a mango plantation. The perfect present for someone who has everything—and you'll feel good too!

Don't panic if you're strapped for cash. Draw on your own talents to bake, make or sew a gift. Totally talentless? Offer your services as a babysitter or petsitter, clean their house, dig their garden, put up shelves, valet their car. Donate a day's lesson to teaching them how to use their computer.

Do buy clothes only if you're sure of the measurements. Buy a garment that's too small and the recipient will think you're hinting they ought to shed a few pounds; buy one that's too big and they might think you regard them as larger than they are. Ideally, buy clothes only if the recipient is with you.

Don't recycle gifts among close family and friends. The hideous vase from Auntie Mary that you offloaded on Cousin John is sure to be recognized by Auntie Mary when she next visits him.

TIP: Remember to remove the price from the present before you wrap it!

— HOW TO MAKE YOUR OWN WRAPPING PAPER —

The choice of gift wrapping available is fantastic but to make it truly personal, why not create your own?

Wallpaper remnants—embossed designs look particularly effective.

Newsprint is not just for wrapping fish and chips. Foreign language newspapers with decorative script such as Chinese, Japanese, or Arabic look very exotic. Comics and magazines—cheap, cheerful, but also colorful and will enliven children's presents.

Mulberry paper has a handmade look. It's made from the bark of the mulberry tree and has visible strands of plant fiber. Available from good art shops.

Bubble wrap is not only protective, it's perfect for a high-tech look, tied with nylon string.

GIVE IT A TRY: Use real tropical leaves to wrap a special gift.
First, wrap the present in brown paper, then add the limp leaves one by one, using double-sided tape to fix them in place. Tie with natural grasses and add a flower. Keep cool until it's time to give the gift.

— HOW TO WRAP THE PERFECT GIFT BOX —

For instructions, see "How to wrap the perfect parcel" on pages 283–285, substituting wrapping paper for brown paper and ribbon for string.

— How to Find the End of the Sticky Tape —

Boil a kettle and hold the tape in the steam for a few seconds to loosen.

— How to Avoid Losing the End of the Sticky Tape —

Stick a small button on the end of the tape, or use a hand dispenser, which dispenses precut pieces of sticky tape.

THINKING OUTSIDE THE BOX: Make the container match the theme of the gift: For a green-fingered friend, place a gardening book, seeds, tools, and gardening gloves inside a basket or flowerpot tied with garden twine. Wrap a baby gift in a baby blanket or terry nappy and secure with big safety pins. An avid cook will love their cook book even more if it's packaged in a mixing bowl, complete with wooden spoon. You get the idea . . .

TIP: Photograph your child unwrapping a gift from Granny or a close relative and enclose the picture with their thank-you letter.

— RIBBONS AND TRIMMINGS —

A luscious final flourish can transform a modest gift into something special. The delectable range of ribbons available means you should have no problem finding one to coordinate with your gift wrap. Consider color, scale, and fabric when making your choice.

— HOW TO TIE A CLASSIC HAND-TIED BOW —

What you need: Double-face ribbon (ribbon that is the same on both sides).

Like tying a bow tie, there's a bit of a knack to tying this bow, but it should only take you a few tries to get it right. Don't give up. Practice on ribbon that is not too floppy or slippery until you've mastered it.

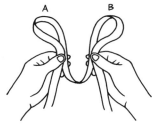

1. Fold the ribbon in half lengthways, then fold it in half again so you have two equal loops. Hold one loop in each hand.

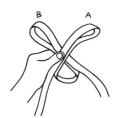

2. Fold loop A over loop B so you are now holding all the ribbon in your left hand.

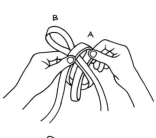

3. Here comes the tricky part . . . With your right hand, push loop A back behind loop B, then pull it forward through the hole in the middle. (figure 3) Pull gently on the two loops to tighten the center and start forming the bow.

4. Tweak and adjust the loops to get your bow looking symmetrical. For a professional finish, trim the tails of the ribbon on the diagonal.

GIVE IT A TRY: Make lots of ribbons in red and green plaid, tie florist's wire around the middle, and use to decorate your Christmas tree.

TIP: To stop a ribbon from fraying when you cut it, paint a few dabs of clear nail polish on the ends.

— How to Make a Double-Looped Bow —

What you need: Wired, double-faced ribbon, florist's wire, double-sided sticky tape.

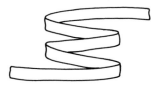

1. On a flat surface, zigzag a length of ribbon into three loops.

2. Pinch the loops together in the center and fasten with florist's wire or strong wire.

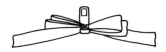

3. Cut a short length of ribbon and attach double-sided sticky tape to each end. Place it over the center of the bow to conceal the wire.

4. Shape the ribbon and cut the tails into swallowtails (see below) for a professional finish.

VARIATION: The more zigzags you make in the ribbon to begin with, the more loops there will be in your final bow.

— How to Make a Swallowtail —

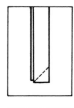

1. Fold the tail end of the ribbon in half lengthways and make a diagonal cut from the "open" end to the folded end.

2. Open out the ribbon and you will see why it's called a swallowtail.

DID YOU KNOW? Hollywood producer Aaron Spelling had a room in his LA mansion reserved solely for the wrapping of gifts.

— How to Make a Rosette —

What you need: Double-faced wired ribbon (the reason why it has to be wired is so that it is easier to mold and the ribbon keeps it shape), florist's wire or strong wire.

This rosette looks divine and very complicated, but it's actually easy to make (shhh, I won't tell, if you won't).

1. Form the ribbon by making a single loop and pinching it between the thumb and first finger of your left hand, leaving some ribbon loose to form the tail.

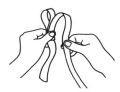

2. With your right hand form another loop of equal size and feed it into your left hand.

3. Continue forming loops and pinching them together in your left hand until the rosette is as full as you would like it. The more loops, the more lavish the bow. An average size would be about 15 loops.

4. Keeping a firm grip on the loops, wrap florist's wire or strong wire around the base where you were pinching them together, and twist to secure it. Leave some wire free if you want to attach your rosette to a gift or a Christmas tree.

5. Fan out the rosette by separating the individual loops, pulling them up and bending them to point in different directions. Trim the tails into swallowtails (see page 276) for a final flourish.

Attach it to a gift, or a display of seasonal cards on a length of ribbon, or make lots and festoon an entire Christmas tree.

VARIATION: Create a different-shaped rosette by gradually increasing the size of the loops as you make them.

TIP: If your wrapping paper is several different colors, make two or three rosettes in complementing shades and join them together for a striking effect.

— HOW TO MAKE A ROSETTE WITH A HALF-TWIST —

This rosette is a variation on the original rosette (see page 277). It is almost as easy.
What you need: Double-faced wired ribbon, florist's wire, decoration—decorative berries/stars etc. (available from garden centers and from stores at Christmas time).

1. Start off as for the original rosette by forming the ribbon into a single loop, then pinch it between the thumb and first finger of your left hand, leaving some ribbon loose for the tail (however long you want it).

2. With your right hand, form another loop of equal size, but before you feed it into your left hand, make a half-twist in the ribbon. This will give the rosette added dimension.

3. Carry on forming loops, giving each one a half-twist as you pass it into your left hand. You'll need to create about 15 loops with a half-twist for an average rosette. Go for more if you want a fuller look.

4. Keeping a firm grip on the loops, wind florist's wire or strong wire around the base where you were pinching them together, and twist to secure. Divide the loops of the rosette down the middle and attach the decoration down through the middle. Give the wire another twist to incorporate it securely into the rosette.

5. Fan out the rosette, spreading out each loop in turn. Trim the tails into swallowtails (see page 276) if desired.

VARIATION: Create a different-shaped rosette by gradually increasing the size of the loops as you make them.

TIP: Omit the decoration if you want a simpler rosette.

ALTERNATIVE TRIMMINGS TO RIBBON: Raffia, lace, tulle, multicolored elastic bands, knitting yarn, old strings of beads or pearls, old belts, ties, or stockings, tape from old cassettes (for a CD).

DID YOU KNOW? Raffia is made from palm tree leaves.

DON'T FORGET: Attach a gift tag to your present with a personal message or greeting. This is particularly important when many presents are being given, for example, at a wedding or birthday. Your tag is the only means of identifying you as the giver.

Keep a list of birthdays, anniversaries, and holidays marked in different colors on your calendar.

TIP: Don't wait for a special occasion to give a gift—surprise someone you love any day of the year!

— HOW TO WRAP A GIFT JAPANESE-STYLE —

"Giving a gift is like wrapping your heart."
—Japanese proverb

In Japan, gift wrapping is part of the expressions of love and thought that go into giving a gift. Not surprisingly, in Japan it is considered impolite to give a gift unwrapped.

The traditional way to wrap gifts in Japan is to use a *furoshiki*—a square-shaped cloth, usually made of silk or cotton. Wrapping gifts in fabric is practical and environmentally friendly— nothing gets thrown away. The gift wrap becomes part of the gift. It's also a great way to wrap awkward shapes like bottles and balls. *Furoshiki* are also fun and easy to wrap with. Once you've tried it, you'll never want to go back to boring old paper and sticky tape.

You can purchase *Furoshiki* online at www.jun-gifts.com. They also crop up for sale on eBay. Or you can make your own version.

How to make a furoshiki
Cut a square of cloth appropriate to the size of gift you are wrapping.
Fold the edges under and stitch down all sides to prevent fraying.

No-sew alternatives
Scarf, handkerchief, table napkin, small tablecloth, or bandanna—any piece of fabric is suitable as long as it's square and not sheer. The advantage of making your own is that you can choose a material to perfectly complement your gift in color and design.

DID YOU KNOW? In Japan the person who brings the gift also unwraps it.

— HOW TO WRAP A BOX JAPANESE-STYLE —

Measure your box: For example, a box 3 in. (height) x 9½ in. (width) x 12½ in. (length) will need a *furoshiki* measuring about 34½ in. x 34½ in.

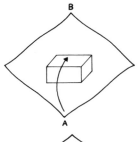

1. Lay the cloth flat with the wrong side facing up. Place the box facedown on the cloth at an angle to the diagonal. The box should not be dead in the center but a little nearer to point A. Fold end A up and over the box.

2. Holding the cloth tight over the box, roll the box over until it is the right way up, taking the cloth with it so it is tucked underneath the box.

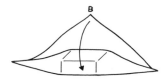

3. Fold end B up and over the top of the box.

4. Take hold of the left and right ends and bring them up to meet in the middle of the box.

5. Tie a square knot (see page 247).

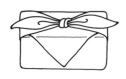

6. The finished box.

TIP: Don't buy lingerie as a gift. You may think that red lacy thong with gold tassels is the sexiest thing ever—but will he?

— HOW TO WRAP A BOTTLE JAPANESE-STYLE —

This is a quick, easy, and original way to "bring a bottle."

For a 12 in. bottle, your *furoshiki* should measure about 30 in. square.

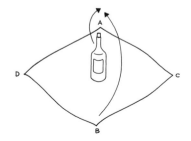

1. Stand the bottle in the middle of the *furoshiki* cloth. Fold end A up to meet end B.

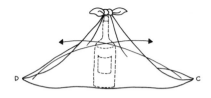

2. Tie ends A and B in a square knot (see page 247) over the top of the bottle. Cross ends C and D in front of the bottle.

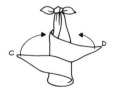

3. Pass ends C and D around to the back of the bottle.

4. Turn the bottle around and bring ends C and D back to the front of the bottle.

5. Tie ends C and D together in a square knot. Tie the bow in the center or just off-center for a chic look.

TIP: Stick to a budget when choosing a gift. Can't stretch to a cashmere sweater? Buy a cashmere scarf or hat.

— How to Wrap a Ball Japanese-Style —

For a ball or round object 8inches in diameter, your *furoshiki* should measure approximately 34½ inches square.

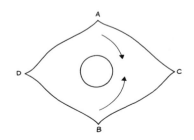

1. Position the ball in the center of the cloth. Fold ends A and B up over the ball into the middle.

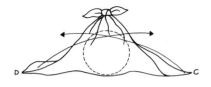

2. Tie a square knot (see page 247) with ends A and B over the top of the ball. Cross ends C and D in front of the ball.

3. Pass ends C and D around to the back of the ball.

4. Turn the ball around and bring ends C and D back around to the front.

5. Tie a square knot in ends C and D to complete the wrapping.

TIP: If the ball is a gift for an avid soccer fan, use a furoshiki in their favorite team's colors.

—THE PERFECT PARCEL —

Brown paper packages tied up with string, these are a few of our favorite things—and they're just what's needed when sending items by mail. Whether boxing baubles or packaging perishables, you can always rely on this classic technique.

— How to Wrap the Perfect Parcel —

What you need: Brown paper (aka kraft paper), rectangular box, string, nylon or vinyl tape (optional)

A rectangular-shaped box is easier to wrap, so if your item is not a regular shape, find a suitable oblong box and pack it inside.

Surround your item with cushioning material, such as crumpled paper, bubble wrap, or Styrofoam peanuts so it won't slide around. If you are sending liquids through the mail, wrap them in plastic and seal with parcel tape. Bed them in with a wadding of absorbent material such as newspaper. At this stage, it's a good idea to slip a piece of paper inside the box with your name, address, and telephone number, just in case your parcel should get lost.

— How to Wrap the Box —

Use brown paper to wrap the box. The amount you need depends on the size of the box.

1. Take the exact measurements of the box. Width: Measure all around the box with a tape measure as if you were measuring a waist, and add 2 inches for the overlap. Length: Measure the length. Measure the height and multiply it by 2. Add that to the first figure.

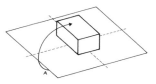

2. Cut the paper to the required length and lay it right side down on a flat surface. Place the box, facedown, in the center of the paper. Wrap one long side of the paper, A, tightly around the box and secure with a short piece of tape.

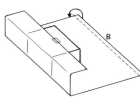

3. Fold over ³⁄₈ inch of the other long side of the paper, B.

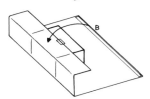

4. Put double-sided sticky tape along the folded edge B. Wrap side B tightly around the box to overlap the other side.

TIP: Can't find a big-enough box? Your local supermarket or DIY store usually have a good supply of boxes in all shapes and sizes.

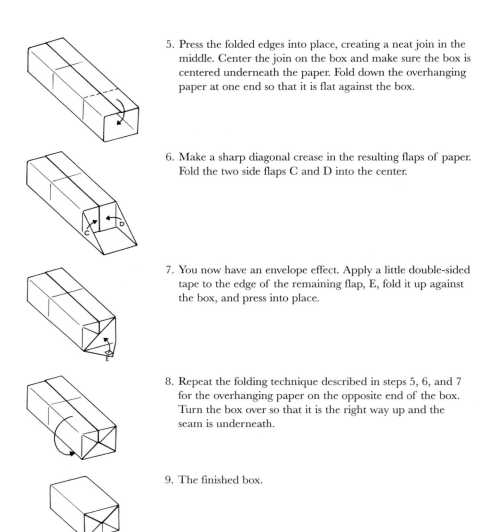

5. Press the folded edges into place, creating a neat join in the middle. Center the join on the box and make sure the box is centered underneath the paper. Fold down the overhanging paper at one end so that it is flat against the box.

6. Make a sharp diagonal crease in the resulting flaps of paper. Fold the two side flaps C and D into the center.

7. You now have an envelope effect. Apply a little double-sided tape to the edge of the remaining flap, E, fold it up against the box, and press into place.

8. Repeat the folding technique described in steps 5, 6, and 7 for the overhanging paper on the opposite end of the box. Turn the box over so that it is the right way up and the seam is underneath.

9. The finished box.

Write the name and address of the person to whom the parcel is being sent on the top of the box, or stick on a label with those details. Use black ink and clear block capitals and include the zip code. Write a return name and address on the back of the box.

To make your parcel doubly secure, if it's being shipped overseas, for instance, seal along all the flaps and edges with nylon or vinyl tape. By all means write FRAGILE or HANDLE WITH CARE on your package, but be aware that they are no guarantee that your parcel will be handled with kid gloves. Most parcels go through automated postal systems that cannot discriminate between sturdy and fragile. Prepare for the worst.

TIP: If you use a felt-tipped pen, you can waterproof the writing by rubbing the end of a candle over it.

— TYING THE PERFECT PARCEL —

Once your parcel is wrapped, the final stage is to secure it with string. Use good quality string, such as hemp or jute. Measure a length of string by taking it twice around the length and width of the box in both directions. Allow about 20 inches extra to make the knot.

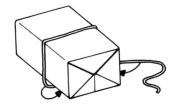

1. Fold the string in half lengthways to find the middle point and place it on top of the box in the center. Wrap the string around the sides of the box, turning the box over in the process.

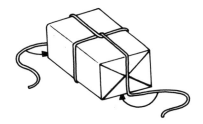

2. Now that the box is upside down, bring the strings to meet in the middle. Twist the two ends together, then take them off at right angles and bring them back up the other sides of the box to the top, turning the box back up the right way in the process.

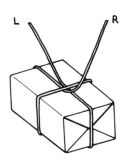

3. Now that the box is the right way up, tie the two ends under the first length of string, and again above it, then snip off the excess. Tie a square knot (see page 247). Ask a friend to put their finger on the first knot of the square knot while you tie the second to make it as tight as possible.

4. The finished box.

FINISHING TOUCH: Make an elegant seal in sealing wax to give your parcel the polished, personal look of packages from days gone by.

TIP: Wet the string before tying the parcel and as it dries, it will shrink tight around the box, keeping the contents more secure.

– Christmas –

"Every Christmas, I feel like a little child. But we always have turkey."

—Joey Bishop

— PICKING THE PERFECT CHRISTMAS TREE —

For many people, a real Christmas means a real Christmas tree. But with over 600 varieties of conifer, how can you tell the trees from the wood?

Tree	Color	Needle type	Information	Needle retention
Norway Spruce	Dark green color	Short, soft needles on long branches	Choose a tree that is freshly cut for longer needle-retention.	1–2 weeks; more if frequently watered.
Scots Pine	Dark green to bluish green	Stiff, long, elegant needles	Particularly noted for its long-lasting pine-forest scent; well suited to carry either light or heavy decorations.	4–6 weeks
Noble Fir	Bluish green to gray-green	Short, soft, curl upward	Slow-growing so can be expensive. The shape and sturdiness of its branches make it perfect for supporting decorations.	6–12 weeks
Douglas Fir	Dark-green to blue-green	Short, soft	Sweet orange scent; its branches are ideal for making wreaths and garlands but do not hold decorations well.	6–12 weeks
Blue Spruce	Silvery blue	Short, stiff	Symmetrical shape; strong scent; a good tree to keep all year round in the garden.	2–3 weeks

TIP: The scent of a Christmas tree is the very essence of Christmas, but scents vary between varieties. Sniff the needles to check that your tree has a clean, fresh scent.

— BUYING YOUR TREE —

Measure the height and width of the area where the tree will stand
before you go out to buy your tree. Also, measure the dimension of your tree stand.
Take all these measurements—and a tape measure—with you when you
go tree shopping.

Select a tree that looks fresh and green, with no brown needles or dull patches.

Choose a tree with sturdy branches if you have a lot of heavy ornaments.
Take a shatterproof ornament with you to test the strength of the branches.

Go for a tree with good needle retention if you like to put up your tree early.

Trees are sold either in a pot with roots, or cut. A tree with roots won't
need much watering. If you choose a cut tree, make a fresh cut with a saw of
about ½ inch before putting it in a water-holding stand. Leave a cut tree
out in the open until needed. Put it in a bucket of water before bringing it inside.

— DECORATING THE PERFECT CHRISTMAS TREE —

Site your tree away from radiators or other heat sources, such as an open fire or sunny window. Don't put it somewhere it may be knocked over.

Place the tree securely in its holder and turn it so that its best side is facing into the room.

Start by arranging the lights on the tree. These are a vital part of your decorative scheme, so be generous and allow at least 40 lights per 12 inches of tree height. Lights are available in a dazzling variety of shapes and colors. Pick a set to complement your theme. Also ensure that the color of the wire matches your tree. A green tree can be ruined by ugly white wire trailed around it.

Untangle the lights and test them *before* putting them on the tree. Replace any bulbs if necessary.

Unplug the lights and start winding them from the highest branches, around and around the tree, ending at the back of the base of the tree. Aim to create a silhouette of the tree in lights. Switch the lights on again to check that they are all still working and reposition any lights which don't enhance the silhouette.

In theory, your top decoration should go on next, but you might prefer to leave the fairy/angel/star as your final decorative flourish. Just check that it isn't top-heavy as the weight could cause the tree to overbalance.

Tinsel time now . . . drape the tinsel, beads, or chains evenly over the tree. Create swags or garlands, or arrange them from the top point of the tree like spreading maypole ribbons. Experiment until you create an effect you're happy with.

TIP: Store small ornaments in old egg cartons. Bigger ornaments fit well in those polystyrene trays you buy fruit in at the supermarket.

Bedeck the tree with beautiful ornaments. Start with the largest and place them at intervals around the tree. Fill in the gaps with smaller ones. Avoid strict regiments of ornaments—vary the positions, colors, and sizes across the tree for a balanced look. Take a step back now and again to get an overall view, and make any necessary adjustments.

Summon the children and have a grand "switching on the lights" ceremony!

— How to Keep Your Christmas Lights Tangle-Free —

Trying to force lights back into the box they came in is like trying to force toothpaste back into the tube. Don't even attempt it. Instead, wind lights carefully around a long cardboard tube and store.

— TOPSY-TURVY TREE —

Are you fed up with your toddlers or your pet cat wrecking your tree? Maybe you're living in cramped quarters and don't have room for one? Or, perhaps you're just up for doing something a bit different this year? Answer yes to any of the above and here is your solution: Hang your tree upside down.

Yes, you heard me right. And, no, it's not as crazy as it sounds. Topsy-turvy trees are not a new innovation. The tradition dates back to the 12th century when people suspended a fir tree from the ceiling beams in their home as a symbol of their Christian faith.

If your room is not blessed with beams, suspend it from a stairwell or anywhere with a high ceiling (or go for a smaller tree). Place it in the front window and it will be sure to draw crowds of astonished passersby, all wondering if they haven't had one too many glasses of mulled wine.

Both real and artificial trees are suitable. If you choose real, go for one with good needle retention. Suspend the tree by the trunk and ensure it is secure. Decorate once in position. Shatterproof ornaments are a boon. Switch on the fairy lights and gaze in awe as your tree floats ethereally in space. Magical.

TIP: Before decorating, spray your tree with a light covering of glitter hair spray to give it a glitzy look and help needle retention.

— HOW TO MAKE A FIR TREE SNOWFLAKE —

Make a frame by wiring together three equal lengths of bamboo cane, then wire the branches onto the frame to create a snowflake shape. Suspend with decorative cord or ribbon.

TIP: Entwine battery-operated fairy lights through the branches so your snowflake twinkles at night.

— HOW TO CONVINCE THE KIDS THAT SANTA CLAUS HAS BEEN —

'Twas the night before Christmas . . . Grab a bag of flour from the cupboard, put on the largest pair of boots in the house, and make a trail of footprints leading from the fireplace to the presents under the tree by sprinkling flour around your feet on the floor as you walk.

Christmas morning . . . Enjoy the looks of surprised delight on the children's faces!

— MAKING A MISTLETOE KISSING BALL —

Kissing under the mistletoe is a time-honored Christmas custom, but one measly sprig isn't going to kick-start a romance. Think big! Think great balls of mistletoe! Kissing balls have been around for more than 200 years, and tradition dictates—listen up, guys—no girl can be refused a kiss beneath one.

What you need: Strong decorative cord, florist's wire or strong wire, ball of florist's foam, fresh sphagnum moss, mistletoe, ribbon (optional).

Attach decorative cord to the top of a ball of florist's foam (available from florists and garden centers) using florist's wire bent into hairpin shapes. This will be used to hang the ball. Cover the ball in fresh sphagnum moss using more florist's wire or a hot glue gun. Bind several sprigs of mistletoe together with florist's wire and stick it into the moss. Continue until the moss is completely covered. Hang the ball in a conspicuous spot, such as a doorway. Mistletoe dries out quickly, so hang it in a cool place, if possible. Pucker up in readiness.

TIP: Tie a brightly colored ribbon around the cord to add an extra decorative touch. (See "How to tie a classic hand-tied bow" on page 275).

VARIATION: Make a smaller version by sticking mistletoe sprigs directly into a potato. The moisture in the potato will help keep it fresh.

WARNING: Mistletoe berries are poisonous, so keep away from children and pets.

DID YOU KNOW? In Scandinavian tradition, if two enemies met under the mistletoe they would lay down their arms and break off fighting for the day.

— HOW TO MAKE PERFECT MULLED WINE —

How better to stave off the winter blues than with a warm and cheering glass of spicy mulled wine? There are many variations on this theme, but this recipe is guaranteed to hit the spot on a cold and frosty night.

DID YOU KNOW? The word mulled *means "heated with spices."*

Serves 6

2 unwaxed oranges	1 dried bay leaf
6 cloves	2 star anise
1 unwaxed lemon	Pinch of freshly grated nutmeg
1 cinnamon stick (approx. 2 in.)	25 fl. oz. bottle full-bodied red wine
12 fl. oz. water	4 fl. oz. brandy (optional)
3–4 tbsp. raw, cane sugar	Cranberries, to garnish

1. Keep one orange whole and stud it with the cloves. Slice the other fruit thinly. Break the cinnamon stick into pieces.

2. Pour the water into a large saucepan with the sugar, spices, and fruit (including the whole orange). Warm the mixture, stirring from time to time, until the sugar has dissolved. Bring the heat up to simmering point and continue warming for about 15 minutes.

3. Add the red wine. Choose a decent red wine with a hearty, full fruit flavor and lots of body. A merlot, burgundy, or cabernet sauvignon are ideal. Warm the liquid but don't let it boil or the alcohol will evaporate!

4. Take the pan off the heat. Now's the time to stir in the brandy—if you want an extra kick. Taste, and add more sugar according to taste. Put a lid on the pan and allow to infuse for about 30 minutes. Strain, and ladle into a punch bowl or heatproof glasses. Decorate with star anise, orange slices, and berries, and serve with warm mince pies.

Cheers!

TIP: Substitute 2½ fl. oz. of water with .2½ fl. oz. of weak tea for an extra-special brew!

CALLING ALL DRIVERS: For a nonalcoholic version, use spiced berry cordial (various brands available) and freshly squeezed orange juice instead of the alcohol.

TIP: When the festivities are over, save on vacuuming by wrapping the tree in an old sheet before carrying it out of the house.

— PACKING YOUR SUITCASE —

"The scientific theory I like best is that the rings of Saturn are composed entirely of lost airline luggage."

—MARK RUSSELL

— HOW TO CHOOSE A SUITCASE —

Buy a case that is suitable for your purpose. Aim for something strong but lightweight. A suitcase that feels heavy before you even start packing might tip you over the baggage allowance and make you liable to pay excess baggage fees.

A rollerboard suitcase has built-in glide wheels and a pull-out handle to save pulling your arms out of their sockets.

It's false economy to choose a cheap bag. Buy the best you can afford, one that is robust enough to cope with the rough handling by baggage handlers.

Avoid suitcases with pockets and clips sticking out on the outside, which might catch on luggage carousels, etc.

Go for a suitcase with pockets, dividers, and packing straps on the inside to keep your belongings organized and secure.

A discreet and anonymous-looking suitcase is less likely to attract the attention of an opportunist thief than expensive designer bags. The same goes for rip-off designer luggage, which is often indistinguishable from the real thing.

— HOW TO PACK THE PERFECT SUITCASE —

Make a list of all the items you want to take. Now halve it!

Spread everything you want to take on the bed and divide it into piles—shirts, sweaters, T-shirts, etc. Now halve it again!

Buy small plastic bottles and decant your shampoos and lotions into them. Free trial-size samples of toothpaste, deodorant, body lotion, etc., also come in handy.

Tighten the lids on all toiletry bottles, wrap adhesive tape around the lids, and pack in a zip-up, watertight plastic bag, see-through if possible.

String your jewelry chains through a straight drinking straw to ensure a tangle-free journey.

If you're traveling with someone else, mix clothes in each other's bags, so if you're unfortunate enough to lose your luggage, you'll still have a change of clothes.

Place a card with your name, home address, and telephone number INSIDE your suitcase. If you must have a label on the outside of your suitcase, write your business address rather than your home address. Airports are prime targets for burglars on the lookout for the addresses of houses guaranteed to be empty.

For air travel, use a bag with a hard outer shell as your hand luggage and it doubles as a foot-rest on the plane, reducing the risk of your ankles swelling.

TIP: Keep the list of items you're taking with your documents, so if your suitcase goes missing you have a record of what it contains.

— How to Keep Your Clothes Wrinkle-Free —

The secret to keeping your clothes wrinkle-free is tissue paper, and lots of it. The tissue should be white, acid-free paper, which is stronger than regular tissue paper and the dyes won't run. Place the tissue between any folds you make in the clothes, between the pleats of skirts, stuffed into the sleeves of jackets, and between every layer of clothing in the suitcase. This might strike you as an extravagant waste of tissue, but it does make all the difference, and remember, you can reuse it.

Do all your folding on the bed before you start to pack.

To fold shirts, use the techniques described on page 36, but remember to pack tissue paper into the folds. Fold the flares of a flared skirt into the middle of the back of the skirt with tissue paper at the creases.

Fold the upper part of a dress like a shirt and the bottom part like a flared skirt, using tissue paper in the folds.

Roll a pleated skirt lengthways into a tubular shape, then place the waistband end into the toe of a stocking and pull it all the way up over the skirt. Remove any belt on a pair of trousers, and fold in half lengthways (with tissue in between).

— Interlocking —

The best system of packing your clothes to keep them wrinkle-free is "interlocking." Here's how to do it. NOTE: In order to show the order of packing more clearly, the illustration omits the tissue paper spread between folds and layers of clothes.

Place heaviest items such as books, shoes, and toiletry bag in the base of the case so they will not crush your clothes.

Wrap shoes in individual see-through plastic bags to prevent soiling your clothes. Pack heavy shoes soles up.

Underwear and socks: Wrap socks and underwear in plastic bags and tuck inside shoes.

Place a towel or coat on top so you have a flat surface on which to start packing your clothes.

Trousers and long skirts: Start by placing a long garment such as a long skirt or a pair trousers

TIP: Take half the clothes and twice the money.

across the case so that the waistband is against the inside edge and the hem (if a skirt) or the legs (if trousers) hang over the rim of the case. Place a few sheets of tissue paper on top.

Place the next long item of clothing using the same method, but lay it in the opposite direction to the previous garment packed so the waistbands are at opposite ends. Place a few sheets of tissue paper on top. Continue layering trousers, skirts, and long dresses in this way, at opposite ends, with tissue paper in between.

Coats and jackets: Button them up (folding the sleeves neatly toward the center) and place them faceup, the opposite way, dangling over the edge of the case.

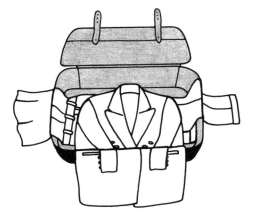

Shirts, sweaters, and dresses next, layered with tissue paper. If you don't have enough of these items to fill up the middle area, pack it with more underwear, etc. Casual clothes, such as T-shirts, can be rolled up and put in this area. Cover with a layer of tissue paper.

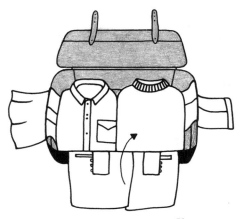

TIP: To reduce the risk of fire and to save electricity, unplug electrical items before you go away. If you empty and unplug the fridge, be sure to defrost it first and leave the door propped open.

Fold back the jackets one at a time, putting
tissue paper at the crease.

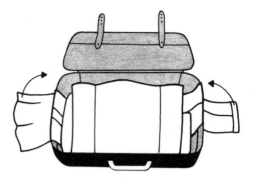

Fold the trouser legs and skirts back into the case, with tissue paper at the crease.
Tuck any leftover socks, shoes, and underwear into the gaps around the sides. Place belts along
the length of the case. Don't roll them as they may crack.

You might want to place a fold-up nylon bag over everything to form a protective layer. It can
also serve as a laundry bag at your destination and then an extra bag to bring home souvenirs.

Connect the packing straps.

Don't overfill your case or you will put stress on seams and fastenings and the case might
explode open. If you have to sit on the case to close it, it's too full. On the other hand, don't
pack too loose or everything will shift about. Use a smaller case.

Close the case, lock it, and as an extra precaution against accidental opening, attach a strap
tight around the girth.

Tie colored tape or put a distinctive sticker on both sides of the case as a means of identifying
your case in a crowd.

*DID YOU KNOW? There is a store in Scottsdale, Alabama, the Unclaimed Baggage Center, that sells items
from unclaimed baggage and lost and unclaimed cargo.*

At your destination: Unpack as soon as possible. If, perish the thought, any of your clothes have creased, hang them in the bathroom while you shower. The steam will smooth out any creases.

When you return home: Empty your suitcase entirely before storing; a single sock left inside can leave a distinct whiff. Tuck a scented drawer liner or dryer sheet inside to keep it smelling sweet.

— HOW TO PACK THE PERFECT BACKPACK —

The most efficient and fastest method is the "Roll and Pack" (not to be confused with the "Shake and Vac"). This is the system used by the armed forces—and if anyone knows about packing, it's them.

Everything is rolled.

Start with well-ironed clothes and lay them out on a flat surface.

Always roll from the hem up to the neck.

Fold trousers in half, leg over leg, then start rolling from the bottom of trousers to the waist.

Fold T-shirts and tops in half, sleeve to sleeve, and roll from hem to neck.

The tighter you roll, the more you'll pack in.

If you roll the clothes over tissue paper, they will have fewer creases.

A delicate article such as a silk shirt can be rolled inside a sweater or cotton shirt with tissue paper in between.

Fill the spaces with shoes, underwear, etc.

Heavy items like hiking boots should go in the bottom of the backpack.

TIP: If you have mostly casual clothes or man-made fibers, this method also works well for packing your suitcase.

TIP: If you're going backpacking, don't start out with a full backpack, as you will inevitably acquire things along the way and need room for them.

—CONVERSION CHARTS—

"If they ask you to convert Fahrenheit to Celsius, remember that it's easier just to put on a sweater."

—ANONYMOUS

— CONVERTING MEASUREMENTS —

Multiply by

Inches to centimeters	2.540
Centimetres to inches	0.3937
Feet to meters	0.3048
Metres to feet	3.281
Miles to kilometers	1.609
Kilometers to miles	0.6214
Ounces to grams	28.35
Grams to ounces	0.03527
Pounds to kilograms	0.4536
Kilograms to pounds	2.205

Celsius to Fahrenheit:
Multiply by 9, divide by 5, add 32.
Fahrenheit to Celsius:
Deduct 32, multiply by 5, divide by 9.

— CONVERTING WEIGHTS —

Metric	Imperial
5 g	¼ oz.
15 g	½ oz.
25 g	1 oz.
50 g	2 oz.
85 g	3 oz.
110 g	4 oz.
140 g	5 oz.
180 g	6 oz.
200 g	7 oz.
225 g	8 oz.

One teaspoonful is 5 ml.
One tablespoonful is 15 ml.

— APPROXIMATE CONVERSIONS —

A millimeter is about the diameter of a paper clip wire (0.001 meter)
A centimeter is a little more than the width of a paper clip (about 0.4 in.)
A meter is a little longer than a yard (about 1.1 yards)
A kilometer is a little further than ½ mile (about 0.6 mile)
A liter is a little larger than a quart (about 1.06 quarts)
A gram is a little more than the weight of a paper clip
A kilogram is a little heavier than two pounds (about 2.2 pounds)
A hectare is about 2½ acres
A metric ton is about 1 ton (about 2,500 pounds)

DID YOU KNOW? In 1999, a U.S. spacecraft crashed into the planet Mars because NASA forgot to convert imperial units to metric units. Oops.

INDEX